Understanding Documentary Bills and Credits

A practical guide for importers, exporters, forwarders and bankers

Frank W Dow ACIB

Croner Publications Limited
Croner House
London Road
Kingston Upon Thames
Surrey KT2 6SR
Telephone: 081-547 3333

Published by
Croner Publications Ltd,
Croner House,
London Road,
Kingston Upon Thames,
Surrey KT2 6SR
Telephone: 081-547 3333

British Library Cataloguing in Publication Data
Dow, Frank W.
Understanding documentary bills and credits:
a practical guide for importers, exporters,
forwarders and bankers.
1. International banking. Documentary credits
I. Title
332.7'7

ISBN 1-85452-052-0

Printed by Whitstable Litho Ltd, Whitstable, Kent

Contents

Acknowledgements

It is easy when writing a book of this nature to allow one's own prejudices and bad habits to manifest themselves in the text, and to give published credence to long-held misconceptions. I do not say that the work is entirely free of such blemishes, but in the elimination of much which would have caused me great embarrassment I incurred a vast debt of gratitude to the following:

Mr Bernard Wheble, who checked the accuracy of the information given with great thoroughness, offered a wealth of helpful advice, and provided me with much material to which I would not otherwise have had access. All this was done despite the very heavy workload which he already carries in connection with his activities on behalf of the United Nations and the International Chamber of Commerce.

My wife, Maggie, who went through the text with equal thoroughness in ruthless pursuit of clichés, repetitions, mis-spellings, jargon, and gobbledeygook, and then later checked both the galley proofs and the page proofs.

Mr Michael Coney, Managing Director of AFL Afri-Freight Ltd, freight forwarders of Hounslow, for his enthusiastic co-operation and advice.

Cotecna International Ltd for their helpful advice on the procedures involved in pre-shipment inspection of goods, and for provision of and permission to reproduce specimens of their documentation.

Commercial Union Assurance Co plc, for advice and provision of specimen documents.

Girobank plc, Hapag-Lloyd AF, Hamburg, and Lloyds of London for provision of specimen documents.

Acrow Engineers (PVT) Ltd, of Harare, Zimbabwe; Federation of Sussex Industries and Chamber of Commerce, Brighton; Habselyem

Kotottarugyar, clothing manufacturers of Budapest, Hungary; Industrieel Assurantie Kantoor BV, of Eindhoven, Netherlands; Mandarin Publishers Ltd, of Hong Kong; Voss Ltd, laboratory instrument manufacturers of Burgess Hill, Sussex for permission to reproduce documents.

Halewood Chemicals Ltd, of Staines, Middlesex; and ICI Agrochemicals, of Haslemere, Surrey for help given or offered.

The management and staff of National Westminster Bank, Maldon branch, for believing my continued assurances that solvency would one day return.

Standard Chartered Bank for making it all possible by giving me the experience to even contemplate such a venture.

Material from publication No. 322 (ICC copyright © 1978) and publication No. 400 (ICC copyright © 1983) is reproduced by permission of the publisher, International Chamber of Commerce, Paris (France).

The full texts are available from ICC United Kingdom, Centre Point, 103 New Oxford Street, London WC1A 1QB or ICC Publishing, 38 Cours Albert 1er, 75008, Paris, France.

Introduction

As an instrument designed to provide a compromise between the conflicting interests of buyers and sellers in trade transactions, it is difficult to imagine anything which could adequately replace the documentary letter of credit. Thousands of importers, exporters, bankers and forwarders are handling credits each working day in every country in the world, yet time and again the essential basic understanding of the concept of the credit is simply not there. As a result, someone suffers. That someone may be the buyers who receive the wrong goods, or the right goods at the wrong time (which is sometimes worse), or it may be (and most frequently is) the sellers, who have to wait for cripplingly long periods of time to receive payment for their goods.

The blame for such inconveniences almost invariably falls upon the banks. Yet nearly every letter of credit and application for the issue of a credit carries wording to the effect that it is issued subject to the "Uniform Customs and Practice for Documentary Credits" (UCP) issued by the International Chamber of Commerce (ICC). Similarly, a high proportion of collections are stated to be subject to the ICC's "Uniform Rules for Collections" (URC). How many exporters and forwarders can honestly say that they or their staff have a working knowledge of what those rules say? Sadly, the majority have never read them and do not even have a copy available to be consulted.

The record of the banks in this field is far from unblemished, however. As the banking system lurches from one debt crisis to the next, as competition for a dwindling volume of business intensifies, as new hi-tech systems are purchased, each costing more than the last, as increasing inflation fuels even higher wage demands, so the inevitable slimming down process causes the banks to look at areas where money can be saved. All too often, training, particularly of the technical sort, presents itself as a ready target. Consequently, bank staff themselves frequently lack the most basic understanding of what they are doing and why they are doing it.

This, however, is no new situation. The motor manufacturers who, when the factory docket arrives on the desk announcing that a batch of new vehicles has been completed and is in the compound awaiting despatch notes, only then realise that this is an export consignment against a letter of credit and take the trouble to read the terms of that credit; the bank which glibly adds its confirmation to its own paper; the timber importers who attach 16 pages of detailed specification to their credit application with the instruction that these form an integral part of the credit; the forwarders who cannot understand why a bank should reject their house bill of lading under a credit; all these and many more have been with us for many years. Too many years.

It is the aim of this book to try to bring these varying and often conflicting interests together in a deeper understanding of how the documentary letter of credit and, to a lesser extent, the documentary bill for collection, works. Only by achieving this is there any hope of reducing the high incidence of rejected drawings under credits, and the vast quantities of unwanted goods offered for sale at huge discounts simply to get rid of them.

The target audience is large. The book is not written from the particular standpoint of any one of the parties involved in the international trade transaction but is intended to be read by all who need to know: export/import clerks, bank clerks, forwarders, students, etc. It does not set out to be an exhaustive guide to trade documentation; many books have appeared on this subject and have admirably achieved their objectives. We will, however, be looking at various documents and examining their function and format, but only from the point of view of their effect on the achievement of the underlying purpose of the documentary credit or bill – the exchange of correct goods for prompt payment.

One apology must be made. Many aspects of international trade are truly international, and this includes the various codes drawn up by the International Chamber of Commerce to standardise actions and interpretations in certain situations on a global basis. Sometimes, however, and this has happened recently in Sweden, Switzerland and Italy, domestic laws, and in particular bill of exchange legislation, can affect the international aspect of a transaction. It is impossible in a work of this size to examine in detail all the possible variations in attitudes within the courts to a particular problem. What it is hoped will be achieved is that far fewer such transactions will come before the courts at all. However, as this book is written in English in the United Kingdom any venture into the legal background to international trade will be based largely upon English law and statute.

Above all, the book is intended to equip the reader with the knowledge and understanding to deal with practical situations as they arise. The variety of these situations can be quite astonishing, and no work of this kind could possibly provide a codified answer to each and every problem, not least because many of them have not yet arisen and are therefore not identified as problems at all. It is hoped that the book will be readable.

The world of international commerce is dynamic and change is under way even as these words are written. Although from time to time, as the situation indicates it as desirable, the book will be updated, it must be left to the reader to keep abreast of developments. In this, such publications as Croner's *Export Digest* and the periodic issue by the International Chamber of Commerce of significant opinions of their Banking Committee relating to letters of credit are invaluable.

1
Methods of payment in international trade

Before looking at the two methods of settlement in international trade which most concern us – the bill for collection and the documentary letter of credit – it will be useful to examine the options which are available to buyers and sellers and the factors which influence their decision to prefer one method over another. Sometimes the domestic regulations in one or other of the countries involved will dictate that a particular method be used, and this is often the case where a documentary credit is opted for. Normal trade usage, either within a country, a trading community or an individual company, also often plays a part. More frequently, however, the most influential factor is the degree of trust which exists between the principals in the transaction, since different methods of settlement provide correspondingly different degrees of protection to the interests of one or the other of them.

Countertrade

Countertrade does not fit easily within this statement, but since it is usually supplemented by one of the other forms of settlement it is perhaps not really necessary to attempt to achieve such a fit. There are many different forms of countertrade, ranging from straightforward barter transactions (the simple exchange of one form of goods for another) to bilateral trade agreements between countries. It is not within the scope of this book to discuss this in detail and it is mentioned as a means of settlement merely for the sake of completeness.

Open account trade

In a domestic sales transaction, potential buyers can easily satisfy themselves as to the quality of goods, either by physical examination of them
before purchase or by reliance upon the reputation of the seller. In
international trade, however, the limitations of geography generally prevent such a mutually desirable situation from being possible. Physical
examination of goods is expensive and inconvenient, and in any case is
rarely a guarantee that those will be the goods which actually arrive. It
can, of course, be delegated to an agent, but often the difficulty in identifying a suitable person in another country to fulfil this role nullifies any
advantage which is to be obtained. Furthermore, with increasing distance
comes decreasing facility to check on the reliability of a trading partner,
so the second option is not necessarily available either.

This is not to say, however, that normal trade with perfect mutual trust
between the participants does not take place in the international context.
When it does, it is most likely to fall into one of three groups:

(a)   buyers and sellers have been dealing together for a long time
       and have developed the kind of relationship which engenders
       absolute trust;
(b)   buyers and sellers are situated in countries which are geographi-
       cally close, thus allowing the domestic type of transaction to
       which reference has already been made to take place;
(c)   or buyers and sellers are constituent parts of the same inter-
       national group.

Whatever the reason for the existence of such a special relationship, the
method of settlement which, in the absence of any outside influences
such as exchange control regulations, is likely to be chosen is open
account trading. This, like any other trade account, is an agreement
whereby goods up to an agreed limit can be ordered and will be
dispatched, settlement being made by means of a single payment at an
agreed time to cover all goods for which invoices have been received
from the seller up until that time. The sellers are in no doubt that they
will receive payment when due, and the buyers are confident that the
goods, when received, will be correct and of the quality required, or in
the case of any dispute will be replaced or taken back and the money
refunded without question.

However strong the relationship, where an open account system of settlement is in use there is no excuse for complacency in either party, since the potential risk is obviously high. Changes in market conditions or ownership, political or economic developments—any of these can affect the underlying basis for the trust which gave rise to the relationship. International traders need to be in touch with the world situation and to be capable of assessing the likely effects of developments on their own business interests. If, for instance, suppliers in Canada export to a manufacturer in West Germany whose principal market place for the finished product is in Turkey, then any events in Turkey may affect the Germans' ability to meet their obligations to Canada. The fullest financial information on the strength of a trading partner should therefore be obtained and regularly updated. Given the special relationships which normally exist in open account trade, such information should be freely given without question by the company concerned, but there is still no harm in seeking a periodic report from one of the recognised credit rating agencies.

Payment in advance

Such, then, is the situation where the level of trust between trading partners is high. What of the other extreme? It is to be hoped that no-one would venture into international trade without making at least some attempt to establish the reputation and creditworthiness of their partners, and some may say that those who are not cautious deserve little sympathy when things go wrong. For this reason, the use in international trade of cash in advance as a method of settlement is relatively rare, other than small percentages which are sometimes payable in advance under major capital contracts. On the occasions when it does arise, the reason is more often to be found in the sellers' doubts about the buyers' country rather than about the buyers themselves. Obviously, under this system of settlement the sellers are under no risk whatever; the buyers, however, must have absolute trust in the sellers and it becomes even more important to make full financial enquiries about them before parting with any cash.

It might be thought that such a statement is not worth the making, yet some of the largest frauds in recent times have been successful simply because the buyers made no attempt to establish just how honest were the people with whom they were dealing. Nor are we talking only of the small or occasional trader; very often the victims are governments.

Frequently, of course, the inducement to do business is a cheap offer, and this factor makes governments of less-developed countries particularly vulnerable. It is a sad fact that for exporters, importers and indeed, banks, there are only two substitutes for adequate training. One is extremely good luck; the other is bitter experience.

The documentary collection

Both methods of settlement discussed so far deal with extremes; open account represents almost the ideal situation for the buyer and advance payment provides similar advantages for the seller. Between the two come the compromise solutions which will form the subject of the remainder of this book: the documentary bill for collection and the documentary letter of credit. Both methods involve the intervention of an agent and because of the nature of the transaction, which basically involves the remittance of money, and because of their worldwide networks of correspondent agreements, the banks have traditionally filled the role of that agent. With the bill for collection the principals are the sellers, with the credit it is the buyers. But whichever is used, it should always be remembered that it is very often the law of agency which is cited in any dispute, rather than specific laws or other rules dealing with either bills or credits.

Where the level of trust between buyers and sellers is not so high as to make an open account arrangement advisable, yet remains reasonably good, it is very often the collection which will be selected by the parties to achieve settlement of the transaction, whilst going some way towards protecting the interests of both parties. Briefly, since the process will be described in some detail in a later chapter, the sellers despatch the goods and then assemble all the documents which will be required by the buyers in order to import and take delivery of those goods on arrival. The documents, often though not invariably accompanied by a demand for payment addressed to the buyers – a bill of exchange, are then handed to the sellers' bank together with full instructions for their disposal. These instructions are repeated by the bank to its own agent in the buyers' country, which will then release the documents to the buyers in accordance with the instructions received, usually against either payment of the invoice value or against an undertaking to make such payment on an agreed date in the future. Thus the interests of both parties are protected to an extent; the sellers, through their agent the bank, retain control of the documents which are necessary to the buyers before they can take delivery, while the buyers are not obliged to pay before having had an opportunity to inspect those documents and possibly the goods themselves.

To the sellers, the greatest disadvantage of the bill for collection as a method of settlement is that it is slow. The effects of this defect can frequently be overcome, however, by arranging with the bank which is handling the collection to provide finance, on agreed terms, to cover the period during which payment is outstanding. Advantages of a collection to the sellers are that it is a relatively simple and, where bank finance is not required, cheap method. For the buyers, the main advantage is that payment can be deferred at least until arrival of the documents, which can then be inspected before a decision is reached, and frequently, either by agreement or by custom, until arrival of the goods themselves.

The documentary letter of credit

Frequently, the level of security provided to the sellers by the bill for collection is insufficiently high. Although they may retain control of the relative documents they lose physical possession of the goods, although of course retaining legal ownership until payment is received. Legal ownership, however, may be of small consolation to sellers whose goods are eight thousand miles away and must be disposed of by an agent in a forced sale in an unreceptive market. In theory, of course, such goods could be shipped back, but the cost of such an operation is usually prohibitive.

Such exporters are likely to insist on payment being by means of a letter of credit. This is a document issued by the buyers' bank to the sellers promising that they, the sellers, will be paid provided that they comply with all the terms and conditions stipulated by the buyers as expressed in the letter of credit. Thus, the sellers' reliance on the standing and integrity of the buyers is replaced by a promise from a bank that payment will be made under certain specified conditions, and this before the goods have been shipped or, perhaps, even produced.

To the sellers, this system brings the undoubted and obvious advantage of certainty of payment subject to certain conditions. It brings other advantages to both parties, however, which are perhaps not quite so obvious. Before investigating these advantages it is necessary to consider how the system actually proceeds after the issue of the credit.

Having received the credit, the sellers ship the goods and put together the required documents in the same way as they would have done for a collection, except of course, that any special requirements regarding documents in the letter of credit must be borne in mind. These are then presented to a bank in the sellers' own country, which carefully checks the documents against the terms of the credit and, if they are in order, pays the sellers. Two more advantages to the sellers are therefore immediately apparent:

(a)   the documents are checked before they leave the exporting country, and therefore if anything is found to be wrong it can very often be put right quickly, whereas with a collection the chances are that such discrepancies remain undetected until documents are checked by the buyers;

(b)   payment may, if the credit terms make it possible, be made to the sellers immediately upon presentation of documents in their own country after shipment of the goods.

For the buyers, the advantages in using a credit lie in the ability to control the circumstances under which suppliers will receive payment by making presentation of correct documentation a prerequisite for that payment to take place. By careful consideration of the dates which are specified in the credit for certain events to occur, they can also attempt to control the time at which goods are received and the time at which the documents themselves are received, both potentially important factors as we shall see later. Finally, because the issue of the letter of credit is instigated by the buyers, the banks intervening in the operation are acting as their agents and not as those of the sellers, as is the case with a bill for collection.

Disadvantages to the sellers in the use of a credit are few. The most important is that the method, once set up, is comparatively inflexible and altered circumstances, which might not be considered sufficiently important to frustrate the contract where any other payment method is used, may render the credit null and void and therefore deprive the sellers of all their advantages at a stroke. To the buyers the greatest disadvantage is probably that payment will have to be made with effect from the time when documents are presented to the issuing bank with no facility for awaiting arrival of the goods as is often the case when using a collection. The credit is also relatively expensive; security must usually be paid for.

Inflexible though the credit may be when things go wrong, an advantage to all concerned is its extreme flexibility in catering for different circumstances. The credit in its many forms will be looked at more closely in a later chapter, but, where security of payment is an important factor, there are few occasions when a letter of credit in one form or another cannot be adapted to meet the particular requirements of that occasion.

Summary

These, then, are the options available to partners in international trade when agreeing between themselves how settlement will be made. In ascending order of security offered, at least to the sellers, they are open account, bill for collection, documentary letter of credit and cash in advance. From the point of view of the banks, both bills and credits provide a good steady income from handling commissions, with credits being the more lucrative, but also the most expensive to operate in terms of intensity of labour involved and carrying by far the greater risk. Both also offer opportunities for further business in the form of export finance for bills, and import finance for both but especially for credits because of the earlier payment, mentioned above, which is often implied by this method of settlement. Such considerations, however, will form the subject material of later chapters.

2
The international trade contract

Before we can adequately deal with operations in either documentary collections or documentary credits there are areas of which a basic understanding is essential if what follows is to make any sense. One of these is the contract between buyer and seller which underlies every trade transaction.

The trade contract is rarely a formal document drawn up by lawyers and signed, witnessed and sealed before being locked away in a safe, although standardised forms of contract are the norm in certain trades. The pace of international trade would not allow such elaborate procedures and they are seldom necessary in any case. This does not mean, however, that no contract exists, and it is just as binding as its more formal cousin. The conditions of the contract are usually expressed in two or three documents, which, when taken together and accepted either in writing or by implication through a particular course of action, contain all the terms of the agreement between the parties. Those documents may include the initial specification in the buyer's enquiry, the *pro forma* invoice issued by the seller, and the buyer's confirmation of order, the last two constituting the legal offer and acceptance respectively.

In any international trade transaction, the difference between the price quoted for goods delivered at their destination is going to differ considerably from the price charged for those goods in the domestic market of the producing country. This is because of the additional costs which must be incurred in getting those goods from producer to consumer where the consumer is in a different country. Such costs will include the cost of inland transport used for delivery of the goods to the port of shipment, dock dues and the like (both here and at the port of destination), forwarding charges, the cost of ocean transport, import duty, inland transportation to the buyer, and insurance cover for the entire journey. Similar considerations will apply where goods are sent by air, road, rail, or a combination of any of these.

It is important at the time when the contract is entered into that both parties know exactly what their responsibilities are for making the arrangements for completion of each stage. More important from our point of view is that both parties know exactly which charges they will be responsible for paying. It is evident that the type of contract which is agreed between buyer and seller will have an effect both on the amount which is eventually charged on the invoice and on the documents which must be supplied by the sellers. For instance, if under the contract it is the sellers' responsibility to insure the goods in transit, then it will be necessary for an insurance document to be included in the documents eventually presented to the buyers. The terms applicable to a particular contract will be stated in the relevant sellers' invoice, and should be followed by the name of a place to allow identification of the exact point at which the responsibilities of the sellers end and those of the buyers commence.

Incoterms

With such a bewildering variety of responsibilities and costs to be borne, it can be seen that the potential areas for dispute in international contracts are vast. It is fortunate, therefore, that we have an organisation such as the International Chamber of Commerce (ICC), one of whose many functions is to standardise procedures worldwide in just such difficult areas as this. This standardisation has been achieved by the creation and publication of a range of contracts for use by participants in international trade. At the time of writing the current edition of these rules, the *International Procedures for the Interpretation of Trade Terms* (officially abbreviated to "Incoterms") published in 1980, is about to be replaced by the 1990 version which is in the final stages of preparation. The remainder of this chapter is therefore based upon these new rules, with comment and comparison with the previous rules where appropriate.

Use of these contracts is not mandatory; traders are free to reach whatever agreement suits their particular purposes when contracting with each other. However, where an ICC contract term is adopted any later dispute can readily be settled by reference to the appropriate responsibilities of each party under that particular form of contract. A particularly important aspect of Incoterms is that they specify the point at which the risk in the goods passes from the sellers to the buyers, thus making it relatively easy to determine whether or not the buyers are obliged to pay for goods which have been lost in transit.

Ex-works...(named point) (ExW terms)

The two extremes which are possible are where the sellers pay all costs involved in transporting the goods to the buyers, and where the buyers pay all those costs. For the purposes of international invoicing the basic selling price of goods reflects the first situation where the buyers are responsible and the ICC has followed previous usage in calling this type of contract ex-works. Variations on this term such as "ex-mill", "ex-go-down", etc, all amount to the same thing: the buyers are responsible for collecting the goods from the sellers' premises or such other place as may be named in the contracts and thereafter those goods are entirely their responsibility. In effect the buyers' foreign status is ignored and they are regarded no differently from domestic buyers. The sellers' main responsibility is to make the goods available at the agreed time, in suitable packing, to allow the collection to take place. Responsibility for the risk and expense in the goods passes from sellers to buyers at the time when the sellers make the goods available to the buyers, not at the time when the goods are collected by the latter. The most common instance of regular use of the ex-works contract occurs where exporting and importing countries are connected by road and the buyers dispatch their own lorry to collect the goods from the sellers' factory.

Free alongside ship (FAS terms)

It is both convenient and logical to consider Incoterms in the order in which the responsibility of the sellers builds up gradually to the point at which they are obliged under the contract to make all arrangements necessary for the delivery of the goods at their ultimate destination. Where the traditional method of sea carriage is being used it is the duty of the buyers to nominate the ship on which the goods will be conveyed, but because of the difficulties which the buyers may encounter in arranging transportation of the goods to that ship at the port where it is loading cargo, it is often convenient for the sellers to undertake these arrangements.

Where this is so, the contract terms are designated as free alongside ship (FAS). From the sellers' point of view, this is little different from an ex-works contract, except that the point of delivery is changed to the quayside at the port of loading nominated by the buyers. Their responsibilities regarding documentation change slightly, in that they are required to provide the buyers with a dock receipt or similar document as evidence that they have performed their tasks as required under the contract. The buyers' foreign status is still ignored, however: besides paying transportation costs from that point, the buyers must obtain any export documents which may be required and arrange for customs clearance of the goods and for their loading on board the carrying vessel. This is because they have in effect made a domestic purchase in a foreign country and technically therefore become the exporters themselves.

Free carrier ... (named place) (FCA terms)

Under FCA contract terms the sellers assume the major additional responsibility and expense of clearing the goods for export, which includes the obtaining of any export licence which may be required and attendance to customs formalities in their own country. FCA terms are particularly useful because they leave to the sellers all the arrangements which they are best suited by their geographical situation to make, and because they may be utilised for any mode of transportation or for combined transport. Transfer of risk, and responsibility for costs, takes place on delivery to the carrier at the place named in the contract except in the following circumstances:

(a) *Goods by rail* where they constitute a full wagonload, in which case the sellers are responsible for the loading of the wagon.

(b) *Goods by road or inland waterway* where they are loaded at the sellers' premises, in which case the sellers are responsible for loading the goods on to the carrying vehicle or vessel or into the buyers' container.

The sellers must provide the buyers with the carriers' usual document of receipt as evidence that they have fulfilled their obligations under the contract.

For convenience the buyers may sometimes ask the sellers to make arrangements for carriage of the goods, even though the contract terms are

FCA. When this occurs, and if the sellers agree to such an arrangement, they do so at the risk and expense of the buyers.

Free on board (FOB terms)

Under an FOB contract the sellers' responsibility is to deliver the goods at their own expense to the ship nominated by the buyers, clear the goods for export and pay for their loading on board the vessel. Although the full cost of loading is borne by the sellers it is interesting that the actual point at which the risk in the goods passes from the sellers to the buyers is where they cross the ship's rail. Technically, therefore, if the hawser of a crane breaks the resulting insurance claim will be under the sellers' policy if the goods hit the dock and under the buyers' policy if they hit the deck; what happens if they hit the rail is a legal nicety which the present writer has not investigated, but in practice where the contract terms are FOB the buyers would normally have insured the goods on a "warehouse to warehouse" basis and would therefore claim under that policy. These terms will be discussed in detail in Chapter 5, which deals with marine insurance.

As evidence of fulfilment of their obligations, the sellers must provide the buyers with documentary evidence of the loading of the goods on to the ship. In practice, this would normally be a "shipped" bill of lading but in some cases might be a lesser document such as a mate's receipt. It is worth noting that in all cases where documentary evidence of delivery at any point is required, that the document must be "clean", ie it must not contain any notation to the effect that the goods or packaging appear to be defective in any way and if this is not so the sellers are technically in breach of contract. Bills of lading and the clauses which may appear in them relating to the condition of the goods, form the subject of Chapter 3.

FOB terms are an ancient and traditional form of contract and are often quoted even though the circumstances of a particular shipment indicate that an FCA contract would be more appropriate. They are, for instance, not suitable for anything other than shipment by sea or inland waterway, and even then the use of a container or a trailer, or delivery to the carriers at any point other than the port of loading may make them inoperable.

Cost and freight (CFR terms – historically C&F terms)

Where shipment by sea is concerned, the next major cost which must be

allocated is the sum of money which will be charged by the owner of
the carrying vessel in consideration for delivering the goods to their port
of destination; normally this will include any charge made for unloading
them from the ship at that point. This charge is referred to as *freight* and
where it is to be the sellers' responsibility to pay it the contract is designated as cost and freight (CFR). It is an obligation of the sellers under
such a contract to provide the buyers with the transport document customary for the named destination. Payment of the freight must also be
evidenced, either by means of annotation of the bill of lading or by the
carrier's signed receipt. It is interesting to note that, although the sellers'
responsibilities for payment of costs are thereby extended to the port of
discharge, the risk in the goods still transfers to the buyers when the
goods cross the ship's rail at the port of loading, ie the point of FOB.

The remarks above regarding continued incorrect use of the FOB contract, apply equally to the CFR contract, often designated by its historical
abbreviation of C&F. Again it is only suitable for shipment by sea and is
inappropriate where goods are containerised or are received by the carriers other than at the port of loading. In this case the more appropriate
contract terms are likely to be CPT, described below.

Carriage paid to ... (named point of destination) (CPT terms)

CPT contract terms are to FCA what CFR are to FOB, ie they carry the
same basic responsibilities for the sellers with the additional obligation to
arrange and pay for shipment of the goods to their named destination
and to provide the buyers with transport documents applicable to the
mode of transport used. Like the FCA terms, they are capable of being
used for any mode of transportation and it can already be foreseen that
they will replace the CFR contract entirely.

Cost and insurance (C&I terms); cost, insurance and freight (CIF terms); carriage and insurance paid to ... (named destination) (CIP terms)

It is convenient at this point to consider the case where the sellers are
required under the contract to insure the goods for their journey. Such
insurance cover relates to marine risks only; war and other special risks
are not included and if required by the buyer may be charged for in

addition to the basic contract price. The basic contract responsibilities to which the requirement for the sellers to insure the goods may be added are FOB, CFR and CPT. In the case of the first, the contract is then said to be on cost and insurance terms (C&I), in the case of the second cost, insurance and freight (CIF), and in the case of the last carriage and insurance paid to ... (named destination). C&I contracts are not in fact covered by Incoterms, but are mentioned because they are reasonably commonplace, particularly where the exporting country has introduced protectionist measures insisting that all exports are covered by its own national insurance company. In all cases the risk in the goods still passes from sellers to buyers as they cross the ship's rail at the port of loading.

Delivered ex-ship (DES terms)

It will have been noticed that between FOB and CIF contracts the sellers' responsibility for costs increased whilst their assumption of the risk in the goods remained static. In certain trades, particularly where bulk cargoes are concerned, it is the custom for this risk of the sellers to be extended to whatever point is specified. The first of these to be considered is where the sellers' responsibilities end when they make the goods available for collection by the buyers, still in the ship but alongside the quay at the port of discharge. Such a contract is expressed as delivered ex-ship (DES). It is the buyers' responsibility to arrange for the discharge of the goods from the ship and their clearance through customs. It has already been mentioned that the amount paid to the carrier in freight normally includes the cost of discharge of the goods, and this is certainly true for general cargo carried in liner vessels (the meaning of this term is covered in Chapter 3). With bulk cargoes, however, there is often a need for specialised equipment such as grabs, conveyors or pumping or suction machinery, which is both expensive and more readily provided by the buyers, who are also better placed to see to the hiring of labour to assist in the discharge. In DES contracts it is the sellers' responsibility to insure the goods up to the point where delivery is made to the buyers.

Delivered ex-quay (duty paid/unpaid) ... (named destination point) (DEQ terms)

One step further in the proceedings sees the cargo discharged from the ship and ready for collection on the quay by the buyers. Where the sellers have agreed to carry the risk and expense up to this point, the contract is stated to be on delivered ex-quay (DEQ) terms, and this may be qualified as "duty paid" or "duty unpaid" according to whether or not the sellers have agreed to accept this additional responsibility and expense. If such is the case, the sellers have effectively imported the goods into the buyers' country and are then making a domestic sale in that country.

Delivered duty unpaid ... (named point) (DDU terms)

Here the sellers are obliged to undertake all the costs and risks involved in bringing the goods to the point of destination named in the contract, save only any duty or taxes payable in order for the goods to be imported. DDU terms are applicable to any means of transportation.

Delivered duty paid ... (named point) (DDP terms)

We now reach the furthest extreme regarding the sellers' responsibility, that where they agree to deliver the goods to the buyers' warehouse free of any extra charge, having been responsible for inland carriage in the buyers' country in addition to all the expenses up to the point of ex-quay duty paid. Such a contract is described in Incoterms as delivered duty paid (DDP) but in practice is far more likely to be identified by the quotation on the invoice of a "delivered" price, or by the somewhat archaic expression "franco". As with the ex-works contract, it is commonest where two countries are connected by road, but in this case it is the sellers', rather than the buyers', vehicle which carries the goods to their destination.

Delivered at frontier ... (named point) (DAF terms)

Finally, we must consider a contract which has been designed principally to cater for overland international trade. We have already seen that the ex-works and DDP contracts are frequently used for road transport where either the sellers or buyers have agreed to be responsible for the whole journey. It is, however, possible to move the point of transfer of responsibility to one of the intervening frontiers en route by using the delivered at frontier (DAF) contract. The actual point of transfer in this case is between customs barriers, ie after clearance for export but before the customs border of the adjoining country.

These, then, are the 13 types of contract provided for in Incoterms, with one extra, the C&I contract, added for good measure. The benefits accruing from specifying that Incoterms will apply cannot be over-emphasised, since each party will then know exactly what is expected of them. With differing local interpretations of commercial terms, for instance the varying meanings of the term FOB in the United States, such understanding is essential. Naturally, having opted for a particular contract, it behoves sellers to then make sure that the price quoted reflects all the costs which they will have to bear as a result. Since at the time of writing the 1990 version of Incoterms has not yet come into force it is likely that some time will elapse before the new terms are universally adopted, and it is therefore worthwhile to mention the ousted terms from the 1980 version which will no doubt continue to be encountered in the interim:

(a)   carriage paid (DCP) replaced by CPT terms
(b)   ex-quay (EXQ) replaced by DEQ terms
(c)   ex-ship (EXS) replaced by DES terms
(d)   FOB airport (FOA) replaced by FCA terms
(e)   free on rail (FOR)/free on truck (FOT) replaced by FCA terms
(f)   free carrier (FRC) replaced by FCA terms.

Documentation

Thus far, we have been concerned only with the aspects of the contract which relate to the actual movement of the goods and the division between the contracting parties of the costs and responsibilities relating to such movement. There are, however, many other aspects which should be covered in the contract. One of these is the question of sup-plementary documentation. It is, of course, the buyer's responsibility to ensure that all the required documents are called for in the contract. At best, an omission will cause inconvenience; at worst, it could mean that the goods cannot be imported at all. The different types of document used in international trade are examined in detail at a later stage, but only buyers in individual countries can know for certain which docu-ments they require for their own purposes and which are required by the authorities in those countries. For the latter, a regularly updated publi-cation such as Croner's *Guide for Importers* is invaluable for British importers, while for forwarders, bankers, and many others, the compan-ion *Guide for Exporters* gives similar information for every other country in the world. The same information can usually be obtained from other sources, such as the consulates of the countries concerned, but updating, language and work pressures all combine to make such sources generally unsatisfactory.

Whatever the source of the information, the document must be called for in the contract. It is of little use including additional requirements in any letter of credit which may be issued at the buyer's behest as a result of the contract, since if those requirements are sufficiently onerous the sellers may quite legally choose to ignore both contract and credit. They may, in fact, even have rights against the buyers for breach of contract for not having provided a letter of credit in accordance with the terms of the agreement.

Goods

Similarly, the full specification of the required goods must be given by the buyers at the contract stage. Sellers are under no obligation to hold a contract price if the specification is altered at a later stage. Once again, the most common time for such a change to be made, surreptitiously, is in the letter of credit, so it is essential when sellers receive such instruments that they examine them carefully and compare them with the contract terms.

Bank charges

Finally, a word about bank charges. They are not usually very high in comparison to the value of the consignment, but nonetheless are a frequent source of dispute between sellers and buyers as they are almost invariably overlooked at the contract stage. Consequently, when they arise, there is no guidance, either from Incoterms or from the contract itself, regarding who is responsible for their payment. Common sense suggests that each party should bear that portion of any bank charges which relates to their own side of the transaction, but the law of agency says that principals are responsible for reasonable costs incurred by their agents; since in a collection transaction the seller is the principal, and in a credit transaction the buyer is the principal, and all the banks involved are acting as agents forming a continuous chain from the principal, it follows that, legally speaking, all bank charges are for the seller under a collection and for the buyer under a credit. All too frequently, however, the choice of a particular method of settlement is not the result of a freely negotiated agreement but is imposed by one or other of the parties acting from a position of strength. When this is the case, resentment is often engendered in the other party, and so the seeds of dispute are sown.

Leaving aside financing charges for the moment, the charges which will accrue to a collection will be the commissions (plus any out-of-pocket expenses) charged by each bank involved, with a minimum of one (where a bank uses its own overseas branch as collecting agent and charges merely for the one service—an increasingly rare occurrence these days) and a possible maximum of four (where a domestic bank uses a local branch of a recognised international bank as its agent, which in turn passes the item to its branch in the buyer's country, which may well present for settlement through the buyer's bank), plus any stamp duty which may be payable on the bill of exchange, and any reimbursement commission if the contract stipulates payment in the currency of a third country.

A letter of credit will certainly attract opening commission, probably advising commission and negotiation commission, with possibly confirmation commission and reimbursement commission as well. In all cases any additional services provided, such as telex costs and postal charges, will probably be added.

It is important that agreement is reached at the contract stage regarding who is to pay these charges and any financing fees. Only when such agreement has been reached is it possible for sellers to know exactly what their profit on a transaction will be, and for buyers to know the true cost of the goods which they are purchasing.

These, then, are the aspects of the international trade contract of which every person involved in the handling of a bill or credit transaction should be aware. No attempt has been made to investigate the intricacies of contract law in this chapter, and for the most part there is no need to do so, but in the remainder of this book such reference will be made when it has a direct bearing on the subject under discussion.

3
Marine bills of lading

It is necessary to consider the marine bill of lading separately from other documents because of its immense importance as a security document. This importance arises because, apart from being a receipt for the goods and in many cases evidence of the contract of carriage, it has one quality which is unique among transport documents in that it can be a document of title to the goods which it covers.

Negotiability

This is made possible by the bill of lading's quality of negotiability. Just as title to the proceeds of a cheque which is made out to the order of the payee can be transferred by simple endorsement, so can title to the goods covered by a bill of lading be transferred, if the consignee is shown as "order". Since the carrier will not deliver the goods without production of the bill of lading, its transfer for value amounts to a sale of the goods and, furthermore, if a buyer refuses to pay for them, the holder of the bill of lading can obtain possession of the goods.

Features of a bill of lading

Please refer to the example of an ocean bill of lading illustrated overleaf.

| SHIPPER | Bill of Lading | Page 2 |

B/L No.

Ref.-No.

| CONSIGNEE |

Hapag-Lloyd AG
EURO-PACIFIC
Westbound Service

| NOTIFY ADDRESS (carrier not responsible for failure to notify; see clause 21 hereof): | **Place of receipt: |

| *Local vessel: | *From: | **Place of delivery: |

| OCEAN VESSEL: | PORT OF LOADING: |

| PORT OF DISCHARGE: | *For transhipment to: |

| Marks and Nos. Container Nos. | Number and kind of packages; description of goods | Gross weight kilos | Measurement |

Particulars furnished by shipper of goods

ORIGINAL

Total No. of containers/packages:

Movement:

Freight/Charge indicator:

All agreements or freight engagements for the shipment of the goods are superseded by this Bill of Lading, except the conditions of the applicable tariff which are available from the carrier and which are deemed to be incorporated in this Bill of Lading. In case of inconsistency of any conditions of the applicable tariff with the terms stated on page 1 and 2 of this Bill of Lading the latter shall prevail unless otherwise expressly provided for herein. All the terms of this Bill of Lading, whether written, typed, stamped, or printed, are accepted and agreed by the merchant to be binding as fully as if signed by the merchant any local customs or privileges to the contrary notwithstanding.
IN WITNESS WHEREOF the number of original Bills of Lading stated below all of this tenor and date has been signed, one of which being accomplished the others to stand void.

| Freight payable at: | Place and date of issue: |

| Number of original Bs/L: | For the carrier: |

*Applicable only when document used for transhipment (see clause 2 b)
**Applicable only when document used for INTERMODAL transportation (see clause 2 c)

62 15 30 01 80 Printed in the Federal Republic of Germany

Face (page 1) of bill of lading

Bill of Lading

Page 1

Hapag-Lloyd Aktiengesellschaft — Ballindamm 25 · 2000 Hamburg 1 –

Gen. Agent in USA: United States Navigation (Pacific), Inc., P O Box 7913, San Francisco, Calif. 94120 (for P. O. B.); One Maritime Plaza, San Francisco, Calif. 94111

Received for Shipment the goods mentioned on page 2, in apparent good order and condition unless otherwise indicated in this Bill of Lading to be carried to the port of discharge or, if so provided for, to the place of delivery mentioned on page 2 and there to be delivered on payment of the charges thereon and on due performance of all obligations at the merchant. If the goods in whole or in part are shut out from the ship named herein for any cause, the carrier shall have the liberty to forward them under the terms of this Bill of Lading on the next available ship of this line or at carrier's option of any other line.

It is agreed that the custody and carriage of the goods are subject to the terms stated on page 1 and 2 herein, which shall govern both the relations, whatsoever they may be, between the merchant and the carrier, master and ship in every contingency, whensoever and wheresoever occurring and whether the carrier be acting as bailee, warehouseman or in any other relation whatever and also in the event of deviation of or unseaworthiness of the ship at the time of loading or inception of the voyage or subsequently and none of the terms of this Bill of Lading shall be deemed to have been waived by the carrier unless by express waiver in writing. If any part of any term of this Bill of Lading contract is not enforceable or is inconsistent with the law applicable to this Bill of Lading contract, that circumstance shall not affect the validity of any other term hereof. This Bill of Lading contract shall be governed by Law of the Federal Republic of Germany. The titles of the following articles have been printed for the convenience of the merchant only and said titles shall not be considered binding for purposes of construing or interpreting any clause.

DEFINITIONS

1. In this Bill of Lading, the word 'ship' shall include any substituted vessel, and any craft, lighter or other means of conveyance owned, chartered or operated by the carrier; the word 'carrier' shall include the ship, her owner, operator, master, demise charterer, and if bound hereby the time charterer; the word 'shipper' shall include the person named as such in this Bill of Lading and the person for whose account the goods are shipped; the word 'merchant' shall include the shipper, the consignee, the holder of this Bill of Lading, the receiver and the owner of the goods.

[The remainder of this page consists of dense multi-column fine print covering the standard Bill of Lading terms and conditions, including sections titled: RESPONSIBILITY AND JURISDICTION; SERVANTS, AGENTS AND CONTRACTORS; VOYAGE; OPTIONS OF THE CARRIER; GOVERNMENT ORDERS; DESCRIPTION OF GOODS; SUPPLY OF CARRIER'S CONTAINERS; OPTIONS OF STOWAGE; SPECIAL STOWAGE; SPECIAL CARGO; BOTH TO BLAME COLLISION; GENERAL AVERAGE; DISCHARGE AND DELIVERY; RESPONSIBILITY OF MERCHANT IN CONNECTION WITH THE GOODS; FREIGHT AND OTHER CHARGES; STATUTORY EXEMPTIONS; FIRE; IDENTITY OF CARRIER; ADJUSTMENT OF CLAIMS, DECLARATION OF VALUE, TIME LIMITATION; NOTICE OF LOSS OR DAMAGE; FAILURE TO NOTIFY; BREMEN/BREMERHAVEN — the body text being too small to transcribe reliably.]

Reverse (page 2) of bill of lading

Shipper

Frequently the name of the sellers of the goods will appear here, although occasionally the name of a forwarding agent or, if the sellers are merchants, the name of the actual manufacturers may be substituted. This is the counterparty to the carriers in the contract of carriage and it is important to remember that the carriers owe no contractual obligation to any other party. Since the shippers are the party to whom the carriers address the bill of lading in its capacity as a receipt for the goods, it is their endorsement which must appear first on an "order" bill of lading to constitute it as a negotiable instrument.

Consignee

As stated above, the word "order" must be inserted here to confer negotiability on the bill of lading. If the name of an actual consignee is substituted, the document (known as a "straight" bill of lading) is no longer negotiable, nor is it a document of title, since the carrier will deliver the goods to the named party without production of the bill of lading. For practical purposes a straight bill of lading is little more than a sea waybill, which will be discussed in the following chapter.

Notify party

Although they will accept the word "order" as the consignee, the carriers still require the name and address of someone whom they can contact when the goods arrive at their destination, since goods remaining on the quay or at a container depot for undue time waste valuable space, which, of course, costs money. It is also worth noting that, *prima facie*, the notify party is considered to be the party responsible for the goods after they have been loaded on board the carrying vessel (see section on FOB contract terms, Chapter 2) and this can have embarrassing consequences for banks who have their own name inserted as notify party, having deluded themselves that this will give them extra security.

Name of carrying vessel

Often there is also the provision for the name of a local vessel which carries the goods to a main port for shipment on the ocean vessel. In this instance, and in the case where the preamble to the bill of lading states "received for shipment" rather than "shipped" or "loaded" (see below), the name of the ocean vessel can only be taken as an indication of intention, unless there is a separate signed and dated endorsement on the document stating that goods have been loaded on that vessel.

Port of loading; port of destination

Note that the carriers reserve the right to vary the destination of the goods if they see fit (". . . or as near thereto as she may safely come"). This right is one which is frequently exercised in time of war, or where strikes or port congestion make a call at the intended port of destination an uneconomic or unsafe proposition.

Marks and numbers

Packages usually have stencilled on them in large characters an abbreviated form of the consignee's name to assist in identification at the port of destination. The name of the port of destination and port of transhipment, if applicable, is similarly stencilled so that cargo for discharge at a particular port is readily identifiable in the ship's hold. Finally, each package within a consignment is given an individual number for identification purposes. When goods are received at the docks for loading, marks and numbers are copied from the packages themselves on to a mate's receipt or similar document, and it is from this that the details inserted on the bill of lading are derived. The bill of lading is thus the definitive document and it is important that all other documents agree with it in respect of marks and numbers.

Number and type of packages

If the carriers notice that either the goods or the packages are defective or damaged in any way, they will protect themselves by clausing the bill of lading appropriately, making it a claused or "dirty" bill of lading. This obviously makes it unattractive to any subsequent holder and may also affect the insurance cover. Many disputes have arisen in the past over what constitutes a dirty bill of lading and the problem has been addressed by the ICC in Incoterms, and in *Uniform Customs and Practice for Documentary Credits* (see Chapter 12 Article 34). They stress that to be considered as not clean, a bill of lading must specifically refer to an observed defect in the goods or packing. Clauses which simply describe the packing, such as "secondhand drums", clauses which reserve the carriers' rights where specific types of packing are used (cartons are a frequent cause of the use of this clause) and clauses whereby the carriers disclaim responsibility for weight, quality, number of pieces, etc ("shipper's load and count") do not turn a clean bill of lading into a dirty one. To this list should be added the various clauses which carriers often use which relate to particular trade routes or ports; these seldom affect the cleanness of the bill in any way.

There are some clauses, however, which must be regarded as transforming the bill of lading into a dirty one. Where such clauses are to be expected from the particular trade, such as "surface rust" if the goods are unprotected steel girders, then sellers and buyers are well advised to agree between them at the contract stage that such clauses are acceptable and to incorporate a provision to this effect in any letter of credit which may be involved.

A relatively common practice among shipowners has been the provision of a clean bill of lading where it would otherwise have been claused, in exchange for the provision of an indemnity stating that the shippers will reimburse the carriers in respect of any claims which may be made against them for goods delivered in a damaged condition. This practice is potentially damaging to the interests of the buyers and of any intermediate endorsee of the bill, and is considered by many to be illegal, since the bill of lading usually contains a statement that the goods have been received in "apparent good order and condition". Since this could involve the carriers and the shippers in being sued jointly or individually for misrepresentation, it is difficult to see who benefits from the procedure in the long term, and it should be discouraged as much as possible. Certainly no bank should ever agree to add its counter-signature to such an indemnity, as has sometimes happened, since it could be the agent of the buyer and may well also be an intermediate holder of the bill.

Description of goods

This need not be detailed, provided that it does not contradict the description given in the commercial invoice, and also provided that the regulations of the importing country do not call for a full description to appear on the bill. Upon the description given, the carriers will base the rate of freight which they apply to the consignment and it will usually include the gross and nett weights and cubic measurements of the packages. This information is required by the carriers both for calculation of freight and for safe stowage of the goods in the ship.

Freight

The money payable to the carrier for transportation of the goods – freight – is payable even if the ship and goods fail to arrive at the destination. The bill of lading will state whether it has been paid (*prima facie* evidence of CFR, CIF, DDP, etc contract terms) or is to be paid at destination, either by those words or "freight forward", "freight collect", etc (contract terms ex-works, FAS, FOB, FCA, etc). Many countries insist that full freight details appear on the bill of lading.

Number of original bills of lading

Bills of lading are usually issued in a set of two or more "originals" plus any number of copy or non-negotiable bills of lading for record purposes. Historically, this was to cater for the uncertainty of international mails when all such material was sent by sailing ships, which were far more susceptible to delay or even total loss than are more modern forms of transport. One original would be (and often still is) dispatched to the consignee and the second similarly mailed two or three days later to ensure that it would be transported on a different conveyance. The originals are equal in all respects and the goods will be delivered against production of any one of them. It is important, therefore, to account for the whereabouts of all of the original bills of lading in the set if title to the goods is to be retained. At the present day, there is really very little advantage in perpetuating this anachronism, which is wasteful of material, time and money, but tradition, as always, dies hard, and banks and trades alike persist in calling for multiple originals where one would in fact be sufficient. In any case, some countries insist on a particular number of originals being issued for their own imports.

Signature of the master or agent

Most carriers have appointed agents for various purposes, including the signing of bills of lading, in every port at which their vessels call. Each of these agents will probably have a number of persons who are authorised to sign. Normally the signature, or rather, the capacity in which it is given is only important when a dispute exists as to whether a particular document is a carrier's bill of lading in the traditional sense, or a house bill of lading issued by a forwarding agent. This matter is discussed further in Chapter 4.

Date

The date of a "shipped" bill of lading is taken to be the date of shipment of the goods. It should be remembered that carriers are frequently very accommodating in the matter of dating bills of lading where their customer, the shipper, is contractually obliged to ship the goods by a certain date. Banks, however, are often in a position to check on the apparent authenticity of the date given and, if it is obviously a misrepresentation, may well reject documents if presented under a letter of credit, since, as we have seen, they are acting as agents for the buyers and must do all they can to protect that party's interests.

"Shipped"/"received"

Many bills of lading bear the word "shipped" printed on them, and this may be taken as evidence that the goods are actually on board the named vessel. Where the bill of lading merely states that goods have been received for shipment it can be converted into a "shipped" bill by the insertion of an appropriate clause by the carrier. This clause should confirm the name of the ship, include the place and date of shipment and be separately signed or otherwise authenticated by the carrier. In practice, however, ship and place of loading are often omitted, the assumption being that confirmation of shipment is as described elsewhere in the bill of lading.

Terms in common use to describe bills of lading

Charter party bill of lading (illus. pp 33-4)

When a ship has been hired to perform a specific task or voyage, the document forming the contract between the hirer and the owner is called the *charter party*. There are two distinct types of charter, the *time charter* and the *voyage charter*. Time charters usually cause little or no problem, since they are frequently the result of fleet owners supplementing the tonnage available to them in order to cover short-term deficiencies due

Page 2

CODE NAME: "CONGENBILL" . EDITION 1978

Shipper

ULSTER MEAT EXPORT CO. LTD.
Antrim Road
BELFAST

BILL OF LADING
TO BE USED WITH CHARTER-PARTIES

B/L No. A 1.

Reference No.

ORIGINAL

Consignee
To the order of
ALEXANDRIA COMMERCIAL AND
    MARITIME BANK

Notify address

HASSAN HASSAN
Trading Partnership,
P.O. Box XL239
CAIRO

Vessel   **Port of loading**
'PACIFIC MARCHIONESS' DUN LAOGHAIRE

Port of discharge
ALEXANDRIA / Egypt

Shipper's description of goods   **Gross weight**

3765 cartons of fresh frozen   Gross Wt.   Nett Wt.
bnoless (boneless) beef
forequarters   103,681 Kgs.   99,784 Kgs.

Clean on Board
L/C no.: 86159
Carrying temperature not warmer than -20 degrees C
Freight Prepaid

(of which XXXXXX   on deck at Shipper's risk; the Carrier not
being responsible for loss or damage howsoever arising)

Freight payable as per
CHARTER-PARTY dated ...... 4th July, 1986.

FREIGHT ADVANCE.

Received on account of freight:

        - nil -

Time used for loading .... days .... hours.

S H I P P E D at the Port of Loading in apparent good order and
condition on board the Vessel for carriage to the
Port of Discharge or so near thereto as she may safely get the goods
specified above.

Weight, measure, quality, quantity, condition, contents and value unknown.

IN WITNESS whereof the Master or Agent of the said Vessel has signed
the number of Bills of Lading indicated below all of this tenor and date,
any one of which being accomplished the others shall be void.

FOR CONDITIONS OF CARRIAGE SEE OVERLEAF

Freight payable at	Place and date of issue
FREIGHT PREPAID	DUN LAOGHAIRE, 7th July, 1986.
Number of original Bs/L	Signature
3 (three)	

Printed and Sold by S. STRAKER & SONS LTD.
23A Lime Street, London, E.C.3
By Authority of the Baltic & International Maritime Conference
Copenhagen

Example of face of charter party bill of lading

BILL OF LADING
TO BE USED WITH CHARTER-PARTIES
CODE NAME: "CONGENBILL"
EDITION 1978
ADOPTED BY
THE BALTIC AND INTERNATIONAL
MARITIME CONFERENCE (BIMCO)

Conditions of Carriage.

(1) All terms and conditions, liberties and exceptions of the Charter Party, dated as overleaf, are herewith incorporated. The Carrier shall in no case be responsible for loss of or damage to cargo arisen prior to loading and after discharging.

(2) General Paramount Clause.
The Hague Rules contained in the International Convention for the Unification of certain rules relating to Bills of Lading, dated Brussels the 25th August 1924 as enacted in the country of shipment shall apply to this contract. When no such enactment is in force in the country of shipment, the corresponding legislation of the country of destination shall apply, but in respect of shipments to which no such enactments are compulsorily applicable, the terms of the said Convention shall apply.

Trades where Hague-Visby Rules apply.
In trades where the International Brussels Convention 1924 as amended by the Protocol signed at Brussels on February 23rd 1968 – the Hague-Visby Rules – apply compulsorily, the provisions of the respective legislation shall be considered incorporated in this Bill of Lading. The Carrier takes all reservations possible under such applicable legislation, relating to the period before loading and after discharging and while the goods are in the charge of another Carrier, and to deck cargo and live animals.

(3) General Average.
General Average shall be adjusted, stated and settled according to York-Antwerp Rules 1974, in London unless another place is agreed in the Charter.

Cargo's contribution to General Average shall be paid to the Carrier even when such average is the result of a fault, neglect or error of the Master, Pilot or Crew. The Charterers, Shippers and Consignees expressly renounce the Netherlands Commercial Code, Art. 700, and the Belgian Commercial Code, Part II, Art. 148.

(4) New Jason Clause.
In the event of accident, danger, damage or disaster before or after the commencement of the voyage, resulting from any cause whatsoever, whether due to negligence or not, for which, or for the consequence of which, the Carrier is not responsible, by statute, contract or otherwise, the goods, Shippers, Consignees or owners of the goods shall contribute with the Carrier in general average to the payment of any sacrifices, losses or expenses of a general average nature that may be made or incurred and shall pay salvage and special charges incurred in respect of the goods.

If a salving ship is owned or operated by the Carrier, salvage shall be paid for as fully as if the said salving ship or ships belonged to strangers. Such deposit as the Carrier or his agents may deem sufficient to cover the estimated contribution of the goods and any salvage and special charges thereon shall, if required, be made by the goods, Shippers, Consignees or owners of the goods to the Carrier before delivery.

(5) Both-to-Blame Collision Clause.
If the Vessel comes into collision with another ship as a result of the negligence of the other ship and any act, neglect or default of the Master, Mariner, Pilot or the servants of the Carrier in the navigation or in the management of the Vessel, the owners of the cargo carried hereunder will indemnify the Carrier against all loss or liability to the other or non-carrying ship or her Owners in so far as such loss or liability represents loss of, or damage to, or any claim whatsoever of the owners of said cargo, paid or payable by the other or non-carrying ship or her Owners to the owners of said cargo and set-off, recouped or recovered by the other or non-carrying ship or her Owners as part of their claim against the carrying Vessel or Carrier. The foregoing provisions shall also apply where the Owners, operators or those in charge of any ship or ships or objects other than, or in addition to, the colliding ships or objects are at fault in respect of a collision or contact.

For particulars of cargo, freight, destination, etc., see overleaf.

Reverse of charter party bill of lading

to such causes as repairs and maintenance. Voyage charters, however, are, as the name suggests, entered into with the intention of covering one or a limited number of voyages only, and bills of lading issued while they are in force are subject to their terms. They are not, therefore, evidence of the full conditions of the contract of carriage, since the charter party may perhaps provide for deviation from the voyage under certain circumstances, a possibility which is undesirable from the point of view of holders of bills of lading who are waiting to receive their goods.

It is interesting that the 1990 revision of Incoterms requires the sellers, where they are obliged to provide a transport document under the contract and that transport document is a charter party bill of lading, to provide additionally a copy of the charter party itself. Whilst this may or may not satisfy holders of the bill of lading, it is unlikely to change the attitude of banks, who will be unwilling to take on the additional responsibility of examining the small print of the charter party to ascertain the degree of risk which it imparts to the transaction.

Combined transport bill of lading

This is increasingly used nowadays when many goods are shipped in containers. Container depots have been established in many areas remote from the docks and the carrier takes the goods in charge and delivers them at these depots. The bill of lading therefore covers one or more trips by rail, road or inland waterway besides the main ocean voyage. A combined transport bill of lading will normally state merely that the goods have been received for shipment rather than shipped and the name of any vessel given on them can only be taken as evidence of intent rather than fact. Where it is essential under the contract to provide a "shipped" bill of lading, a combined transport bill can be satisfactorily converted by the addition by the carriers' agent of a clause to the effect that goods have actually been shipped. This clause should confirm the name of the carrying vessel, and be separately signed and dated by the carriers in addition to the date and signature which are already on the bill in its capacity as a receipt for the goods. To avoid the difficulties and inconvenience which often attend the securing of the addition of this clause, it is common sense that where such mode of transport is intended, buyers and sellers at the contract stage agree that the terms of the contract shall be one of the three types specifically intended to cover multi-modal transport, ie FCA, CPT or CIP. If this is done, and the method of settlement is to be a letter of credit, buyers should be careful that they do not spoil the whole thing by allowing their bank to then issue a credit calling for "shipped" bills of lading. Too many bank application forms for credits bear this requirement as a pre-printed clause: this does not mean that it cannot be deleted.

House bill of lading

See the section in Chapter 4 on "Other transport documents".

Liner bill of lading

A liner vessel is one which sails regularly between specified ports, departing and arriving on published dates regardless of whether or not she is filled with cargo. Such a service is obviously preferable in most circumstances to that offered by a "tramp" vessel which can await a full cargo before sailing and can deviate from the voyage if sufficient inducement is offered. For some cargoes, however, particularly bulk ones or those requiring specialised accommodation, or where the contemplated voyage is not covered by a liner service, the only practical form of transport is a tramp ship, often operating under a voyage charter, and the already-mentioned problems with bills of lading issued under such circumstances should be remembered.

Liner owners often group together in "conferences"—associations which allocate sailing frequencies, ports of loading and ports of destination between their members, reach agreement on rates of freight to be applied to particular goods (freight tariff) and offer inducements to shippers to use only conference line vessels. At first sight this seems to smack of restrictive practice but some insurance for owners against the possibility of being obliged to sail a half-empty ship to the other side of the world is essential and the conference is intended to provide such security. The terms "conference" and "liner" are not synonymous, since not all liner operators are conference members, though the "pirates" encounter fierce opposition from those who are.

Ocean bills of lading

These are issued by the carrier responsible for the main ocean voyage. Where goods are carried to the ocean vessel in feeder vessels, bills of lading issued by the owners of these vessels, even if they purport to be

Hapag-Lloyd Aktiengesellschaft Hamburg/Bremen	Bill of Lading Page 2 FOR MULTIMODAL TRANSPORT OR PORT TO PORT SHIPMENT

SHIPPER: PRINCETON PIPES LTD. MALDON, ESSEX.	VOYAGE-NO. W88	B/L-NO. 12345
	SHIPPER'S REFERENCE	

CONSIGNEE:
ORDER

Hapag-Lloyd
Europe – North America Services

NOTIFY ADDRESS (carrier not responsible for failure to notify; see clause 22 hereof): EASTERN TUBE SUPPLIES LTD., P.O.BOX 890045 BUFFALO, N.Y.	Place of receipt (Applicable only when document used for MULTIMODAL transport; see clause 2c): RAINHAM FREIGHT TERMINAL

*Local vessel:	*From:	Place of delivery (Applicable only when document used for MULTIMODAL transport; see clause 2c):
OCEAN VESSEL: NURNBERG EXPRESS	PORT OF LOADING: LIVERPOOL	BROOKLYN CONTAINER YARD NEW YORK
PORT OF DISCHARGE: NEW YORK	*For transhipment to:	

Container Nos, Seal Nos; Marks and Nos. CNTR.NO.0987654321 SEAL NO. 1234 ETSL NEW YORK 1/34	Number and kind of packages; description of goods 34 CARTONS PLASTIC TUBING FREIGHT PREPAID	Gross weight (kg) 185	Measurement (cbm) 8.5

COPY NOT NEGOTIABLE

ABOVE PARTICULARS AS DECLARED BY SHIPPER

Total No. of containers/packages: 1 CONTAINER	Shipper's declared value (see clause 3 hereof): $	Received by the carrier from the shipper in apparent good order and condition (unless otherwise noted herein) the total number or quantity of containers or other packages or units indicated (see Box opposite), stated by the shipper to comprise the goods specified above, for carriage subject to all the terms hereof (INCLUDING THE TERMS ON PAGE 1 HEREOF AND THE TERMS OF THE CARRIER'S APPLICABLE TARIFF) from the place of receipt or the port of loading, whichever is applicable, to the port of discharge or the place of delivery, whichever is applicable. In accepting this Bill of Lading the merchant expressly accepts and agrees to all its terms, conditions and exceptions whether printed, stamped or written, or otherwise incorporated, notwithstanding the non-signing of this Bill of Lading by the merchant. IN WITNESS WHEREOF the number of original Bills of Lading stated below all of this tenor and date has been signed, one of which being accomplished the others to stand void.
Movement:		

Freight and Charges:	Prepaid	Collect	
Ocean freight			
Multimodal Through Freight			
Origin Landfreight			Freight payable at: LONDON
Destination Landfreight			Place and date of issue: LONDON 15TH.MAY 1990
Origin Terminal Charges			
Destination Terminal Charges			Number of original Bs/L: TWO (2)
			For the carrier:
Appropriate columns to be marked with "X"			

* Applicable only when document used for transhipment (see clause 2 b)

150002 51 Printed in the Federal Republic of Germany

Completed "received" liner bill of lading

"through" bills of lading (see below), are of no value since they will not be accepted in exchange for the goods at the port of destination, nor indeed can they be evidence that the goods are even on board the ocean vessel. The only exception to this rule is where the owner of the local vessel is an accredited agent of the owner of the ocean vessel, but even then the bill of lading must be the ocean carrier's standard form and, to be acceptable as a "shipped" bill of lading, must bear the same additional clause as a combined transport bill relating to actual shipment on the ocean vessel (see page 37).

Short form bills of lading

These do not contain the full terms of the contract of carriage. Provided that they are not defective in any way, however, they remain documents of title and are almost universally accepted as good tender under contracts and letters of credit. A glance at the mass of densely-packed small print on the reverse of a standard bill of lading will make the reason for the genesis of the short-form alternative obvious to anyone familiar with printing and typesetting costs; the principle of the short-form bill is similar to the clause on the back of a bus ticket (another transport document) which says that the full terms of carriage will be made available at the request of the holder, a request which is, of course, seldom necessary.

Stale bills of lading

A bill of lading is usually considered to be stale when it is received at the port of destination later than the arrival date of the goods, although local regulations may require its presentation even earlier. Goods which are uncollected beyond a specified period after discharge incur charges called *demurrage* which must be paid by the holder of the bill of lading before they will be released. The level of such charges varies considerably, usually in line with the degree of congestion normally experienced in that particular port. Where they are high, even a short demurrage period may make the total cost of the goods an unattractive proposition to the buyers, causing them to seek avoidance of the contract. It should be noted that the staleness or otherwise of a bill of lading is irrelevant where it is presented under a letter of credit, for reasons which will be discussed in Chapter 13.

Through bills of lading

These cover voyages where goods must be transhipped from the ocean vessel to another vessel in order to reach their destination. The ocean carrier takes responsibility for the transhipment and for the selection of the oncarrying vessel. The term is also sometimes used to describe combined transport bills of lading.

Summary

From the above, the reasoning may be seen behind the common stipulation, both in contracts and in letters of credit, for presentation of a full set of clean, shipped, ocean bills of lading made out to order and endorsed in blank:

(a) a full set because if one of the originals is in the possession of someone else, they may get possession of the goods first;

(b) clean, because an unclean bill bears a clause which states that the carriers have observed the goods or the packaging to be defective in some way on delivery to them;

(c) shipped, because it is often important to the buyers to know that their goods are on board a specific vessel and will, all being well, arrive at a predeterminable time;

(d) ocean, because that is the bill of lading which must be presented at the port of destination in order to secure possession of the goods;

(e) to order, because that gives the bill of lading its quality of negotiability;

(f) endorsed in blank, because that enables the holder of the bill to obtain the goods when they arrive at their destination.

A number of countries impose special regulations relating to bills of lading covering goods which they are importing. Often these relate to the minimum amount of information which must appear on the bills, but sometimes the requirements are more unusual. Also, a number of countries require all bills of lading relating to their imports to be presented to their embassy or consulate in the exporting country for legalisation. As has been mentioned before, *Croner's Reference Book for Exporters* is invaluable in determining what, if any, special regulations apply to any particular country.

To sum up this chapter, we will briefly trace the life history of a bill of lading which conforms with the above description. Goods, space for which will previously have been booked by the shippers on that vessel, are presented at the advertised place for receiving cargo. In exchange, the carriers will issue a dock receipt, wharfinger's receipt, or the like, a copy of which will be retained by the carriers. It will state the number of packages received and their visible marks and numbers, and will comment on their apparent condition. The shipper will then prepare the bill of lading and submit it to the carriers for signature after the goods have been loaded on the carrying vessel.

The carriers will carefully check the details declared by the shippers against those on their copy of the dock receipt and will add to or amend the bill as appropriate, at the same time adding any clauses applicable to the particular type of goods or packing (not necessarily derogatory though almost invariably protective of the carriers' interests). They will then sign the original copies (not a contradiction in this context), date the bill, usually with the sailing date of the ship, and release it to the shippers against payment of the freight due, unless freight is to be paid at destination. The bill will then be endorsed in blank by the shippers and sent, possibly through the banking system if a collection or a letter of credit is the agreed method of settlement, to the buyers, who on arrival of the ship will present it to the carriers and receive the goods in exchange.

4
Other transport documents

The house bill of lading (illus. p 42)

House bills of lading are generally understood to be those issued by forwarding agents and much argument has taken place in the past regarding whether or not they may be accepted as good tender under a letter of credit which calls for presentation of a marine bill of lading. They become necessary when a forwarder is arranging shipment of goods for more than one client on the same vessel and between the same ports of loading and discharge, although for convenience and consistency forwarders often cover all shipments in this way.

When forwarders have a number of such consignments they consolidate them, which means that, so far as the carriers are concerned, all goods are declared on one bill of lading which shows the forwarders as shippers. To satisfy their individual clients, they then issue their own "bills of lading" which have similar functions to the carriers' bills but with subtle differences. They act as receipts for the goods addressed to the shippers by the forwarders instead of by the carriers (the word "carrier" is used in its literal rather than its legal sense here, but the legal implications will be discussed a little later). They may evidence the conditions of the contract between the shippers and the forwarders but not the conditions on which the true carrier is handling the goods. And they act as a means of transferring to a third party the right to take delivery of the goods from the forwarder on arrival at their destination. However, they convey no rights against the true carriers, who, of course, will require presentation of a signed original of their own bill of lading before releasing the goods. Legally, the owner of the goods is the party named as shipper on the marine bill of lading, or the consignee or endorsee of that bill.

The effect of these differences is to reduce the attractiveness of these

BILL OF LADING

Shipper		B/Lading number
ABLE COFFEE MACHINERY LTD		00000000

Shipper's Reference

11111111

Consignee (If 'Order', state Notify Party and Address)
TO ORDER

Notify Party (No claim shall attach for failure to notify)
AFRICAN COFFEE EXPORTERS LTD BLANTYRE, MALAWI

Afri-Freight Ltd
Ketts House
30-32 Staines Road
Hounslow
Middlesex
TW3 3JS
United Kingdom
Tel: 01-572 5371
Telex: 264237 AFLLDN
Fax: 01-570 8228

Place of Receipt	Port of Loading
	FELIXSTOWE

First Vessel	Port of transhipment
CHIARA	

Second Vessel	Port of Loading

LUSAKA Tel. 215012 Tlx. 40720, NAIROBI Tel. 23071/22000 Tlx. 22823
KAMPALA Tel. 57328 Tlx. 61324, KITWE Tel. 214981 Tlx. 53250
DAR ES SALAAM Tel. 29403 Tlx. 41625

Port of Discharge	Final Destination	Freight Payable at	Number of original Bs/L
DURBAN	BLANTYRE	LONDON	THREE

Marks and Numbers	Number and kind of packages: description of goods	Gross Weight	Measurement
A.C.E. BLANTYRE MALAWI VIA DURBAN NO.1	1 PALLET said to contain 10 CARTONS COFFEE MACHINERY	260KGS	0.910CBM

FREIGHT TO DURBAN, CHARGES AT DURBAN AND ON-CARRIAGE TO BLANTYRE PREPAID.

LETTER OF CREDIT NUMBER - said to be - 12345/6789

SHIPPED IN ACT...
14 MAR 19..
AFRI-FREIGHT LTD.

PARTICULARS OF GOODS ARE THOSE DECLARED BY SHIPPER

TO OBTAIN DELIVERY THIS BILL OF LADING, DULY ENDORSED, MUST BE DELIVERED TO —

AFRI - FREIGHT (M) LTD. BLANTYRE, MALAWI

Freight Details, Charges etc:

RECEIVED by the Carrier the Goods as specified above in apparent good order and condition unless otherwise stated, to be transported to such place as agreed, authorised or permitted herein and subject to all the terms and conditions appearing on the front and reverse of this Bill of Lading to which the Merchant agrees by accepting this Bill of Lading, any local privileges and customs notwithstanding.

The particulars given above as stated by the shipper and the weight, measure, quantity, condition, contents and value of the Goods are unknown to the Carrier.

In WITNESS whereof one (1) original Bill of Lading has been signed if not otherwise stated above, the same being accomplished the other(s), if any, to be void. If required by the Carrier one (1) original Bill of Lading must be surrendered duly endorsed in exchange for the Goods or delivery order.

LONDON 14 MAR 19..

Place and date of issue _____

Signed on behalf of the Carrier: Afri-Freight Ltd

AFRi-FREIGHT LTD.

by _____

Example of a house bill of lading

documents to banks who may be in part relying on their rights against the goods when either providing export finance against collections, issuing letters of credit, or financing imports by trust receipt facilities and the like. Although there are many notable exceptions, generally speaking, forwarding agents are less likely to be well known names than ship-owning companies, and banks may feel that they are relying on the goodwill of an organisation concerning which they have no knowledge and no means of acquiring information at short notice. Their natural tendency in these circumstances is to exercise the caution for which they are renowned and reject the document.

Forwarding agents

With modern methods of transportation of goods, particularly container-isation and multi-modal transport, the use of forwarding agents has become increasingly common, since such entities are geared to extract the maximum benefit from these methods. At one time forwarders were merely agents who, for a fee, would take on the responsibility of making all the necessary arrangements for the dispatch of goods; they have now risen in the hierarchy of the transport world to the status of contractual carriers. This is quite possible under English law, where to be a common carrier, a company (or individual) merely has to agree to accept full liability for the goods from the point at which it takes delivery of them to the point at which they are delivered to the holder of the house bill of lading. Thus, whereas the traditional bill of lading was signed "for the master", it is now far more common to find it signed "for the carrier" or simply signed under the name of the issuer.

The problem remains, however, that there is in many countries very little statutory control over who can call themselves a forwarding agent. Many are, quite literally, one-person concerns, often established by people who have previously worked for larger forwarders or for ship-ping companies and who are using the expertise acquired during such employment to make their own way in business. Thus the banks' worry about the people with whom they are dealing when presented with a house bill of lading is not lessened by the document being signed for the carrier.

FIATA

The answer must lie within the forwarding industry, which effectively is the only area in which measures can be taken to remedy the situation. Significant steps have already been taken in this direction by the Zurich-based International Association of Freight Forwarders (FIATA—Federation Internationale des Associations de Transitaires et Assimiles). The members of FIATA are national forwarders' associations, which in turn are associations of individual companies. FIATA has developed a standard forwarding agents' bill of lading (FBL) using standard conditions of carriage, which affiliates of its member organisations are entitled to use upon the granting of a licence. Before such a licence is issued, the National Association must have satisfied itself upon various relevant subjects such as capital adequacy of the licensee, the standard of expertise of its management and employees, and, most importantly, the level of indemnity insurance cover carried by the company in relation to its average turnover.

The FBL, as used by FIATA licensees, is a very distinctive document, currently a deep blue in colour and bearing the globe and ribbons FIATA logo prominently in its centre. Its format was arrived at in full consultation with the International Chamber of Commerce, and the ICC symbol, accompanied by that of the national association concerned, is prominent towards the top of the document. The licence number of the issuer is also given. The issuer accepts carrier's liability under internationally agreed rules for the performance of the contract of carriage for loss of or damage to the goods during such performance. There should be no doubt as to the acceptability of this document, but unfortunately disputes do still occur from time to time, since the wording of the ICC's *Uniform Customs and Practice for Documentary Credits* appears to disqualify it where a credit calls for presentation of a marine or ocean bill of lading. The ICC has ruled in favour of the FBL's acceptability, and has published that ruling (*Opinions of the ICC Banking Commission on Queries Relating to Uniform Customs and Practice for Documentary Credits 1984-1986*, ICC Publication No. 434). Most rejections, however, result from reliance on the UCPs themselves, which have yet to be amended. This question will be further considered in Chapter 12.

Even with full acceptance of the FIATA FBL, however, there still remains the large number of forwarding agents who do not use it, either through failure or inability to obtain a licence or because they consider that their own document should be acceptable to all concerned without further assurance from FIATA. The banks, understandably, are reluctant to maintain any sort of credit rating table to enable them to decide whether a particular forwarder's house bill should be acceptable or not.

Consignor		Customs Reference/Status	B. Lading number
ABLE COFFEE MACHINERY LTD			00000000 **GB**
		Shipper's Reference	11111111
FBL		F/Agent's Ref	

Consignee (If Order, state Notify Party and Address)	
TO ORDER	NEGOTIABLE FIATA COMBINED TRANSPORT BILL OF LADING issued subject to ICC Uniform Rules for a Combined Transport Document (ICC publication 298) **ICC**

Notify Party	
AFRICAN COFFEE EXPORTERS LTD BLANTYRE, MALAWI	AfriFreight Ltd Ketts House 30-32 Staines Road, Hounslow Middlesex TW3 3JS United Kingdom

AFL

FIATA Licence No. 1010

Tel: 01-572 5371
Telex: 264237 AFLLDN
Fax: 01-570 8228

LUSAKA Tel. 215012 Tlx. 40720, NAIROBI Tel. 23071/22000 Tlx. 22823
KAMPALA Tel. 57328 Tlx. 61324, KITWE Tel. 214981 Tlx. 53250
DAR ES SALAAM Tel. 29403 Tlx. 41625

Pre-Carriage By	Place of Receipt by Pre Carrier
Vessel/Trailer CHIARA	Port of Loading FELIXSTOWE
Port of Discharge DURBAN	Place of Delivery by On-Carrier BLANTYRE

Marks and Numbers	Number and Kind of Packages	Description of Goods	Gross Weight	Measurement
A.C.E. BLANTYRE MALAWI VIA DURBAN NO.1	1 PALLET said to contain 10 CARTONS COFFEE MACHINERY		260KGS	0.910CBM

FREIGHT TO DURBAN, CHARGES AT DURBAN AND ON-CARRIAGE TO BLANTYRE PREPAID.

LETTER OF CREDIT NUMBER - saID TO BE - 12345/6789

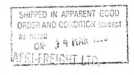

SHIPPED IN APPARENT GOOD ORDER AND CONDITION (except as noted ON- 14 MAR

AFRI-FREIGHT LTD

according to the declaration of the consignor

The goods and instructions are accepted and dealt with subject to the Standard Conditions printed overleaf.

Take in charge in apparent good order and condition, unless otherwise noted herein, at the place of receipt for transport and delivery as mentioned above

One of these Combined Transport Bills of Lading must be surrendered duly endorsed in exchange for the goods. In Witness whereof the original Combined Transport Bills of Lading all of this tenor and date have been signed in the number stated below, one of which being accomplished the other(s) to be void

Freight Amount	Freight Payable at LONDON	Place and date of issue LONDON
Cargo Insurance through the undersigned ☐ not covered ☐ COVERED	Number of Original FBL's THREE	Stamp and signature
For delivery of goods please apply to AFRI - FREIGHT (M) LTD, BLANTYRE, MALAWI		

Face of completed FIATA Combined Transport Bill of Lading (FBL)

Standard Conditions (1984) governing FIATA COMBINED TRANSPORT BILLS OF LADING

Definitions «Merchant» means and includes the Shipper, the Consignor, the Consignee, the Holder of this Bill of Lading, the Receiver and the Owner of the Goods. «The Freight Forwarder» means the issuer of this Bill of Lading as named on the face of it

The headings set forth below are for easy reference only

CONDITIONS

1. **Applicability**
Notwithstanding the heading «Combined Transport Bill of Lading», the provisions set out and referred to in this document shall also apply if the transport as described on the face of the Bill of Lading is performed by one mode of transport only

2. **Issuance of the «Combined Transport Bill of Lading»**

2.1 By the issuance of this «Combined Transport Bill of Lading», the Freight Forwarder
a) undertakes to perform and/or in his own name to procure the performance of the entire transport, from the place at which the goods are taken in charge to the place designated for delivery in this Bill of Lading
b) assumes liability as set out in these Conditions

2.2 For the purposes and subject to the provisions of this Bill of Lading, the Freight Forwarder shall be responsible for the acts and omissions of any person of whose services he makes use for the performance of the contract evidenced by this Bill of Lading

3. **Negotiability and title to the goods**

3.1 By accepting this Bill of Lading the Merchant and his transferees agree with the Freight Forwarder that, unless it is marked «non-negotiable», it shall constitute title to the goods and the holder, by endorsement of this Bill of Lading, shall be entitled to receive or to transfer the goods herein mentioned

3.2 This Bill of Lading shall be prima facie evidence of the taking in charge by the Freight Forwarder of the goods as herein described. However, proof to the contrary shall not be admissible when this Bill of Lading has been negotiated or transferred for valuable consideration to a third party acting in good faith

4. **Dangerous Goods and Indemnity**

4.1 The Merchant shall comply with rules which are mandatory according to the national law or by reason of international Convention, relating to the carriage of goods of a dangerous nature, and shall in any case inform the Freight Forwarder in writing of the exact nature of the danger, before goods of a dangerous nature are taken in charge by the Freight Forwarder and indicate to him, if need be, the precautions to be taken

4.2 If the Merchant fails to provide such information and the Freight Forwarder is unaware of the dangerous nature of the goods and the necessary precautions to be taken and if, at any time, they are deemed to be a hazard to life or property, they may at any place be unloaded, destroyed or rendered harmless, as circumstances may require, without compensation, and the Merchant shall be liable for all loss, damage, delay or expenses arising out of their being taken in charge, or their carriage, or of any service incidental thereto
The burden of proving the Freight Forwarder knew the exact nature of the danger constituted by the carriage of the said goods shall rest upon the person entitled to the goods

4.3 If any goods shipped with the knowledge of the Freight Forwarder as to their dangerous nature shall become a danger to the vehicle or cargo, they may in like manner be unloaded or landed at any place or destroyed or rendered innocuous by the Freight Forwarder, without liability on the part of the Freight Forwarder, except to General Average, if any

5. **Description of Goods and Merchant's Packing**

5.1 The Consignor shall be deemed to have guaranteed to the Freight Forwarder the accuracy, at the time the goods were taken in charge by the Freight Forwarder, of the description of the goods, marks, number, quantity, weight and/or volume as furnished by him, and the Consignor shall indemnify the Freight Forwarder against all loss, damage and expenses arising or resulting from inaccuracies in or inadequacy of such particulars. The right of the Freight Forwarder to such indemnity shall in no way limit his responsibility and liability under this Bill of Lading to any person other than the Consignor

5.2 Without prejudice to Clause 6 (A) (2) (c), the Merchant shall be liable for any loss, damage or injury caused by faulty or insufficient packing of goods or by faulty loading or packing within containers and trailers and on flats when such loading or packing has been performed by the Merchant or on behalf of the Merchant by a person other than the Freight Forwarder, or by the defect or unsuitability of the containers, trailers or flats, when supplied by the Merchant, and shall indemnify the Freight Forwarder against any additional expenses so caused

6. **Extent of Liability**

A 1) The Freight Forwarder shall be liable for loss of or damage to the goods occurring between the time when he takes the goods into his charge and the time of delivery

2) The Freight Forwarder shall, however, be relieved of liability for any loss or damage if such loss or damage was caused by:
a) an act or omission of the Merchant, or person other than the Freight Forwarder acting on behalf of the Merchant or from whom the Freight Forwarder took the goods in charge;
b) insufficiency or defective condition of the packaging or marks and/or numbers;
c) handling, loading, stowage or unloading of the goods by the Merchant or any person acting on behalf of the Merchant;
d) inherent vice of the goods;
e) strike, lockout, stoppage or restraint of labour, the consequences of which the Freight Forwarder could not avoid by the **exercise of reasonable diligence**;
f) any cause or event which the Freight Forwarder could not avoid and the consequences whereof he could not prevent by the exercise of reasonable diligence;
g) a nuclear incident if the operator of a nuclear installation or a person acting for him is liable for this damage under an applicable international Convention or national law governing liability in respect of nuclear energy

3) The burden of proving that the loss or damage was due to one or more of the above causes or events shall rest upon the Freight Forwarder
When the Freight Forwarder establishes that, in the circumstances of the case, the loss or damage could be attributed to one or more of the causes or events specified in b) to d) above, it shall be presumed that it was so caused. The claimant shall, however, be entitled to prove that the loss or damage was not, in fact, caused wholly or partly by one or more of these causes or events

B When in accordance with clause 6. A 1 the Freight Forwarder is liable to pay compensation in respect of loss or damage to the goods and the stage of transport where the loss or damage occurred is known, the liability of the Freight Forwarder in respect of such loss or damage shall be determined by the provisions contained in any international Convention or national law, which provisions
(i) cannot be departed from by private contract, to the detriment of the claimant, and
(ii) would have applied if the Claimant had made a separate and direct contract with the Freight Forwarder in respect of the particular stage of transport where the loss or damage occurred and received as evidence thereof any particular document which must be issued in order to make such international convention or national law applicable

7. **Paramount Clause**
The Hague Rules contained in the International Convention for the unification of certain rules relating to Bills of Lading, dated Brussels 25th August 1924, or in those countries where they are already in force the Hague-Visby Rules contained in the Protocol of Brussels, dated February 23rd 1968, as enacted in the Country of Shipment, shall apply to all carriage of goods by sea and, where no mandatory international or national law applies, to the carriage of goods by inland waterways also, and such provisions shall apply to all goods whether carried on deck or under deck

8. **Limitation Amount**

8.1 When the Freight Forwarder is liable for compensation in respect of loss of or damage to the goods, such compensation shall be calculated by reference to the value of such goods at the place and time they are delivered to the Consignee in accordance with the contract or should have been so delivered

8.2 The value of the goods shall be fixed according to the current commodity exchange price, or, if there be no such price, according to the current market price, or, if there be no commodity exchange price or current market price, by reference to the normal value of goods of the same kind and quality

8.3 **Compensation shall not, however, exceed 2 SDR (SDR = Special Drawing Right) units per kilo of gross weight of the goods lost or damaged, unless, with the consent of the Freight Forwarder, the Merchant has declared a higher value for the goods and such higher value has been stated in the CT Bill of Lading, in which case such higher value shall be the limit. However, the Freight Forwarder shall not, in any case, be liable for an amount greater than the actual loss to the person entitled to make the claim.**

9. **Delay, Consequential Loss, etc.**
Arrival times are not guaranteed by the Freight Forwarder. If the Freight Forwarder is held liable in respect of delay, consequential loss or damage other than loss of or damage to the goods, the liability of the Freight Forwarder shall be limited to double the freight for the transport covered by this Bill of Lading, or the value of the goods as determined in Clause 8, whichever is the less

10. **Defences**

10.1 The defences and limits of liability provided for in these Conditions shall apply in any action against the Freight Forwarder for loss of or damage or delay to the goods whether the action be founded in contract or in tort

10.2 The Freight Forwarder shall not be entitled to the benefit of the limitation of liability provided for in paragraph 3 of Clause 8 if it is proved that the loss or damage resulted from an act or omission of the Freight Forwarder done with intent to cause damage or recklessly and with knowledge that damage would probably result

11 **Liability of Servants and Sub-contractors**

11.1 If an action for loss of or damage to the goods is brought against a person referred to in paragraph 2 of Clause 2, such person shall be entitled to avail himself of the defences and limits of liability which the Freight Forwarder is entitled to invoke under these Conditions

11.2 However, if it is proved that the loss or damage resulted from an act or omission of this person, done with intent to cause damage or recklessly and with knowledge that damage would probably result, such person shall not be entitled to benefit of limitation of liability provided for in paragraph 3 of Clause 8

11.3 Subject to the provisions of paragraph 2 of Clause 10 and paragraph 2 of this Clause, the aggregate of the amounts recoverable from the Freight Forwarder and the persons referred to in paragraph 2 of Clause 2 shall in no case exceed the limits provided for in these Conditions

12. **Method and Route of Transportation**
The Freight Forwarder reserves to himself a reasonable liberty as to the means, route and procedure to be followed in the handling, storage and transportation of goods.

13. **Delivery**
If delivery of the goods or any part thereof is not taken by the Merchant, at the time and place when and where the Freight Forwarder is entitled to call upon the Merchant to take delivery thereof, the Freight Forwarder shall be entitled to store the goods or the part thereof at the sole risk of the Merchant, where upon the liability of the Freight Forwarder in respect of the goods or that part thereof stored as aforesaid (as the case may be) shall wholly cease and the cost of such storage (if paid by or payable by the Freight Forwarder or any agent or sub-contractor of the Freight Forwarder) shall forthwith upon demand be paid by the Merchant to the Freight Forwarder

14. **Freight and Charges**

14.1 Freight shall be paid in cash without discount and, whether prepayable or payable at destination, shall be considered as earned on receipt of the goods and not to be returned or relinquished in any event

14.2 Freight and all other amounts mentioned in this Bill of Lading are to be paid in the currency named in the Bill of Lading or, at the Freight Forwarder's option in the currency of the country of dispatch or destination at the highest rate of exchange for bankers sight bills current for prepayable freight on the day of dispatch and for freight payable at destination on the day when the Merchant is notified of arrival of the goods there or on the date of withdrawal of the delivery order, whichever rate is the higher, or at the option of the Freight Forwarder on the date of the Bill of Lading

14.3 All dues, taxes and charges or other expenses in connection with the goods shall be paid by the Merchant

14.4 The Merchant shall reimburse the Freight Forwarder in proportion to the amount of freight for any costs for deviation or delay or any other increase of costs of whatever nature caused by war, warlike operations, epidemics, strikes, government directions or force majeure.

14.5 The Merchant warrants the correctness of the declaration of contents, insurance, weight, measurements or value of the goods but the Freight Forwarder reserves the right to have the contents inspected and the weight, measurements or value verified. If on such inspection it is found the declaration is not correct it is agreed that a sum equal either to five times the difference between the correct figure and the freight charged, or to double the correct freight less the freight charged, whichever sum is the smaller, shall be payable as liquidated damage to the Freight Forwarder for his inspection costs and losses of freight on other goods notwithstanding any other sum having been stated on the Bill of Lading as freight payable.

15. **Lien**
The Freight Forwarder shall have a lien on the goods for any amount due under this Bill of Lading including storage fees and for the cost of recovering same, and may enforce such lien in any reasonable manner which he may think fit

16. **General Average**
The Merchant shall indemnify the Freight Forwarder in respect of any claims of a General Average nature which may be made on him and shall provide such security as may be required by the Freight Forwarder in this connection

17. **Notice**
Unless notice of loss of or damage to the goods and the general nature of it be given in writing to the Freight Forwarder or the persons referred to in paragraph 2 of Clause 2, at the place of delivery before or at the time of the removal of the goods into the custody of the person entitled to delivery thereof under this Bill of Lading, or if the loss or damage be not apparent, within seven consecutive days thereafter, such removal shall be prima facie evidence of the delivery by the Freight Forwarder of the goods as described in this Bill of Lading

18. **Non delivery**
Failure to effect delivery within 90 days after the expiry of a time limit agreed and expressed in a CT Bill of Lading or, where no time limit is agreed and so expressed, failure to effect delivery within 90 days after the time it would be reasonable to allow for diligent completion of the combined transport operation shall, in the absence of evidence to the contrary, give to the party entitled to receive delivery, the right to treat the goods as lost

19. **Time Bar**
The Freight Forwarder shall be discharged of all liability under the rules of these Conditions, unless suit is brought within nine months after
(i) the delivery of the goods, or
(ii) the date when the goods should have been delivered, or
(iii) the date when in accordance with Clause 18, failure to deliver the goods would, in the absence of evidence to the contrary, give to the party entitled to receive delivery, the right to treat the goods as lost

20. **Jurisdiction**
Actions against the Freight Forwarder may only be instituted in the country where the Freight Forwarder has his principal place of business and shall be decided according to the law of such country

Reverse of FIATA FBL (requires shippers' endorsement)

Since we are talking of international trade, such a list would have to be world-wide in its scope, and the problems of compiling it and of keeping it updated would be insuperable. The simplest solution, therefore, from the banks' point of view, is to reject all house bills of lading.

Some forwarders have reacted to this attitude by designing their house bills of lading to resemble as closely as possible the traditional form of marine bill, complete with house flags and funnel symbols, in the hope that by making the document appear to be what is required it will be accepted without further query. Some have gone to the lengths of calling the service which they offer by a suitably nautical brand name followed by the word "Line", and it has even been known for forwarders to sign their house bills "For the Master", though this amounts to misrepresentation and could leave them open to legal action.

In many cases, the tell-tale sign of a house bill of lading is the nomination upon it of a clearing agent at the port of discharge to whom application must be made in order to obtain delivery of the goods. It is the task of clearing agents to present to the ship's agents the true ocean bill of lading in order to obtain the goods which were shipped by their principals, the forwarders. Only then are they in a position to release individual consignments to holders of the relative house bills of lading. The principle of transfer of ownership of goods by mere endorsement of the bill of lading makes it difficult to exclude from the bill such vital information as the name of the clearing agent, since in its absence the bill is useless.

The answer, from the exporters' point of view, is to arrange for presentation of a particular house bill of lading to be allowed under the contract, and a similar provision to be made in any covering letter of credit. A slightly more risky method, in the present circumstances, is to ensure that any forwarder they are proposing to employ is a licensed issuer of the FIATA FBL: the more enlightened and well-informed banks should accept this document without question. If neither alternative is possible, it must be made clear to the forwarders that nothing but a marine bill of lading issued by the actual carrier of the goods will suffice. This may make the forwarders' charges slightly higher, but this is infinitely preferable to the possible alternative of having to wait for an indefinite period before receiving payment for the goods.

Whatever its shortcomings as a security document, in practice the house bill of lading is used in the same way as the marine bill of lading to facilitate transfer of control of goods by simple endorsement. None of the transport documents which remain for our consideration has this capability. Some may evidence the conditions of the contract of carriage; all act as a receipt, issued by the carrier to the shipper, for the goods; none, however, can be a document of title. Because of their comparatively low worth, the potential for disputes is correspondingly reduced and less time need therefore be spent in discussing their attributes and shortcomings.

Most non-negotiable transport documents take the form of waybills. All indicate that the sellers have performed their obligations under the contract as far as those obligations relate to the dispatch of goods. All show a named consignee for the goods, and this is the basis of the contract of carriage, with the carriers' obligation being to deliver the goods to that named consignee.

Sea waybill

The sea waybill, at first glance, looks very similar in layout to a bill of lading. The same information is given, in the same places; it may bear the same clauses as the bill of lading, and it is signed, dated, and freight is denoted as either paid or to collect in the same way. It clearly distinguishes itself, however, by announcing in bold print at the top that it is a non-negotiable sea waybill. It was first introduced on the shorter sea routes where use of the traditional bill of lading was rendered impractical by the time constraints involved in getting an original document to the port of destination by the arrival date of the goods. One solution was to arrange for an original bill of lading, in an envelope addressed to the buyers, to be sent with the goods in the "ship's bag", but as this was tantamount to releasing the goods to the buyers it was but a short step to the use of the waybill in which the goods are normally consigned to the buyers anyway.

Air waybill

The air waybill is a very different document in appearance, though not in effect. Again the goods are deliverable to a named consignee, with provision for the details of the goods to be declared by the shippers. Freight particulars are usually shown in some detail, not always the case with sea transport documents, and separate columns are provided for charges which have been paid by the shippers and those which are to be collected from the consignees. To understand fully the detailed aspects of the journey which the goods will make often requires an intimate knowledge of the international codes used to denote particular airports and individual airlines. Sometimes such knowledge can be dangerous, since it may reveal firstly that the goods will not complete the entire journey in the same aircraft (transhipment by any mode of transport being generally considered as undesirable because of the unknown risks involved) or secondly that the carrier is not the party which has issued the air waybill.

The main problems encountered with air waybills arise where the document is examined for acceptability under the UCP. Unfortunately these rules, admirable though they are in most respects, attempt to cover all transport documents other than marine bills of lading and parcel post receipts in one catch-all article which prompts frequent rejection of air waybills under letters of credit for such reasons as the document not being signed by the carriers or their agents (required by UCP), being issued by forwarding agents who are not the carriers or their agents (in which case, technically they are not air waybills at all, but air consignment notes), and not evidencing actual dispatch of the goods. The latter information is normally provided by the addition of a rubber stamp stating that the goods were on board a particular flight, identified by that flight's number. Apart from any considerations relating to the ease with which a rubber stamp can be obtained, many which are used by those who are entitled to do so are unsigned and may not even name the party making the statement. Their value as evidence of dispatch is therefore dubious.

The whole position regarding the requirements of UCP in respect of air waybills will be discussed in a later chapter; suffice it to say here that in the writer's experience they occasion very little real trouble. Far more problems and cases of actual fraud and forgery occur where a marine bill of lading is the transport document. It must be said, though, that since the vast majority of air cargo is handled by freight forwarders, they could do a great deal to alleviate the problems encountered by applying flight stamps which convey the impression that someone has made a statement which is true and which they are not ashamed to be identified with, and by obtaining the carriers' signature in the appropriate place on the waybill or signing it on their behalf. It is easy to sympathise with the forwarders' attitude because, since the air waybill is not a document of title, it is difficult for any reasonable person to see why so much fuss is made about it, particularly by banks. Nonetheless, the rules exist, and until they are changed the inevitable outcome of non-compliance is that their

Understanding Documentary Bills and Credits

PANALPINA

PANALPINA INTERNATIONAL TRANSPORT LTD.		CRN	HOUSE AIR WAYBILL
Registered Consolidator of IATA (International Air Transport Association) VAT 243 6843 52			475265

Shipper's Name and Address	Not Negotiable	AIR CONSIGNMENT NOTE PA LHR
MIAMI FABRICS PRINCESS HOUSE EASTCASTLE STREET LONDON W.1.	PANALPINA INTERNATIONAL TRANSPORT LTD UNIT 63/65G, BUILDING 521, SOLENT ROAD HEATHROW AIRPORT HOUNSLOW MIDDLESEX TW6 3HL TELEPHONE: 01-759 0351 TELEX: 262443	

Shippers Ref:-

If the carriage involves an ultimate destination or stop in a country other than the country of departure, the Warsaw Convention may be applicable and the Convention governs and in most cases limits the liability of carriers in respect of loss of or damage to cargo. Agreed stopping places are those places (other than the places of departure and destination) shown under requested routing and/or those places shown in carrier's timetables as scheduled stopping places for the route. Address of first carrier is the airport of departure.

Consignee's Name and Address		
MANDARIN PUBLISHERS LTD 6TH FLOOR TOPPAN BLDG. 22A WESTLAND ROAD, QUARRY BAY H.K.	Accounting Information	Agents IATA Code 91-4-7059
	REF:475265	

Consignees Order No:-

Airport of Departure (Address of First Carrier) and requested Routing	Currency	Weight/charges prepaid/collect	Other Charges prepaid/collect	Declared Value for Carriage	Declared Value for Customs
LONDON HEATHROW AIRPORT	UKL	XXX	XXX	NVD	NVD

Airport of Destination	Flight/Day
HONG KONG	MAWB No.121.22116581 BR382/18/6

Marks, Numbers and Types of Packing

NINETY TWO PACKAGES/ADDRESSED/INVOICES ATTACHED
1 @184x22x22 cms 6 @ 184 x23x23 cms
6 @ 184x24x24 cms

DIMS: 18 @ 184x28x28 cms
19 @ 184x26x26 cms
16 @ 184x25x25 cms
6 @ 184x29x29 cms
2 @ 184x30x30 cms
18 @ 184x27x27 cms

Number of Packages	Actual Gross Weight Kilos	Rate Class	Commodity Item No.	Chargeable Weight	Rate/Charge	Total	Nature and Quantity of Goods (Inc. Dimensions or Volume)
92	1674K			1964VOL	1.12	2199.68	BLACK KNITTED POLYESTER INTERLOCK FABRIC PRINTED TO APPROVED DESIGN IN METALLIC GOLD
			LETTER OF CREDIT NO: 320/100903				
			FREIGHT PREPAID				
			PARTIAL SHIPMENT ALLOWED				
92	1674K					2199.68	

We hereby declare that according to information received from the Carrier, the goods mentioned were despatched on,...................................
Flight.BR382.......Air Waybill.121-2211 6581.........
Date.18.6......and a copy of the Air Waybill has been forwarded to the Consignee on the same Aircraft.

PREPAID		COLLECT
Freight	2199.68	
Handling	80.00	
Insurance		
Cartage		
Packing		
EEC/Consular		
Other		

Carrier certifies goods described herein were received for carriage subject to Carrier's Trading Conditions 1985 Edition (copy on application) the goods then being in apparent good order and condition except as noted hereon. FOR AND ON BEHALF OF BRITISH CALEDONIAN AIRWAYS

16/6/86   LONDON
Executed on............................
(Date)   (Place)

Signature of Issuing Carrier or its Agent.......... PANALPINA
PANALPINA INTERNATIONAL TRANSPORT LTD.

Total Ancillary	80.00	C.O.D.	
		C.O.D. Fee	
TOTAL PREPAID CHARGES 2279.68		TOTAL COLLECT CHARGES	

1. ORIGINAL FOR SHIPPER   THIS IS NOT A TAX INVOICE

Example of a completed (house) air waybill

customers, the exporters, do not get paid when they should.

Road transport

The usual document where goods are sent by road is the international consignment note, known universally as the CMR from the initials (Convention Marchandises Routiers) appearing prominently on its face. Many road hauliers, however, issue their own documents, calling them variously road receipts, truck receipts and the like. The CMR carries the advantage that it is issued subject to a standard set of conditions of carriage laid down by international agreement, whereas the private document may not convey any information on the terms of the contract. The CMR's use, however, is restricted to those countries, all in Europe, which are signatories to the agreement, comprising all mainland nations except Albania, Turkey and the USSR, plus the United Kingdom.

Rail transport

A similar standard document for goods sent by rail is the CIM (Convention Internationale Marchandises Chemin de Fers).

Parcel post

No such standard document exists where goods are dispatched by parcel post, although in most cases carriage will be on the globally-recognised conditions laid down by the Universal Postal Union.

Forwarders' documents

Finally, mention must be made of two other FIATA creations. The first is the Forwarders' Certificate of Receipt (FCR) (illus. p 53), which is a non-negotiable document designed to cover forwarders' handling of traffic for which the FBL would not be appropriate, such as overland, short-sea or inland waterway consignments. The second is the Forwarders' Certificate of Transport (FCT) which is designed for multi-modal transport where the facility to transfer title to the goods is required but where a carrier's document is not a necessity. The latter is issued in a set of originals, as is the FBL, but contains an express statement that the issuer is acting as a forwarder and not as a carrier. As with the marine bill of lading and

LETTRE DE VOITURE INTERNATIONALE   (CMR)   **INTERNATIONAL CONSIGNMENT NOTE**

Sender (Name, Address, Country) Expéditeur (Nom, Adresse, Pays) 1	Customs Reference/Status Référence/désignation pour mise en douane 2
Aldgate Warehouse Wholesale Ltd 65/66 Whitechapel High St London E1	Senders/Agents Reference Référence de l'expédieur/de l'agent 3 BM211644

Consignee (Name, Address, Country) Destinataire (Nom, Adresse, Pays) 4	Carrier (Name, Address, Country) Transporteur (Nom, Adresse, Pays) 5
Habselyem Kötöttárugyár Budapest. XX. Török F.U. 116. Hungary	Hungarocamion Budapest

Place & date of taking over the goods (place, country, date) Lieu et date de la prise en charge des marchandises (Lieu, pays, date) 6	Successive Carriers Transporteurs successifs 7
London, 9.9.1985 ~~Budapest~~xxxxxxxxx	

Place designated for delivery of goods (place, country) Lieu prévu pour la livraison des marchandises (lieu, pays) 8	
Budapest XX, Hungary	This carriage is subject, notwithstanding any clause to the contrary, to the Convention on the Contract for the International Carriage of Goods by Road (CMR) Ce transport est soumis nonobstant toute clause contraire à la Convention Relative au Contrat de Transport International de Marchandises par Route (CMR)

SF

COPY 1 SENDER
COPY 2 CONSIGNEE
COPY 3 CARRIER

*NB FOR
DANGEROUS
GOODS

INDICATE
1 CORRECT
TECHNICAL
NAME
(PROPER
SHIPPING
NAME)
2 HAZARD
CLASS
3 U N
NUMBER
4 FLASH
POINT
(IF ANY)
IN C

Marks & Nos. No & Kind of Packages, Description of Goods* Marques et Nos, No et nature des colis, Désignation des marchandises* 9	Gross weight (kg) 10 Poids Brut (kg)	Volume (m³) 11 Cubage (m³)
Tricotex Budapest Hungary 415 Rolls Cloth	6225	40 circa
Contract No. 164.19.5.3104 xcxcxcxcxcxcxcxcxcxcxcxcxcxc		
Trailer VR3585/XY9313		

Carriage Charges Prix de transport 12	Senders Instructions for Customs, etc Instructions de l'Expédieur (optional) 13
c&f Budapest	

Reservations Réserves 14	Documents attached Documents Annexés (optional) 15
...GOODS... and unexamined	Invoices packing lists
	Special agreements Conventions particulières (optional) 16

Goods Received/Marchandises Reçues 17	Signature of Carrier/Signature du transporteur 18	Company completing this note Société émettrice 19
	for Hungarocamion: HUNGAROCAMION Co. Budapest U.K. Sole Agent	London, 9.9.1985 ...SHIPPING... Place and date, Signature 20

Approved by FTA, RHA, SITPRO UK 1981

730

Completed International Consignment Note (CMR)

Suppliers or Forwarders Principals		Customs Reference/Status	FCR Number	G
THE HERNE BAY SUPPLY CO.			01234	B
4 BIRCHINGTON ROAD, HERNE BAY, KENT.	**FIATA FCR**	Shipper's Reference		
	FORWARDERS	Forwarder's Reference		
Consignee	**CERTIFICATE**	04/12/FATA		
BATONS SPORTS INC.	**OF RECEIPT**			
998 BONAVISTA BOULEVARD, LOS ANGELES, CALIFORNIA 93618, U.S.A.	**ORIGINAL**			

Marks and Numbers	Number and Kind of Packages	Description of Goods	Gross Weight	Measurement
R S I LOS ANGELES 1/30 Container no. UFCU-53118-6	30 cases	Sports equipment	1224 kgs.	34.51 cb.

Contents, weight and measurement according to the declaration of the consignor.
The goods and instructions are accepted and dealt with subject to the General Conditions printed overleaf.

We certify having assumed control of the above mentioned consignment in external apparent good order and condition.

* Forwarding instructions can only be cancelled or altered if the original Certificate is surrendered to us, and then only provided we are still in a position to comply with such cancellation or alteration.

at the disposal of the consignee ☐

With irrevocable instructions*

to be forwarded to the consignee ☐

Instructions authorizing disposal by a third party can only be cancelled or altered if the original Certificate of Receipt is surrendered to us, and then only provided we have not yet received instructions under the original authority.

Special remarks

Instructions as to freight and charges

PREPAID

Place and date of Issue

LONDON 2.6.90

Stamp and signature

Example of FIATA Forwarder's Certificate of Receipt (FCR)

the FBL, delivery of the goods will only take place on surrender of a proper-ly endorsed original FCT.

Summary

It will be evident that only the first and the last of the documents which have been dealt with in this chapter are of any use where some measure of control over the goods is required as security, whether that security is sought by the sellers or by a bank. Where a non-negotiable transport document is dictated by the mode of transport used, the only method of retaining control over goods until payment is made by the buyers is to consign them to the sellers' agents in the buyers' country, and the agency most frequently used in this connection is the bank itself. Banks, however, are in the business of handling money and documents, not goods, and are understandably reluctant to become more deeply involved in trade transactions. The charges they make for such services reflect this attitude. As we have seen in a previous chapter, in FOB, CFR and CIF contracts the risk in the goods passes from sellers to buyers at the point of FOB, and if a bank is named as consignee or even as notify party in a transport document, then, *prima facie*, that is where the risk lies as far as the carrier is concerned. Furthermore, if the goods are not taken up on arrival, it falls to the bank to make arrangements for their clearance, storage and insurance. Herein lies the reason for the banks' reluctance to be involved unless they require for their own security that the goods be consigned to them.

From the point of view of the sellers, this underlines what was said several times at the beginning of this book: there is no security so good as a knowledge of the standing and integrity of the person with whom one is dealing and this applies especially if full advantage is to be taken of modern methods of transportation.

5
Marine insurance

The scope of this subject is immense and it is fortunate that a detailed knowledge is not necessary within the present context of its application to collections and letters of credit. As with any other form of insurance, its basic aim is to provide compensation where a loss is suffered due to circumstances beyond the control of the insured loser. The sellers and buyers of the goods are clearly the parties primarily concerned with the covering of such risks, but banks may also have an interest where they are in any way relying on goods as security for lending or for the issue of credits. As the arrangers of marine insurance cover on behalf of others, forwarders also need a basic understanding of the principles involved.

Marine insurance is divided into two broad categories, hull and cargo. Hull insurance is the insurance of the ships themselves, and does not concern us here. Cargo insurance may be taken out with an insurance company, or with underwriters. "Underwriters" usually means the Corporation of Lloyds in London or similar organisations elsewhere. It should be noted that some countries insist that imports are insured with their own national insurance companies making CIF contracts impossible with those countries.

Marine insurance is subject to many of the conditions normally applying to other forms of insurance. For example, the insured party must have an insurable interest: that is, they must actually be at risk. All known facts which may affect the underwriters' decision to insure (and, of course, the premium charged) must be disclosed, and all parties must exert the "utmost good faith" (often expressed as the Latin phrase *uberrimae fidei*) which involves eventualities ranging from inadequate packing to fraudulent claims.

Extent of cover

No claim will be met if the loss was caused by a risk not covered. This would seem to be obvious but is not always as simple as it sounds. If a policy covers the risk of fire but not war risks and goods are destroyed by a fire started by an act of war, a claim will probably not succeed. The extent of the cover to be taken out will depend on the contract and on the custom in a particular trade. It is not possible to insure against loss of market due to delay of the carrying vessel, nor against inherent vice, such as natural decay of fresh produce. Basic cargo insurance covers the goods against loss due to sinking, fire, storm, water damage, piracy, barratry (dishonest acts of the ship's master or crew), pilferage, breakage from mishandling, and jettison (where cargo is thrown overboard to save the ship). These risks are known as particular average and may be varied to suit particular trades. For instance, breakage is usually deleted from the risks covered where the commodity shipped is ordinary glass, since the risk is so great that the premium would be prohibitively expensive.

General average

Also covered is general average. A voyage of a ship is considered as a joint venture involving all who have an interest in the safe arrival of the ship at its destination—basically the shipowner and the individual owners of the cargo. If any of these makes a financial sacrifice which is for the general benefit of the rest, such as salvage costs for the ship or the value of jettisoned cargo, then each of the others is expected to make a *pro rata* contribution to those costs based on the extent of their interest.

War clauses; strikes clauses

War and strikes must be specifically insured against and additional premium will be charged. It will not usually be possible to cover these risks where war or strike conditions actually exist at the time the insurance proposal is made.

Institute cargo clauses

Standard clauses governing the contract of marine insurance have been drawn up by the Institute of London Underwriters (comprising both Lloyds underwriters and companies) and similar clauses are used by other organisations such as the American Institute of Underwriters. The clauses currently in force are designated A, B and C. Broadly speaking:

(a)   clauses A cover all claims for risks covered and attract the highest premiums;

(b)   clauses B cover total loss of individual packages, each package being treated as a separate insured risk;

(c)   clauses C cover loss of the whole consignment only and provide the cheapest cover available, being particularly suitable for very durable cargoes such as iron and steel.

These clauses approximate to the old "All Risks", "WA" (with average) and "FPA" (free of particular average) clauses, respectively, but these terms are now obsolete and should not be used.

Franchise

Like any other insurance, marine insurance may be subject to a franchise, ie in return for a reduction in premium, the insured party bears an agreed proportion of the amount of any claim. Such arrangements are common where the nature of the goods would give rise to numerous small claims, such as wine in bottles, crockery and the like.

Lloyds

The Corporation of Lloyds is effectively a market place for marine insurance, where the sellers are syndicates of underwriters and the buyers are accredited Lloyds' brokers acting on behalf of customers. Different syndicates cover different types of risk and brokers will take propositions to the appropriate syndicate. If the amount is large a syndicate may not feel able to accept the entire risk but will mark the proposal with the proportion which they are prepared to cover (they literally "write under", hence their name). The broker must then approach other syndicates until the entire risk is covered. To become members of Lloyds, individuals must undergo exhaustive investigation of their financial position and must put up a bond from an acceptable bank for a substantial sum of money.

Insurance documents

Insurance documents come in two forms, policies and certificates. Marine policies may be the custom in certain countries, such as Japan, or may be issued where the seller does not engage in international trade to an extent where it becomes worthwhile to take out an open cover. Each policy represents a separate contract of insurance and, because to arrange such a contract for every shipment which they make would be onerous and time consuming, regular exporters often seek a more convenient arrangement. This may still produce a policy, perhaps by an arrangement whereby the exporters are appointed by the insurers as their policy-issuing agents. With this authority, the exporters can issue policies to themselves for each shipment, sending copies to the insurers with payment of premiums due, as would any other issuing agent.

An alternative to this arrangement is the certificate of insurance, which is issued under two types of contract:

(a)   a floating policy, where the insured pays advance premium for cover up to a certain total amount, then declares individual ship-ments under the policy until the total cover is used up;

(b)   open cover, where all consignments falling within the scope of the agreement are automatically covered and the insured pay a premium at an agreed rate as they declare each shipment.

In the United Kingdom, the initial incentive towards the development of the insurance certificate was the *ad valorem* stamp duty which was at one time applied to all policies of insurance. Thus, the issue of but one policy, in the case of the floating type, and the undertaking to issue a policy only in the event of a claim being made, in the case of the open cover, saved a great deal of money, the spending of which achieved no other purpose than the filling of the coffers of the Treasury, since the majority of export consignments reach their destination unharmed. The duty was abolished but the system set up for its avoidance remains, since it is a very convenient way of arranging cargo insurance. Instead of an individual policy for each shipment, the insured are issued with a supply of signed and numbered certificates, each one usually in triplicate. The details are completed by the insured, the first copy forming the insurance document to be sent to the buyer, the second being sent to the insurers as a declaration to them of the risks they are assuming, and the third being retained by the insured for their records. Payment of premiums may be made with each declaration, or on an open account basis, according to the terms of the agreement.

Policies of marine insurance

This, then is the background to marine cargo insurance. We will now consider the attributes of the two types of insurance document, beginning with the policy (see illustrations on pp 60-1).

Cover usually attaches, ie becomes effective, from the date when the goods leave the sellers' warehouse or from the date of the policy, whichever is the later. As an insurance policy represents an individual contract of insurance, it is essential that it is dated no later than the date of the bill of lading, since if a cause of loss arises between the bill of lading (shipment) date and the policy date the claim will not be met.

Amount insured

The amount insured must be adequate, the figure in general use being the CIF value of the goods plus a ten per cent margin (this figure is in any case stipulated as a minimum level of insurance both by Incoterms and by the UCP). It should be expressed in the same currency as the commercial invoice to guard against adverse fluctuations in exchange rates.

It was stated in Chapter 3 that, because it is based on information taken directly from the goods when they were received for shipment, the bill of lading is the definitive document regarding the actual shipping marks and numbers appearing on the packages. Because these marks and numbers provide positive identification of particular consignments, it is essential that those declared on the policy should agree exactly with the bill of lading, since any difference may cause doubt as to which goods are insured and thus make claims invalid.

The description of the goods as given on the policy need not be

> This policy has been issued in
> **t w o** fold, one of which being
> accomplished the other(s) to stand void.

~~ank approval number 11 764 84~~

Policy nr   30799
Shipment nr   635/53008
Letter of credit nr.:   01/86/5550X

INDUSTRIEEL ASSURANTIEKANTOOR B.V.

Be it known that   PHILIPS EXPORT B.V., or order,

as well in their own Name, as for and in the Name and Names of all and every other Person or Persons to whom the name doth, may or shall appertain, in part or in all, doth make Assurance, and cause themselves and them and every of them, to be insured, lost or not lost, at and from

        interior Holland to Rotterdam (Dutch Port)
        to consignees in Limbe.

upon any kind of Goods and Merchandises in the good Ship or Vessel called: "TRANSVAAL"   o.h.c.   (cl.cl.)

sailing date: 20-06-1986 or h.c.

whereof is Master, under God, for this present voyage   N.N.   or whosoever else shall go for Master in the said Ship or by whatsoever other Name or Names the said Ship, or the Master thereof, is or shall be named or called, beginning the Adventure upon the said Goods and Merchandises from the loading thereof aboard the said Ship, as above; and shall so continue and endure her Abode there, upon the said Ship etc.; and further, until the said Ship with all her Goods and Merchandises whatsoever shall be arrived at as above, and upon the Goods and Merchandises, until the same be there discharged and safely landed; and it shall be lawful for the said Ship etc. in this voyage to proceed and sail to and touch and stay at any Ports or Places whatsoever without Prejudice to this Assurance. The said Goods and Merchandises etc. for so much as concerns the Assured by Agreement between the Assured and Assurers in this Policy, are and shall be valued at:

        JPY 5.624.199,= (FIVE MILLION SIX HUNDRED TWENTY FOUR THOUSAND
        =============== ONE HUNDRED NINETY NINE JAPANESE YEN)
                        so valued on 1555 cartons, containing philips products
                        marked and numbered as per suppliers' invoices.

The insured amount is inclusive of all profit, imaginary or other and cost of freight and insurance.
In case of loss or damage losses to be assessed on the basis of the sound value and the percentage thus found to be applied to the insured value.
Touching the Adventures and Perils which we the Assurers are contented to bear and to do take upon us in this Voyage, they are, of the Seas, Men-of-War, Fire, Enemies, Pirates, Rovers, Thieves, Jettisons, Letters of Mart and Countermart, Surprisals, Takings at Sea, Arrests, restraints and Detainments of all Kings, Princes and People, of what Nation, Condition, or Quality soever, Barratry of the Master and Mariners, and all other Perils, Losses, and Misfortunes that have or shall come to the Hurt, Detriment or Damage of the said Goods and Merchandises and Ship, & c., or any part thereof; and in case of any Loss or Misfortune, it shall be lawful to the Assured, their Factors, Servant, and Assigns, to sue, labour, and travel for, in and about the Defence, Safeguard and Recovery of the said Goods and Merchandises and Ship, & c., or any part thereof, without Prejudice to this Insurance; to the Charges whereof we, the Assurers, will contribute, each one according to the rate and Quantity of his sum herein Assured. And it is especially declared and agreed that no acts of the Insurer or Insured in recovering, saving, or preserving the property insured, shall be considered as a waiver or acceptance of abandonment. And it is agreed by us, the Insurers, that this Writing or Policy of Assurance shall be of as much Force and Effect as the surest Writing or Policy of Assurance heretofore made in Lombard Street, or in the Royal Exchange, or elsewhere in London.

This insurance is governed by English Marine Insurance Law and supplementary customs and further subject to the terms and conditions of the attached clauses, specified as follows:

        Institute Cargo Clauses (A) dated 01.01.1982
        Institute War Clauses (Cargo) dated 01.01.1982
        Institute Strike Clauses (Cargo) dated 01.01.1982
        From warehouse eindhoven to warehouse lime, transhipment risks.

In the event of claim for particular average or loss, the amount insured to be divided as per invoice. In the event of any claim for loss and or damage under this policy, advances shall be treated as increased value of cargo and shall be paid as insured value of cargo.
Now this policy withnesseth that we, the Undersigned Assurers, take upon ourselves the burden of this Assurance, each of us to the extent of the amount underwritten by us respectively, and promise and bind ourselves, each Company for itself only and not one for the other, and in respect only of the due proportion of each Company to the Assured, their Executors, Administrators and Assigns, for the true Performance of the Premises confessing ourselves paid the Consideration due into us for the Assurance by the Assured, at and after the rate as per contract
This insurance has been effected through the intermediary of the Industrieel Assurantiekantoor B.V. at Eindhoven and we have debited their account for the premium, thus discharging the Assured.
In the event of accident whereby loss or damage may result in a claim under this policy and under this policy should be paid abroad, immediate notice to be given to

        Claims payable in Malawi.

In witness whereof we, the Assurers, have subscribed our Names and Sums assured.
All disputes on the subject of this policy or on the insurance covered thereby are to be decided by the competent judge at Rotterdam, subject to appeal to a higher court.

                        Issued at EINDHOVEN, 15th June   1986

                                                                        C 41b

Example of face and reverse side of policy of marine cargo insurance

Industrieel Assurantiekantoor B.V.
For One Hundred Percent.
Assurantie Maatschappij
"Nieuw Rotterdam" N.V. at Rotterdam

tekenen

p.p. PHILIPS EXPORT B.V.

SETTLEMENT OF CLAIMS

In the event of damage, which under this policy may involve a claim apparently in excess of Dutch Guilders 1500,– (or equivalent), **immediate** notice of such damage should be given to the average agent mentioned in the policy. If in the policy no average agent is mentioned or if, on account of the place where the survey should be held, it is not feasible to apply to that average agent, application for survey should be made to:

a) the nearest agent of the Marine Underwriters Association in Holland.
b) the nearest Lloyd's agent or
c) another competent average agent of first class reputation.

Failure to comply with these requirements may prejudice any claim under this policy.

Instructions in case of damage or loss

1. The insurance is continuously effective from the time the goods leave the works until they reach your warehouse. This is, however, subject to the condition of your taking delivery of the goods as soon as they are placed at your disposal. In case there is a delay in the delivery of the goods to your premises (e.g. by customs formalities) the cover may be extended another sixty days (air cargo: thirty days). In any case the cover ends sixty days (thirty days) after discharge. Therefore, in order that we may try to keep the insurance effective on your behalf, it is necessary for you to advise us immediately:

    a) If you do not want to take delivery as soon as the goods are placed at your disposal.
    b) If for other reasons the goods will not arrive at your warehouse within sixty days from discharge.

2. All containers shipped abroad and sealed with a "one seal-lock" have to be inspected on arrival at the port of destination by consignee or his representative (if possible even before customs formalities) in order:

    a) to examine the condition of the "one seal-lock",
    b) to compare the number of the "one seal-lock" with the seal-lock number on the B's/L (or copies).

    In case it appears that the container has travelled unlocked and unsealed or the seal-lock number (mentioned under b.) does not correspond, an **immediate** inspection should be arranged.

3. On discharge the goods should be externally examined at the port. In case there are visible or audible signs of damage, do not give a clean receipt but hold the carriers immediately responsible and invite them to be present at the inspection of the goods. If the damage is likely to be more than 1500 Dutch guilders or its equivalent, call in the surveyor. Unless contrary instructions are given by the surveyor, this inspection should not be postponed until the goods reach your warehouse.

4. If there is a shortage on discharge, ask the carriers for a certificate of short-landing.

5. To avoid loss and damage, do not allow the goods to remain on the quay or in the port sheds any longer than is strictly necessary. Bring the goods into the safety of your warehouse as quickly as possible.

6. When the goods reach your warehouse, they should be immediately unpacked and inspected irrespective of external signs of loss or damage. If loss or damage is ascertained and the amount thereof is likely to exceed 1500 Dutch guilders or its equivalent, call in the surveyor. Keep the container and inner packing for inspection by the surveyor.

7. The surveyor mentioned in nos 2, 3 and 6, is the representative of Underwriters indicated on the back of the insurance policy. If there is no such representative, Lloyd's Agent should be called in.

8. If it is obvious that damage or loss occured while the goods were in care of a local carrier, this carrier should immediately be held responsible.

9. Losses are not payable abroad, unless otherwise stated in the insurance policy.

10. All claims with the supporting documents must be sent **without delay** to the original shippers who will settle the claim on your behalf through the brokers with Underwriters.

     The following is required:

     a) The report of the surveyor (or if the loss is below 1500 Dutch Guilders or its equivalent your own report)
     b) A copy of the invoice.
     c) Copies of your letters to the carriers and of their replies.
     d) Short-landing certificate, if applicable.
     e) Policy of insurance
     f) Information about condition and identification number of the "one seal-lock"

detailed but should include all information which may be relevant to the insurance, eg flashpoint of chemicals, etc.

Risks

The policy must state the risks which are covered (ie Clauses A, B or C, war, strikes, etc), must bear the signature of the insurers, and also the endorsement of the insured, thus enabling subsequent owners of the goods (either in physical possession or as holders of the bill of lading) to claim against the insurer should loss be incurred.

Certificates of marine insurance

Now we turn to the certificate of insurance, be it issued under a floating policy or an open cover. In either case cover is automatic and the date of the certificate is not important, as it is with a policy. Most of the other important aspects of the policy, however, particularly regarding insured value, type of cover, shipping marks and goods description, apply equally where a certificate is used. In addition there are some features of a certificate which are not present in a policy.

Limit per bottom

Firstly, because of the blanket nature of the agreement between the parties to the contract of insurance, at the time of its signature the insurers will have little knowledge of the detail of the risks for which they are taking responsibility. In order that some limiting influence may be exerted over the extent of this risk the certificate may be claused to the effect that no more than a stated total value of goods may be shipped in any one vessel, a restriction known as the "limit per bottom". A similar restriction may also be given relating to locations other than on board ship.

Nature of goods

The certificate will often restrict the nature of the goods which may be declared under the contract, depending on the type of commodity in which the insured party trades. The narrower the scope of goods which may be declared, the easier it is for the insurers to assess their likely risk and therefore a lower premium may well be charged.

LLOYD'S

**CLAIMS SETTLEMENT
INSTRUCTIONS**

1 Lloyd's Agent at. Los Angeles
   is authorised to adjust and settle on behalf of
   the Underwriters, and to purchase on behalf of
   the Corporation of Lloyd's, in accordance with
   Lloyd's Standing Regulations for the Settlement
   of Claims Abroad, any claim which may arise on
   this Certificate.

2 In the event that Clause 1 is not completed
   claim papers should be sent to J. O. B. Long &
   Co . Ltd 999 Lloyd's Street, Insurance Avenue
   London. E C O

Certificate of Insurance No. C 0000/11111

This is to Certify that there has been deposited with the Committee of Lloyd's a continuous Contract effected by *J. O. B. Long & Co.,
Ltd.,* of Lloyd's, acting on behalf of *The Herne Bay Supply Company* with Underwriters at Lloyd's, and that the said Underwriters have
undertaken to issue to *J. O. B. Long & Co., Ltd.,* Policy/Policies of Insurance at Lloyd's to cover, up to *£10,000 (or equivalent in other currencies)*
in all by any one *steamer or sending by air and/or parcel post, Golf Equipment, other interests held covered,* from any port or ports, place or places
in *the United Kingdom* to any port or ports, place or places in *the World;* and that *The Herne Bay Supply Company* are entitled to declare against
the said Contract insurances attaching thereto on or after the *First* day of *January, 1981.* This Certificate is not valid in respect of insurances
attaching after the *Thirty-first* day of *December, 1983.*

for the Committee of Lloyd's
Dated at Lloyd's. London, 29th February, 1982.

Conveyance	From		
"ALEMANIA EXPRESS"	LONDON		
Via To	To	INSURED VALUE (Currency)	
	LOS ANGELES	GBP 24200-00	
Marks and Numbers	Interest	(Twenty four thousand two hundred	
		Pounds Sterlimg only.)	

R S I   30 cases SPORTS EQUIPMENT

LOS ANGELES

We hereby declare for Insurance under the said Contract interest as specified above so valued subject to the special conditions stated below and on the back hereof.

Institute Cargo Clauses (All Risks) excluding rust, oxidisation, discoloration, twisting and bending
Institute Replacement Clause
Institute War Clauses (Cargo) or Institute War Clauses (Cargo) including on-carriage by Air) or Institute War Clauses (Air Cargo) (excluding sendings by Post) or Institute War Clauses for the
   insurance of sendings by Post as applicable
Institute Strikes Riots and Civil Commotions Clauses.

Underwriters agree losses, if any, shall be payable to the order of **HERNE BAY SUPPLY COMPANY** on surrender of this Certificate.

In the event of loss or damage which may result in a claim under this Insurance, immediate notice should be given to the Lloyd's Agent
   at the port or place where the loss or damage is discovered in order that he may examine the goods and issue a survey report.

(Survey fee is customarily paid by claimant and included in valid claim against Underwriters.)

SEE IMPORTANT INSTRUCTIONS ON REVERSE

This Certificate not valid unless the Declaration be signed by

for THE HERNE BAY SUPPLY COMPANY.

Dated 22.2.82

Z. Clements, Director   Signed *Zachariah Clements*

Brokers: J O B Long & Co . Ltd   Authorised Signatory
999, Lloyd's Street, Insurance Avenue. London. E C.O.
                                                                          16667 7

Front and reverse of a completed standard Lloyd's certificate of insurance

For and on behalf of The Herne Bay Supply Co.

Zachariah Clements

Director

IMPORTANT INSTRUCTIONS IN EVENT OF CLAIM

DOCUMENTATION OF CLAIMS

To enable claims to be dealt with promptly, the Assured or their Agents are advised to submit all available supporting documents without delay, including when applicable:–

1. Original policy or certificate of insurance.

2. Original or copy shipping invoices, together with shipping specification and/or weight notes.

3. Original Bill of Lading and/or other contract of carriage.

4. Survey report or other documentary evidence to show the extent of the loss or damage.

5. Landing account and weight notes at final destination.

6. Correspondence exchanged with the Carriers and other Parties regarding their liability for the loss or damage.

IMPORTANT
LIABILITY OF CARRIERS, BAILEES OR OTHER THIRD PARTIES

It is the duty of the Assured and their Agents, in all cases, to take such measures as may be reasonable for the purpose of averting or minimising a loss and to ensure that all rights against Carriers, Bailees or other third parties are properly preserved and exercised. In particular, the Assured or their Agents are required:–

1. To claim immediately on the Carriers, Port Authorities or other Bailees for any missing packages.

2. In no circumstances, except under written protest, to give clean receipts where goods are in doubtful condition.

3. When delivery is made by Container, to ensure that the Container and its seals are examined immediately by their responsible official. If the Container is delivered damaged or with seals broken or missing or with seals other than as stated in the shipping documents, to clause the delivery receipt accordingly and retain all defective or irregular seals for subsequent identification.

4. To apply immediately for survey by Carriers' or other Bailees Representatives if any loss or damage be apparent and claim on the Carriers or other Bailees for any actual loss or damage found at such survey.

5. To give notice in writing to the Carriers or other Bailees within 3 days of delivery if the loss or damage was not apparent at the time of taking delivery.

Note: – The Consignees or their Agents are recommended to make themselves familiar with the Regulations of the Port Authorities at the port of discharge.

NOTE.– The Institute Clauses incorporated herein are deemed to be those current at the time of commencement of the risk.
It is necessary for the Assured when they become aware of an event which is "held covered" under this Insurance to give prompt notice to Underwriters and the right to such cover is dependent upon compliance with this obligation.
Lloyd's Agents referred to herein are not insurers and are not liable for claims arising on this Certificate. The service of legal proceedings upon Lloyd's Agents is not effective service for the purpose of starting legal proceedings against Underwriters.
This Insurance is subject to English jurisdiction.

Printed by The Carlton Berry Co. Ltd

ORIGINAL

Commercial Union Assurance

Marine Centre,
Drury House,
19 Water Street, Liverpool L2 0RL

C U ASSURANCE

Exporters Reference
Contract No. 31442

Marine Open Cover No: M.A.935 – F0065Z
For HALEWOOD CHEMICALS LIMITED.

Insured's Invoice or Reference No.
31442

Certificate of Insurance

INSURANCE CERTIFICATE NO. MAF 32478

Name of Insured
HALEWOOD CHEMICALS LIMITED,
HORTON ROAD, STANWELL MOOR,
STAINES, MIDDLESEX. TW19 6BJ.

Claims payable at destination by nearest branch or agency of
Commercial Union Assurance Company plc.

See list of branches and agencies on reverse of this form or by:-

FROM WAREHOUSE STAINES BY

This is to Certify that the Commercial Union Assurance Company plc,
has insured in the United Kingdom under this Open Cover in the
name of this Insured the interest described and valued herein.

Notwithstanding the description of the voyage stated herein,
provided the goods are at the risk of the Assured, this insurance
shall attach from leaving the warehouse, premises or place of
storage in the interior of the Country of export to interior of
destination country as per Institute Clauses if in accordance with the
Open Cover and unless stated otherwise hereon.

It is a condition of this Insurance that the Insured shall act with
reasonable despatch in all circumstances within their control.

Conveyance &/or Steamers	From	Insured Value (in words)
SEAFREIGHT	LONDON	ONE THOUSAND SEVEN HUNDRED AND NINETY POUNDS
Via/To	To	ONLY
BANJUL	WAREHOUSE BANJUL	Insured Value (in figures) £1,790.00 Sterling

Marks and Numbers	Interest
H.C.L. 31442 G.P.L. BANJUL Nos.1-2	2 Ply Cases PHARMACEUTICALS AS PER PROFORMA INVOICE 6578C

Claims Procedure

Insured or their agents must:—

1. Report claims immediately to C.U.'s agent shown above or overleaf.
2. Claim on carrier, Port Authority or any negligent party for damage or omissions.
3. Apply immediately for survey in the docks by carriers' representative if any loss or damage is apparent at the docks.
4. In no circumstances give clean receipt where goods are in doubtful condition except under written protest.
5. Give notice to carriers' representative within three days of delivery if loss or damage was not apparent at time of delivery.
6. Send all correspondence with carriers or other negligent parties when submitting claim to C.U.

Extension of Cover

If the ordinary course of transit from ship to destination takes more than 60 days (30 days Air) or is in any way interrupted (within control or knowledge of the Insured) this insurance shall terminate unless prompt notice is given to the CU or their agents for extension of cover and such extension, if agreed, shall be subject to an additional premium.

This Insurance is subject to the conditions below
and extended to cover Marine and War Risks Insurance,
including Transhipment Risks.

Conditions of Insurance

The policy to which this insurance attaches is against all risks of
loss of or damage to the subject matter insured in accordance with
the terms, conditions and exclusions set out in the current issue of
the following clauses:

Institute Cargo Clauses (A)
Institute Cargo Clauses (Air)
Institute Classification Clause
Institute Replacement Clause
Duty Clause } as applicable
War & Strikes Riots & Civil Commotions as per appropriate
Institute Clauses.

This insurance is subject to English jurisdiction

Special Policy Conditions.

Signed for Commercial Union Assurance Company plc.

JOHN POPE
UK Divisional Director.

GSF1047(c)
(Liverpool)

Registered in England No. 21487
Registered Office, St. Helen's 1 Undershaft, London EC3P 3DQ

THIS CERTIFICATE IS NOT VALID UNLESS COUNTERSIGNED.
Countersignature by or on behalf of the Insured also
declared to constitute effective assignment thereof.

Place & Date of Issue 3.6.86.	HALEWOOD CHEMICALS LTD.
	Horton Road, Stanwell Moor
Signature E.M. HICKS	STAINES,
	Middlesex

Example of a company certificate of marine cargo insurance

HALEWOOD CI''''''ALS LTD.
Mo::on Road, Stainwall Moor,
'.. ' 'AITS,

Principal CU Marine Settling Agencies

	Country	Location	
U.K.		London	Marine Dept. of Commercial Union Assurance Company plc or Marine Centres at Glasgow, Liverpool, Manchester, Leeds. Birmingham, Bristol, London Marine Centre.
Canada		Toronto	Boyd Phillips & Co. Ltd.
		Montreal	Dale & Co. Ltd.
U.S.A.		New York	Marine Dept. of Commercial Union Assurance Companies or at C.U. Marine Centres at San Francisco.
West Indies	Barbados	Bridgetown	Barbados Commercial Insurance Co. Ltd.
	Trinidad	Port of Spain	Huggins Services Ltd.
Central and	Argentina	Buenos Aires	Ascoli & Weil
South America	Bolivia	La Paz	La Britanica S.A.
	Chile	Valparaiso	Compania de Seguros La Republica S.A.
	Ecuador	Guayaquil	The Sociedad General C.A.
	Guatemala	Guatemala City	G.W.F. Franklin Ltd.
	Guyana	Georgetown	Guyana National Shipping Corporation
Europe	Austria	Vienna	Gellatly Hankey Marine Services / Graham Miller Gesellschaft M.b.H.
	Belgium	Antwerp	J. Haenecour & Co. S.A.
	Cyprus	Nicosia	Commercial Union Assurance (Cyprus) Ltd.
	Denmark	Copenhagen	Hansen & Klein
	Eire	Dublin	Hibernian Insurance Co. Ltd.
	Finland	Helsinki	O.Y. Lars Krogius A.B.
	France	Paris	Commercial Union Assurance Company plc c/o A.T.I.C.A.M.
	Germany	Bremen	Lampe & Schierenbeck
	Gibraltar		Solrac & Co. Ltd.
	Greece	Athens,	Commercial Union Assurance Company plc
	Italy	Milan	Bevington Assicurazioni S.A.S.
	Malta	Sliema	A & V Von Brockdorff (Insurance) Ltd.
	Netherlands	Amsterdam ⎫ Rotterdam ⎬	De Vos & Zoon
	Norway	Oslo	Sev Dahl's Assurancekontor S.A.S.
	Portugal	Lisbon	Rawes & Pinto Basto Ltda.
	Spain	Barcelona	Commercial Union Assurance Company plc
	Sweden	Stockholm	Commercial Union Assurance Svenska A/B.
	Switzerland	Basle	Keller Shipping Ltd
Middle East	Bahrein		Bahrein Technical & Trading Co.
	Dubai		African £ Eastern (Near East) Ltd.
	Kuwait		Kuwait Maritime & Mercantile Co. K.S.G.
	Saudi Arabia	Damman ⎫ Dhahran ⎬ Jeddah ⎪ Riyadh ⎭	Arabian Establishment for Trade
	Syria	Lattakia	Syrian Maritime & Transport Agencies S.A.S.
Africa	Egypt	Cairo	Malcolm Sheppard & Co. (Commodity Surveys) Ltd.
	Kenya	Nairobi	Lion of Kenya Insce. Co. Ltd.
	Mauritius	Port Louis	L & H. Vigier de Latour Ltd.
	South Africa	Johannesburg	Commercial Union Assurance Company of South Africa Ltd. or at any branch office.
	Tanzania	Dar-Es-Salaam	General Agricultural Products Export Corp. (GAP EX).
Asia	Bangladesh	Chittagong	James Finlay & Co. Ltd.
	Hong Kong	Hong Kong	Commercial Union Assurance Company plc
	India	Bombay	Tata Tea Ltd.
		Calcutta	Gillanders Arbuthnot & Co. Ltd.
	Japan	Tokyo	Cornes & Co. Ltd.
	Malaysia	Kuala Lumpur	Commercial Union Assurance (Malaysia) Sdn. Bhd.
	Pakistan	Karachi	Commercial Union Assurance Company plc
	Singapore	Singapore	Commercial Union Assurance Company plc
	Sri Lanka	Colombo	Harrisons & Eastern Export Ltd.
	Thailand	Bangkok	Commercial Union Assurance Company (Thailand) Ltd.
Australia		Melbourne	Associated Marine Insurers Australia Pty Ltd.
New Zealand		Auckland ⎫ Wellington ⎬	Commercial Union General Insurance Co. Ltd.

IMPORTANT

Please follow the claims procedures shown on the face of this certificate.
In the event of di''''lty in contacting a local settling agent please contact
Commercial Union Assurance Company plc in London for advice
Telex 889135   Cable CUMARINE LONDON EC3

Geography of the voyage

Similarly, there may well be limitations placed on the geographical extremes of the voyage to be undertaken by goods declared under the contract, and again the greater the restriction, the less potential risk, and so a further premium reduction may be possible.

All these limits will be agreed at the time that the contract of insurance is signed, and it is for the sellers to decide for themselves whether the resulting contract will be adequate to meet their foreseeable needs during the lifetime of the contract, which may span a number of years. Much of the benefits to be derived from an open cover will be nullified if it is frequently necessary to take out specific insurance for consignments which fall outside the scope of the agreement. Worse is the situation where goods which are outside that scope are shipped in reliance upon it, thereby making the insurance document null and void.

Endorsement by insured party

As with the policy, to enable third parties to the agreement who have obtained an interest in the goods to make valid claims in the event of loss, the certificate requires endorsement by the insured party, unless, as sometimes occurs, it states that claims will be payable to bearer. In addition, because it is a declaration made by the insured, it is usually invalid unless countersigned on its face by them, and the insurers will have specimen signatures of those in the employ of the insured who are authorised to sign.

Expiry date

Finally, where the type of agreement is an open cover, the certificate will normally state the expiry date of the contract of insurance, beyond which date the issue of further certificates is invalid. Because such arrangements are frequently in force for many years, it becomes easy for this date to be overlooked.

Claims

Both policies and certificates will usually state the procedure to be followed in the event of any claims, including the name of the party to be contacted at the port of destination. Frequently use is made of the world-wide network of claims agents maintained by the Corporation of Lloyds, who also provide detailed reports of ship movements which are collated by the Corporation and published daily as Lloyds Shipping Index.

Brokers' cover notes

One last insurance document which must be mentioned is the brokers' cover note, although this will be discussed again in Chapter 12. Insurance brokers are to the world of insurance what forwarding agents are to the world of shipping. In other words, they act as agents who undertake to procure insurance for customers. Because of their deep understanding of the insurance market and because, by bringing new business to particular insurers in quantity they are able to obtain favourable rates of premium which may be passed on to their customers, they perform a valuable service to the insurance community. The problem arises when they issue their own documents which amount to statements that insurance has been, or will be, effected. Such documents are not evidence of the terms, or even the existence, of the actual insurance cover, and are seldom usable by a third party in the event of a claim becoming necessary. Another similarity to the forwarding agent is that in many countries there is little or no control over who may call themselves insurance brokers and thus the trading community, and banks in particular, tend to treat the brokers' cover note with the same circumspection as they display towards the house bill of lading.

6
Commercial and official documents

The commercial invoice (illus. p. 71)

This document is addressed to the buyers by the sellers and contains a detailed description of the goods with their unit and total prices. It will also state the contract terms. This is the minimum information which should appear but, in practice, much more is usually included, either by requirement of the importing country, requirement of the buyers or the convenience of the sellers. Import regulations are so varied on the subject of invoices that it would be futile to attempt to catalogue them in a work of this nature, not least because the information would probably be out of date even before publication. The commonest requirement is for the inclusion of a separately signed statement relating to the value of the goods, or their origin, or a combination of these two. Most of the French speaking countries in Africa require the latter and the declaration must be in French, even though there is no general requirement for the rest of the invoice to be expressed in that language. These countries also require that this declaration be signed by a director of the exporting company. Some Latin American countries require the invoice to be in Spanish, the most notable being Bolivia and Mexico. Another frequent requirement is for a declaration as to the relationship between the sellers and the buyers, although this is often catered for by prescribing the use of a specially designed invoice form which will be considered further below.

Often, where contract terms are, for instance, CIF, the unit prices will be shown as FOB, and freight and insurance costs will then be added to the total FOB price to bring the amount up to contract terms. In many

instances this is a requirement of the importing country. It is good practice for sellers to show their prices in this way as a matter of course,
since it goes some way to explaining the reasons for the frequently large
discrepancy between the domestic price of a product and the selling
price of the same item to an overseas purchaser. In any case, unless the
sellers maintain a separate price list for each of the overseas countries to
which they sell on CFR terms, or beyond, the FOB value of goods
provides a good basis for pricing, since costs up to that point are likely
to be relatively constant.

The customs invoice (illus. pp. 72-3)

It was mentioned earlier that some countries prescribe the form of
invoice which they require to be submitted for imported goods. The
usual motive for this is to ensure the availability of all the information
which they need to evidence compliance with import regulations. Some
merely include a printed version of the certificates of value and origin
mentioned above; some also incorporate information regarding the relationship between buyer and seller; while some call for quite detailed
information concerning the selling price, such as separate figures for the
cost of export packing, inland transport to port of shipment and the like.
The generic term for this type of document used to be customs invoice,
though few countries now actually refer to them by that name. Their use
has diminished considerably in recent years and is now restricted entirely
to countries of the British Commonwealth, particularly in West and
Central Africa (though not Zimbabwe) and in the Pacific and Indian
Oceans. They are still in use, however, in Canada and Malaysia.

The commercial invoice is the document which is most frequently
required to be legalised, or verified, by an independent third party. In
some cases this is linked to pre-shipment inspection of the goods, which
will be considered under inspection certificates later in this chapter. In
other cases the verification is by an authorised chamber of commerce in
the exporting country and is merely to reassure the authorities in the
importing country of the *bona fides* of the sellers. Finally, there is the full
legalisation by a representative of the government of the importing
country, usually the embassy or consulate nearest to the sellers. Where
this takes place, the authorities are reassuring themselves that the money
changing hands is in respect of a genuine shipment of goods, while at
the same time exerting a very strict control over their country's imports.

THE

HERNE BAY

SUPPLY COMPANY

4 BIRCHINGTON ROAD HERNE BAY KENT

TO: Ramona Sports Inc., 998 Bonavista Boulevard, Los Angeles, California 93618, U.S.A.	DATE: 6th. November 1988 INVOICE NO: 903/88 YOUR ORDER NO: 2-BD-290766 1.8.88 TERMS: C.I.F.

SHIPPING MARKS	DESCRIPTION OF GOODS	QTY	UNIT PRICE	TOTAL PRICE
	SPORTS EQUIPMENT		USD	USD
◇ R S I	Cat. ref. AB35576 Trolley	20	140.00	2800.00
	Cat. ref. AB/65954 Bag	100	35.00	3500.00
LOS ANGELES	Cat. ref. CD/00018 Shoes (pairs)	600	18.00	10800.00
(30 cases)	Cat. ref. AC/11912 Umbrella	100	12.00	1200.00
	as per our pro forma invoice dated 5.6.88 and your purchase requisition no. 2-BD-290766 dated 1.8.88.	TOTAL FOB		18300.00
		Plus Freight		3500.00
		Plus Insurance		200.00
	Goods of U.K. origin	TOTAL CIF		22000.00
	Shipped per "Alemania Express" London/Los Angeles 27.10.88. Container no. UFCU-531118-6. Clean on board. Freight prepaid.			

FOR & ON BEHALF OF

THE HERNE BAY SUPPLY COMPANY

Zachariah Clemente

DIRECTOR

Example of a commercial invoice

Invoice and Certificate of Value and Origin for exports to GAMBIA

Seller (Name, Address, VAT Reg. No.)			CCCN No.
HALFWOOD CHEMICALS LIMITED, HORTON ROAD, STANWELL MOOR, STAINES, MIDDLESEX. TW19 6BJ	7"14 ip. and Date (Tax Point) 2 3 JUN 1986 Buyer's Reference TELEX DTD 19th MAY 1986	Seller's Reference 31442	30.03
Consignee GAMBIA PHARMACEUTICALS LTD., 3 LEMAN STREET, BANJUL, THE GAMBIA.	Buyer (if not Consignee)		

Country of Origin of Goods
UNITED KINGDOM

Terms of Delivery and Payment
C.I.F. BANJUL
PAYMENT: By Irrevocable Documentary Credit
No.710/2935 dated 12th May 1986.
(Credit Dept. Opening Section KS)

Vessel/Aircraft Etc. RIVER OSSE	Port of Loading LONDON
Port of Discharge BANJUL	

Marks and Numbers; No. and Kind of Packages; Description of Goods		Quantity	@	Amount (State Currency)
PACK NO.	PHARMACEUTICALS AS PER PROFORMA INVOICE 6578C			
6in1 4in2 2	TETRACYCLINE B.P. 250mg Caps.	10 x 1000	£16.25: 1000	£ 162.50
2	AMPICILLIN B.P. 250mg Caps.	10 x 1000	£31.01 1000	£ 310.10
168in1 32in2 2	ASPIRIN B.P. (ACETYLSALICYLIC ACID) 300mg, White Tabs.	200 x 1000	£2.61: 1000	£ 522.00
2	METRONIDAZOLE B.P. 200mg Tabs.	20 x 1000	£8.98: 1000	£ 179.60
2	GRISEOFULVIN B.P. 125mg Tabs.	10 x 100	£2.42: 100	£ 24.20
2	PENICILLIN V B.P. (POTASSIUM) 250mg Tabs.	20 x 1000	£17.27: 1000	£ 345.40
2	PHENOBARBITONE B.P. 30mg Tabs.	20 x 100	£0.31: 100	£ 6.20
1	PHENOBARBITONE B.P. 30mg Tabs.	5 x 1000	£1.71: 1000	£ 8.55
2	FOLIC ACID B.P. 5mg Tabs.	20 x 1000	£2.16: 1000	£ 43.20
2	AMMON. BICARBONATE B.P.	1 x 5Kg	£9.09: 5kg	£ 9.09
2	AMMON. CHLORIDE 99-100% Fine White	1 x 5Kg	£8.52: 5kg	£ 8.52

(I enumerate the following charges and state if each amount has been included in the total Selling Price to Purchaser)	Selling Price to Purchaser	
	Amount	State if included
1. Value of outside packing/containers	£20.00	Inc
2. Labour in packing goods into outside packing/containers	£10.00	Inc
3. Inland transport and insurance charges to dock/airport area	N/A	
4. Dock and port charges	£ 4.00	Inc
5. Overseas freight	£81.32	Inc
6. Overseas insurance	£16.26	Inc
7. Details of any other charges relating to delivery of goods	—	—
8. Royalties (state full particulars)	—	—
9. Commission and similar charges (state full particulars)	—	—

TOTAL	£1,626.40

EXPORTER'S DECLARATION

Gross Weight (kg)	Cube (m3)
224	0.574

I, THE UNDERSIGNED, being duly authorised in that behalf by the above exporter, and having made the necessary enquiries, HEREBY CERTIFY THAT THIS INVOICE, including continuation sheets, if any, IS MADE IN ACCORDANCE WITH THE VALUE AND ORIGIN CLAUSES SHOWN, and hereby declare that I will furnish to the Customs authorities of the importing country of their nominee, for inspection at any time such accounts and other evidence as may be requested for the purchase of verifying this certificate.

Signature of Witness
J.Al

Name of Signatory
E.M. HICKS

Place and Date of Issue
STAINES, MIDDLESEX.   2 3 JUN 1986

Signature

1. That the amount of all premises and amounts charged and correct...
2. That no component or undercomponent affecting the purchase or of the said goods has been or will be made directly or indirectly between...

It is hereby certified that this invoice shows the actual price of the goods described, that no other invoice has been or will be made, and that all particulars are true and correct.

Form No. 542. Published and Sold by FORMECON SERVICES LTD., Douglas House, Gateway, Crewe CW1 1YN, England. Tel:0270-587811 Telex:36550 Eurofs G

Example of a customs invoice – front and reverse of the form currently used for imports to the Gambia

RECHNUNG FACTU... ..INVOICE FACTURE FACTURA   Continuation

Seller (Name, Address, VAT Reg No.) Vendeur (Nom et Adresse)		Page 2 of/de 2

HALEWOOD CHEMICALS LIMITED,
HORTON ROAD,
STANWELL MOOR,
STAINES,
MIDDLESEX. TW19 6BJ

Invoice No. and Date (Tax Point)
7142   23 JUN 1986   31442

Seller's Reference Référence du Vendeur

Buyer's Reference Référence d'acheteur
TELEX DTD 19th MAY 1986

Consignee Destinataire (Nom et Adresse)

GAMBIA PHARMACEUTICALS LTD.,
3 LEMAN STREET,
BANJUL,
THE GAMBIA.

Origin Code	Marks and Numbers; Number and Kind of Packages; Description of Goods	Quantity Quantité	Or Prix unitaire	Amount (State Currency) Montant (Préciser les Devices)
2	BENZOIC ACID B.P.	1 x 500gm	£2.50: 500gm	£ 2.50
2	SALICYLIC ACID B.P. Powder	1 x 500gm	£4.54: 500gm	£ 4.54
	C.I.F. BANJUL			£1,626.40

SHIPPING MARK   Packed in 2 Ply Cases.
H.C.L.
31442
G.P.L.
BANJUL
Nos.1-2

PACK NO.	MEASUREMENTS	GROSS WEIGHT
Ply Case No.1	89 x 58 x 58cms	138 kilos
Ply Case No.2	89 x 58 x 53cms	86 kilos

E&OE

See Principal Sheet for further details of this Consignment.
Voir feuille principale pour les détails de cet Envoi.

The consular invoice

An alternative to the legalisation of invoices is the requirement for presentation of consular invoices. Whereas the customs invoice usually
replaces the commercial invoice when it is required, the consular invoice
is an additional document, which takes the form of a declaration to the
government of the importing country regarding all the details which they
require concerning the goods shipped. Special forms must usually be
purchased by the sellers from the embassy or consulate of the buyers'
country, which, after completion, must be lodged with the consul for
legalisation. Once widespread, particularly among the Spanish and
Portuguese-speaking areas of the world, their use has dwindled to a
point where they are largely irrelevant in the world of international trade.
At the time of writing, the only countries which still require them are the
Dominican Republic, Honduras, Panama and Paraguay.

The packing list

This document lists the contents of each individual package, identifying
it by the number stencilled upon it. It is of no value where the packages
are of identical size and contain identical goods, or where the goods are
packed in a single packing unit. Its presentation is often stipulated by the
importing country to assist customs officials in identifying packages
which they wish to open for inspection but it is also extremely useful to
the buyers where different types, sizes or qualities of goods are included
in a single shipment, since they can readily refer to it to trace a particular
item, when the alternative would be to open all the packages until the
required one was found (illus. p. 75).

The specification

This gives detailed dimensions, weights, etc of individual items shipped
(eg pieces of timber). It is similar to, and may be combined with, the
packing list.

PACKING LIST

CASE NO	ITEM NO	GOODS	GROSS WEIGHT Kg.	NETT WEIGHT Kg.	CUBIC MEAST Cbm.	QTY
1	AB35576	Golfing trolley	22	11	0.3861	1
2	"	" "	22	11	0.3861	1
3	"	" "	22	11	0.3861	1
4	"	" "	22	11	0.3861	1
5	"	" "	22	11	0.3861	1
6	"	" "	22	11	0.3861	1
7	"	" "	22	11	0.3861	1
8	"	" "	22	11	0.3861	1
9	"	" "	22	11	0.3861	1
10	"	" "	22	11	0.3861	1
11	"	" "	22	11	0.3861	1
12	"	" "	22	11	0.3861	1
13	"	" "	22	11	0.3861	1
14	"	" "	22	11	0.3861	1
15	"	" "	22	11	0.3861	1
16	"	" "	22	11	0.3861	1
17	"	" "	22	11	0.3861	1
18	"	" "	22	11	0.3861	1
19	"	" "	22	11	0.3861	1
20	"	" "	22	11	0.3861	1
21	AB65954	Golf bags	63.4	52.4	0.3003	20
22	"	" "	63.4	52.4	0.3003	20
23	"	" "	63.4	52.4	0.3003	20
24	"	" "	63.4	52.4	0.3003	20
25	"	" "	63.4	52.4	0.3003	20
26	CD00018	Golfing shoes (pairs-assorted sizes)	124.4	113.4	1.5000	200
27	"	" "				200
		plus advertising material of no commercial value	126.2	115.2	1.5247	
28	"	Golfing shoes (pairs)	124.4	113.4	1.5000	200
29	AC11912	Golf type umbrellas, assorted colours Red/white 20 Green/yellow 20 Blue/white 10	46	35	0.2809	50
30	"	Golf type umbrellas, assorted colours Blue/white 10 Blue/yellow 20 Red/green 20	46	35	0.2809	50
		TOTALS	1224.0	894.0	14.3100	

Each wooden case marked ⟨R S I⟩
LOS ANGELES

Example of a packing list, based on the information contained in the commercial invoice illustrated on page 71

The certificate of origin (illus. p. 77)

Certificates of the origin of goods take many forms and are required for many reasons. In their simplest form, they are merely a statement on the commercial invoice as to the country from which the goods originate and may be required simply to reassure the buyers that they are receiving goods which have been made in a country in whose products they have confidence. More often, however, the buyers require a certificate of origin in order to provide evidence to the customs authorities in their country that the goods qualify for a preferential rate of import duty. Such preferential rates often apply between countries which form part of the same trading bloc, such as the European Community or the Caribbean Common Market.

Perhaps the most frequent reason for the provision of a certificate of origin is a government regulation in the importing country which demands its presentation and a very large number of countries have such regulations. The reasons may be statistical, but are more often political.

The form of the certificate of origin may, as has been stated, be a simple statement on the invoice. In some cases, it may be a separate signed document provided by the sellers. Yet again, it may be included in a prescribed form such as a customs invoice. Finally, it may be a document specifically designed for the purpose of evidencing the origin of goods, such as the standard forms used within the EC and that used by the overseas Arab chambers of commerce. It may even be a negative certificate of origin, in that, instead of certifying origin in a particular country, it states that goods do *not* so originate. Obviously, the necessity for such documents changes with the winds and tides of international relations, but at the present time a good example of a negative certificate of origin is that required by many Arab buyers (though, surprisingly, by few governments) that goods do not originate in Israel. This, the so-called blacklist certificate, goes further than the origin of the goods and touches upon whether the sellers have been known to trade with Israel in the past, on the ownership of the carrying vessel and its scheduled ports of call, and even on the insurers and their possible relationships with Israel. This is an extreme example, but is not unique, since the Americans once called for a similar document regarding a list of countries with whom they were then "not on speaking terms".

As with other documents, some countries require the certificate of origin to be legalised by the embassy or consulate in the sellers' country, these being chiefly the Arab countries, with the addition of one or two in Latin America.

1 Consignor BOSS LTD., WATERLOO GARDENS, BURGESS HILL, WEST SUSSEX ENGLAND RH20 7ZN	No. FF 203648	**ORIGINAL**
	456/11	

2 Consignee
LIGHT INDUSTRIES (PTE) LTD.,
10 KIM KEE ROAD,
SINGAPORE 0315
MARKED: CO/7069
LIGHTEN
SINGAPORE
-UP
L/C No. 2/86/1079

EUROPEAN COMMUNITY

CERTIFICATE OF ORIGIN

3 Country of Origin

EUROPEAN COMMUNITES – UNITED KINGDOM

4 Transport Details (Optional)
WEIGHT
VESSEL: "C.R. TOKYO"
E.T.S. 13.6.86
E.T.A. 8.7.86

5 Remarks

6 Item number; marks, numbers, number and kind of packages; description of goods

DOCUMENTARY CREDIT NO. 412/86/1079

					7 Quantity
1/6	ADDR. CONSIGNEE AS ABOVE	12BOXES	1.	1020 MAGNETIC STIRRERS	10
			2.	1065 HOTPLATE/MAGNETIC STIRRERS	5
			3.	2010 MINI LABORATORY STIRRERS	10
			4.	3200 VARISHAKE WRIST ACTION SHAKERS	5
			5.	5200LABORATORY FLOCCULATORS	3
			6.	6000 HOT PLATES	5

ONE LOT OF LABORATORY EQUIPMENT
Ref: Openers' Order CO/7069
As per CV Kurnia Jaya Purchase Order No. 278/KJPO/IV/86

Manufactured by ourselves, BOSS LTD.

8 THE UNDERSIGNED AUTHORITY CERTIFIES THAT THE GOODS DESCRIBED ABOVE ORIGINATE IN THE COUNTRY SHOWN IN BOX 3

FEDERATION OF SUSSEX INDUSTRIES
and CHAMBER OF COMMERCE,
Seven Dials, Brighton BN1 3JS

- 9 JUN 1986

J.W. THUM

Authorised Signatory
Federation of Sussex Industries &
Chamber of Commerce

Place and date of issue; name, signature and stamp of competent authority
Brighton

.... 19 ....

Federation of Sussex Industries and Chamber of Commerce

Example of a standard certificate of origin as used in the European Community

FARING SEWAGE

Faring Sewage Ltd,
Mill Road,
Coventry,
England
Telephone: (0026) 459321
Telex: 1132395

Your Ref

Our Ref   GEF/SJ   25th July 1986

INSPECTION CERTIFICATE

Al Jouf Permanent Staff Housing Scheme
Letter of Credit No 85/1064
Sewage Treatment Plant equipment
including spare parts

This is to certify that all items for the above contract
and as Packing Lists have been subject to our standard works
inspection procedures and were found to be satisfactory
in all respects.

For and on behalf of
Faring Sewage Ltd.

G. E. FIELD
Co. Accountant

Example of a certificate of quality issued by the sellers themselves

Certificate of quality

There are, of course, many other aspects of a consignment of goods upon which the buyers may wish for reassurance: either that the goods are up to the required standard or that they do not contravene the import regulations of their country. The most obvious of these concerns, perhaps, is that relating to the quality of the goods. Here, the standing of the sellers may be significant and a certificate from them to the effect that the goods are of the quality ordered could be sufficient.

Certificate of inspection (illus. p. 78)

If the buyers do not wish to accept the word of the sellers, however, but still desire reassurance as to the quality of the goods, the alternative is to carry out an inspection themselves prior to shipment, or, as most frequently happens, appoint an agent in the sellers' country to do it for them. When this happens, one of the documents called for under the contract will probably be a favourable inspection report issued by that agent. The same will apply to specialised types of merchandise such as foodstuffs, live animals or plants, drugs, alcoholic drinks, chemicals, etc, where the certificate may relate to the fitness of food for consumption, the health of animals and plants, an analysis of drugs or chemicals, or the age and strength of alcohol.

A number of companies exist which specialise in inspection of goods for purchasers in this way and these concerns will usually employ or retain specialists in the various commodities which they may be called upon to inspect. It is important to such companies that they maintain a reputation for impartiality and integrity and this makes them an obvious first choice when buyers require an agent in another country to inspect goods on their behalf.

Pre-shipment inspection and the clean report of findings

A number of developing countries require by law that all imports be subject to Pre-Shipment Inspection (PSI), which is usually in the form of a Comprehensive Import Supervision Scheme (CISS).

The purpose of such schemes is broadly to ensure that the importing country receives value for the foreign exchange it expends on its imported goods; as such, they comprise:

(a)   a physical inspection covering quality and quantity aspects;
(b)   a price evaluation to ensure that the price being charged is within the normal export market price range for the particular country of supply;
(c)   legality checks to ensure that the transaction complies with the laws of the importing country and international trading regulations.

The importing country usually employs one or more inspection agent(s) to act on its behalf in administering the scheme.

In a typical transaction, the inspection agent covering the country of supply of the goods will receive from the importer's bank the appropriate import documentation. Upon receipt the inspection agent will contact the exporter to arrange the pre-shipment inspection. This is normally done by the exporter completing a form which asks for all the information necessary for PSI to take place. As soon as the inspection agent receives the information, the PSI activities can proceed, with all elements taking place concurrently (provided that adequate information has been supplied). If all aspects are satisfactory, and subject to receipt of satisfactory final documents (including an original certified copy of the bill of lading or airway bill), a clean report of findings (CRF) will be issued. This is the means by which the inspection agent informs its principal (the government of the importing country) of the results of its PSI activities. The CRF is also normally required for payment purposes. The format of the CRF may vary from country to country, depending upon the exact information the inspection agent is required to provide, but an example is provided on page 82.

If some aspect of the PSI remains unsatisfactory after consultation between inspection agent and exporter, a non-negotiable report of findings is issued, but this is likely to result in non-payment.

Increasingly, such schemes also include some form of import duty and tariff code assessment to ensure that the importing country receives the correct amount of import duty due on a consignment. This information may be included on the Clean Report of Findings, or a separate report may be produced – an Import Duty Report (IDR). Where an IDR scheme exists, the original of the Report will normally be required by the importer in order to clear his or her goods through customs.

The PSI contract is between inspection agent and the government of the importing country. In the vast majority of schemes, therefore, it is the government which pays the inspection agent's fees, which are more than covered by the economic benefits accruing to the client country; there is normally no direct cost to either importer or exporter.

Up-to-date information on which countries require pre-shipment inspection on all or on certain categories of goods can be found in *Croner's Reference Book For Exporters*.

In conclusion

From the point of view of the buyers, the only really essential documents apart from the transport document and the insurance document, if applicable, are the invoice and possibly the packing list. They may also require certificates, such as those of origin or of inspection, for their own purposes, but it will have been evident that many of the documents which have been dealt with in this chapter are required for no other reason than that the government of the importing country decrees that they are necessary. They are, in fact, official rather than commercial documents.

It is a rather sad fact that, as a general rule, the more regulations a country imposes upon its trading community the lower its position in the world's markets and the less secure its government. It is possible that some of the documents required perform a useful function, but the fact that other countries manage to get along quite well without them casts doubt upon this. In many cases, the apparent paranoia exhibited by governments concerning international trade results from a belief, frequently justified, that they were exploited in the past and a determination that the experience will not be repeated. Unfortunately, the means used, of imposing an ever-increasing burden of regulations on trade, tends to lead to excessive bureaucracy, waste of resources, and to corruption. Far better to give traders the freedom to gain experience in open markets and to rely upon their own skills and on adequate training to avoid the attentions of fraudsters. It is no coincidence that the most successful trading nations are those which have a freely negotiable currency, no exchange control regulations, few import restrictions, low rates of duty and minimal documentary requirements.

COTECNA INSPECTION S.A.
58, rue de la Terrassière 1207 GENEVA, SWITZERLAND

CLEAN REPORT OF FINDINGS
ORIGINAL

No.

ISSUED ACCORDING TO THE IMPORT REGULATIONS OF THE REPUBLIC OF KENYA. THE GOODS WERE INSPECTED IN ACCORDANCE WITH OUR MANDATE AND FOUND ACCEPTABLE AS TO QUANTITY, QUALITY AND PRICE.

Seller		Date
	Code ---	Feal Number
Importer		LC Number ---
	Code	Delivery TOTAL
Description		Quantity

VOID – SPECIMEN ONLY

Invoice No.	Dated	Terms	GBP

Value in Words

Shipping Details		Packing
Shipped at	On Board	
B/L No.	Dated	
Port of Destination		

FOR SOLE USE OF THE KENYAN AUTHORITIES

ISSUED AT: HOUNSLOW HOUSE,
730 LONDON ROAD,
HOUNSLOW, MIDDLESEX,
TW3 1PD, ENGLAND

COTECNA INTERNATIONAL LIMITED
COTECNA INSPECTION S.A. REPRESENTATIVE

Signature

This inspection has been performed and this Report issued to the best of our ability and knowledge but without prejudice or acceptance of liability, and without releasing suppliers and/or shippers and/or other parties involved from their contractual obligations.

Example of a clean report of findings

7
The bill of exchange

Although the role of the bill of exchange in international trade has diminished somewhat in recent years, it is probably true to say that the majority of collections and drawings under letters of credit still involve its use. It is perhaps questionable whether the use of the bill of exchange is always justified, since on occasions where it is expedient to dispense with it (such as where it attracts heavy stamp duty), trade seems to manage quite adequately without it. As a general rule, however, the comprehensive legislation which remains in force in many countries, which is designed to protect the holder of a bill of exchange from loss, makes its use attractive to any party involved in the financing of a trade transaction, whether they be the sellers themselves or an intermediary bank. To the latter, a bill of exchange payable at some date in the future can also be useful as an instrument of liquidity owing to the thriving markets in such documents in many financial centres.

Definition

A good starting point in any study of the bill of exchange is the legal definition of the instrument as set out in the Bills of Exchange Act of 1882 (s.3). This states that a bill of exchange is "an unconditional order in writing, addressed by one person to another, signed by the person giving it, requiring the person to whom it is addressed to pay, on demand or at a fixed or determinable future time, a sum certain in money to or to the order of a specified person or to bearer".

If at first this description makes the reader's head spin, it is worth a second reading, since, in order that a holder of the bill may qualify for the protection given by the Act and referred to above, it is important that it complies with the legal definition in all respects. The courts take the logical view that if a particular piece of paper fails in any way to meet the requirements then it is not a bill of exchange and therefore the further provisions of the Act are irrelevant.

Negotiability

The basis of the bill of exchange is that it is a written request for payment. In this respect it is similar to, and in addition to, the invoice. Unlike that document, however, it can, and frequently does, have an existence completely independent from the other documents to which it relates, since it is a negotiable instrument. The concept of negotiability has been previously referred to in Chapter 3 in connection with bills of lading, but whereas in that case the transfer of title which took place related to goods, in the case of the bill of exchange what is transferred is the right to receive payment of money. The actual transfer is effected in the same way as with a bill of lading, by including the word "order" in the payment instructions followed by endorsement, simple or specific, by the holder.

An important aspect of negotiability is that purchasers of negotiable instruments, provided that they act in good faith and without knowledge of any defect in title of previous holders, can acquire a better title to the instrument than was possessed by the person from whom they obtained it. This is in direct contrast to the situation regarding, for example, stolen goods, which may be traced and recovered from the holders even though they might have purchased in good faith.

Parties

The various parties to a bill of exchange are as follows.

(a)   The *drawers* are the issuers of the bill and therefore evidently the prime creditors in the transaction, usually the sellers.

(b)   The *payees* are the people whom the drawers instruct that the debt be paid to. Normally, of course, this would be themselves, but it may be a third party, particularly where that third party is providing finance to the sellers, such as a bank.

(c) The *drawees* are the debtors, usually the buyers of the goods.

(d) The *acceptors* of a bill are the drawees of that bill where it is payable at a future date, after they have indicated on the bill their promise to pay it when due.

(e) The *endorser* of a bill is anyone who has transferred title to the proceeds of the bill by endorsement, simple or specific. Simple endorsement is achieved initially by the payee signing it on the back. Specific endorsement is where that signature is accompanied by a specific instruction that payment be made to a named party.

(f) The *endorsee* of a bill is anyone to whom title to the bill has been transferred by specific endorsement. Although seldom seen at the present time, it is possible to create more space on the back of a bill of exchange for further endorsements by the attachment of a piece of blank paper called an *allonge*. This is also sometimes used to accommodate the revenue stamps which must be attached to the bill in many countries before it is legally valid.

(g) The *holder* of a bill may be the drawer, payee or any endorsee. Under English law, perfect title is enjoyed by a *holder in due course*. To qualify for the maximum protection afforded by the Act (s. 29) to such holders, they must:

   (i)   hold a bill which is "complete and regular on the face of it"; completeness implies that no essential ingredient is missing, such as the date, the drawers' signature, or any necessary endorsement (the latter even though an endorsement would normally appear on the back, rather than literally "on the face" of the bill). Regularity means the absence of such discrepancies as differing words and figures, endorsements in which the name of the endorser is incorrectly given, and so on;

   (ii) have acquired their rights to the bill before it became overdue;

   (iii) have had no notice that the bill had been previously dishonoured;

   (iv) have taken the bill in good faith;

   (v)   have given value for the bill; and

   (vi) have had no notice of any defect in the title of the person from whom they acquired it.

PRINTED AND SOLD BY
BOWEN & COURT LTD 7 GARDNER INDUSTRIAL ESTATE KENT HOUSE LANE BECKENHAM KENT

No. REFERENCE

At .... TENOR

DATE .... 19 .... For AMOUNT IN FIGURES

Pay this .... of Exchange
to the Order

of .... PAYEE

AMOUNT IN WORDS

Value Received .... which place to Account

To .... DRAWEE

DRAWER'S SIGNATURE

A typical form of bill of exchange. Note that it is not obligatory to use a special form such as this, and the bill could validly be drawn on the seller's own letterhead or, indeed, on a plain sheet of paper.

If holders cannot prove that they can fulfil all of these conditions, they become *holders for value*, which still gives them a certain amount of protection but effectively destroys the bill's negotiability in that they are unable to obtain a better title to it than was possessed by the party from whom they acquired it. Thus, if one of a chain of endorsements on a bill is proved to be a forgery, subsequent holders for value of that bill would be unable to enforce it in the courts against the original drawer or against any endorsers prior to the forgery, though they would still have rights of recovery against subsequent holders. The latter is likely to be of small consolation where the bill was taken for value from the forgers themselves. In these circumstances, holders in due course would have the option of suing any one of the previous holders, or all or any of them collectively, and their claims would be supported by the law.

One of the most significant features of a bill of exchange is the date on which it will be due for payment. This is known as the *tenor* of the bill. It may be payable on demand, in which case it is known as a *sight bill* (illustrated on page 88). If the sellers are granting the buyers time to pay, or, in other words, extending credit to them, these circumstances may be met by making the bill payable on the expiry date of the agreed credit period. In these circumstances it is known as a *usance* bill. In most cases, usance bills are presented to the drawees first for *acceptance*, by which the drawees indicate on the bill their willingness to pay it on its maturity date.

Acceptance

The acceptance to a usance bill must be signed in precisely the same name as that shown on the bill as the drawee. It is desirable, but not essential, that the word "accepted" precedes the signature, the signature in itself being regarded as sufficient acknowledgement of the debt. Thus, individual drawees need merely sign their name across the face of the bill; partners the name of the firm, and company representatives their names under words indicating that they sign on behalf of the company. The date of the acceptance is essential only where necessary to establish the maturity date of the bill, as when it is drawn payable at a stated period after sight, and when this is the case the date should be that of presentation. Acceptance of a bill is perfectly valid if it is indicated on the reverse of the instrument, but the internal rules of discount markets usually require it to be on the face.

PRINTED AND SOLD BY
BOWEN & COURT LTD 7 GARDNER INDUSTRIAL ESTATE KENT HOUSE LANE BECKENHAM KENT

N°

Coventry, 7th. April 19 88 For GBP 6,902-00

At sight Pay this sole of Exchange to the Order

of _____

Six thousand, nine hundred and two British Pounds only

Value Received which place to Account.

To Midwest Farmers Inc.,
262 Main Street,
Lincoln, Nebraska, U.S.A.

for and on behalf of General
Insecticides Ltd.

Director

A completed sight draft. General Insecticides Ltd., have sold goods worth £6902 to Midwest Farmers Inc. The contract provides for immediate payment when the bill is presented to the drawee.

Maturity

The due date of a usance bill may be expressed in a number of ways (illustrated on pages 90-92). It may be payable on a fixed date in the future, or it may be specified as payable at the expiry of a stated period from its date of drawing. In neither of these cases is presentation for acceptance strictly necessary, since the maturity of the bill is known. Such presentation is usually made, however, if for no other reason than reassurance that the debt will be met when due, and is essential if it is desired to *discount* the bill in the market, a process which is discussed in Chapter 18. Far more usually, the usance is stated to be a given period after sight of the bill, which means that the period will not start to run until the drawee has accepted the bill, and dated such acceptance. (Acceptances are illustrated on pages 93-96.)

Qualification as bill of exchange

Technically, until such a bill has been so accepted, it is not possible to determine its maturity date and, therefore, it is not payable at "a fixed or determinable future time". Thus, such a bill is not a bill of exchange within the meaning of the Act, and it is not possible to become a holder in due course of an unaccepted usance bill where the usance is expressed as a particular period after sight. This is perhaps a good point at which to consider the other ways in which a bill of exchange might fall foul of the legal definition, and leave its holders with less protection than they might have thought that they had.

So, to consider the requirements of s.3 of the Bills of Exchange Act 1882 phrase by phrase, the first stipulation which may affect the bill is the word "unconditional". Thus, a clause on the bill such as "pay, subject to satisfactory inspection of goods on arrival" would mean that the instrument would not be a bill of exchange. Note that where a bill of exchange is issued in a set, the whole is regarded as one bill, and the words "pay this first of exchange, second unpaid", or similar, have no such disqualifying effect. "Fixed or determinable future time" has already been mentioned in connection with unaccepted usance bills, but there are other circumstances where these words may be important, such as where the bill is payable "at x days after bill of lading date" or "x days after arrival of goods". In the former case the bill could be validated by the drawees accepting it for payment on a fixed date calculated in ac-

PRINTED AND SOLD BY
BOWEN & COURT LTD   7 GARDNER INDUSTRIAL ESTATE KENT HOUSE LANE BECKENHAM KENT

N°

At   31st. July 1988

Coventry, 7th. April 19 88   For   GBP 6,902-00

Pay this   first

(second unpaid).

of Exchange
to the Order

of   ourselves

Six thousand, nine hundred and two British Pounds only

Value Received   which place to Account

To   Midwest Farmers Inc.,
262 Main Street,
Lincoln, Nebraska, U.S.A.

for and on behalf of General
Insecticides Ltd.

Director

A bill of exchange payable at a fixed date in the future. It has been drawn in duplicate in order that the accompanying documents may be sent in two separate mails.

PRINTED AND SOLD BY
BOWEN & COURT LTD 7 GARDNER INDUSTRIAL ESTATE KENT HOUSE LANE BECKENHAM KENT

No.

Coventry, 7th. April 19 88.   For   GBP 6,902.00

At 30 days date   Pay this   second

(first of exchange not being paid)   of Exchange   to the Order

of

Warwickshire Bank Ltd.

Six thousand, nine hundred and two British Pounds only

Value Received   which please to Account

To   Midwest Farmers Inc.,
262 Main Street,
Lincoln, Nebraska, U.S.A.

for and on behalf of
General Insecticides Ltd.

Director

A bill of exchange payable at a stated period from its date of issue, which is often the date of shipment. It is payable to the order of a bank, indicating that that bank is financing the transaction. This is the second of the two copies issued, and will probably never be used.

PRINTED AND SOLD BY
BOWEN & COURT LTD 7 GARDNER INDUSTRIAL ESTATE KENT HOUSE LANE BECKENHAM KENT

No.

Coventry, 7th. April 79 88. For £ 6,902.00

At 120 days sight Pay this sole of Exchange to the Order

Warwickshire Bank Ltd.

six thousand nine hundred and two British Pounds only

which please to Account

Value Received

To Midwest Farmers Inc.,
262 Main Street, Lincoln,
Nebraska, U.S.A.

for and on behalf of General
Insecticides Ltd.

Director

The commonest form of usance bill of exchange, payable at a stated period from the date when it is presented to the drawee. Technically, at this stage it is not legally a bill of exchange, since its maturity date cannot be determined.

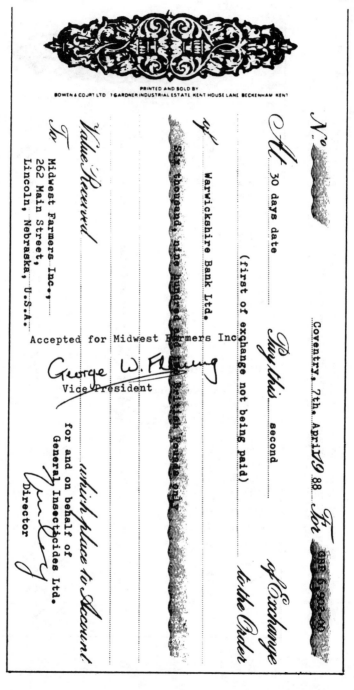

PRINTED AND SOLD BY
BOWEN & COURT LTD   7 GARDNER INDUSTRIAL ESTATE KENT HOUSE LANE BECKENHAM KENT

Nº

At 30 days date

(first of exchange not being paid)

of

Warwickshire Bank Ltd.

Value Received

To   Midwest Farmers Inc.,
262 Main Street,
Lincoln, Nebraska, U.S.A.

Coventry, 7th, April 19 88   For

Pay this   second   of Exchange
to the Order

Six thousand, nine hundred and fifty Pounds only

which please to Account

Accepted for Midwest Farmers Inc.

George W. Fleming
Vice President

for and on behalf of
General Insecticides Ltd.

[signature]
Director

A simple and perfectly valid acceptance. It does not require to be dated since its maturity is determinable without. When due, it must be represented to the drawee for payment.

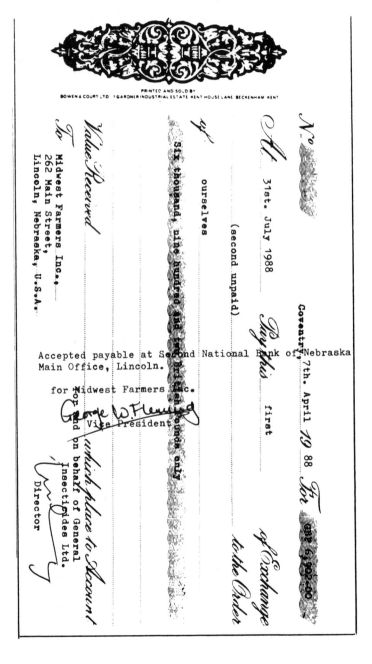

A domiciled acceptance, where the place of payment has been specified as a bank. Provided that the signature is in accordance with the mandate held by the bank, the acceptance is sufficient authority for the amount of the bill to be debited to the acceptors' account at maturity.

An accepted usance bill. The date is essential in order that maturity can be determined.

Nº

Coventry, 7th. April 19 88. For

At .... 120 days sight

Pay this .... sole .... of Exchange to the Order

of .... Warwickshire Bank Ltd.

.... thousand nine hundred ....

Value Received .... which place to Account

To Midwest Farmers Inc.,
262 Main Street, Lincoln,
Nebraska, U.S.A.

ACCEPTED April 16 198

for Midwest Farmers I[nc].

George W. Fleming
Vice President

for and on behalf of General
Insecticides Ltd.

Director

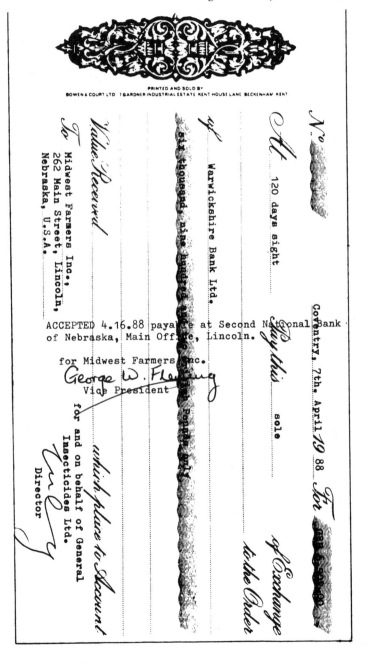

A domiciled and dated acceptance. Note the American style of expressing the date, in which the month precedes the day. This can be confusing where the day is a single figure date.

cordance with the stated tenor, but the last-mentioned event may, of course, never happen, and therefore the bill's usance period could never commence to run. Such dates are conjectural. Finally, the bill must be for "a sum certain in money", a requirement which would disqualify a bill which bears an interest clause such as "payable with interest from date hereof until approximate date of receipt of proceeds by sellers, at the rate ruling in London at maturity", since it is impossible to foretell either what the rate will be at maturity or how long it will take for proceeds to reach the drawers.

Presentation for payment

Once a bill has been accepted its maturity date must be determined in accordance with the laws of the country in which it is payable. Normally, if maturity falls on a non-working day, that maturity is automatically extended until the next working day. It remains the case in some countries of the world, particularly in the British Commonwealth, that days of grace are allowed to the acceptors before the bill may be regarded as overdue, the most common period being three days. It is important, if full rights under the bill are to be retained, to present the bill for payment on the maturity date so calculated, and, what is more, to present it at the correct place. This will be the address of the drawees as stated on the bill if their acceptance was in plain form, ie a simple signature, dated if necessary, across the face of the bill. If, however, the acceptance is a domiciled one it will nominate a place, usually a bank, at which the bill must be presented for payment at maturity and this stipulation must be complied with.

Where a bill of exchange is domiciled for payment by the acceptors' bankers it has exactly the same effect as if they had drawn a cheque on those bankers. Provided that the acceptance is signed in accordance with the mandate which the paying bank holds from its customers, that the bill is in order and that sufficient funds are available to meet it, the bank may pay the bill without reference or advice to the customers.

Protest

Where a bill is dishonoured by either non-acceptance or non-payment, further action may be necessary to preserve the rights of the holders against the acceptors and any other parties to the bill. Usually this takes the form of *protest*, the object of which is to establish beyond doubt for the benefit of the courts that the bill was properly presented at the right place on the correct maturity date. A second presentation is made, this time by a notary public or similar official, although, in the absence of such a dignitary, presentation may be made by any householder in the presence of two witnesses and the resulting deed of protest later sworn in the presence of a notary public. The deed of protest, whatever its source, testifies to the time and place of presentation and to the answer received, if applicable, this answer being, *prima facie*, the reason for refusal of acceptance or payment. From that point on the protest becomes an integral part of the bill of exchange and if the bill is later paid, the notary's charges must be paid in addition to its face amount and any interest or other charges which may be payable as a result of clauses on it. Without such a process being followed it would be almost impossible to satisfy the courts that the bill was properly presented. Under English law, protest must be made not later than the next working day following the bill's maturity date. Protest for non-acceptance is only required where it is necessary to establish a date from which the bill's maturity can be calculated. The date of such protest becomes the equivalent of the date of acceptance for this purpose.

It should be noted that protest of a bill is not always as desirable a course of action as it might at first seem. In many countries the publicity accompanying the protest can spell commercial ruin to the acceptors and bring about their bankruptcy. In extreme cases, particularly in Middle Eastern countries, non-payment of an accepted bill is a criminal offence which attracts the same penalties as outright theft. Careful thought should therefore be given to the particular circumstances surrounding each case. The remedy for such a dilemma is often to be found in a thorough knowledge of the *bona fides* of the buyers at the pre-contract stage. If sellers have confidence in the integrity of the buyers then they may feel that refusal of payment is probably well-justified and any dispute will be amicably and honourably settled without the intervention of the courts.

Another practical disadvantage of protest is that it is expensive. A deed of protest is a legal document which is completed under seal and as such may well be subject to stamp duty in addition to the fees charged by the notary public and other expenses. If the reason for non-payment is lack of funds, then the fact of protest is unlikely to improve the bill's chances of being paid and its cost may well prove to be money thrown away. Furthermore, particularly where the bill must be presented at a place which is remote from the necessary legal facilities, presentation for protest may prove impossible given the time constraints laid down by the law.

Noting

In the United Kingdom and in a very limited number of countries within the Commonwealth, a cheaper form of protection is available by having the unpaid bill *noted*. Presentation must still be made by a notary public but instead of drawing up a legal document to evidence such presentation the notary will merely attach a slip of paper to the bill recording the time and date of presentation, the answer received and the notary's charges. As with the protest, this slip thenceforward forms part of the bill, and the charges must be paid in addition to the face amount before the bill is discharged. The courts will not accept a noted bill as evidence of proper presentation but what noting does achieve is the preservation of the right to take out a full protest at a later date should it prove desirable. Thus, not only are the legal charges reduced but stamp duty on the deed is not due until the decision to protest is taken. Where the refusal of payment is likely to be temporary, this alternative to protest is often much more attractive and it is a pity that a similar option is not available in more countries.

Promissory notes

The legislation enacted by most countries to govern the rights of the various parties to bills of exchange also encompasses promissory notes. Most of the qualities of a bill apply equally to a note. The latter is a fully negotiable instrument, the chief difference being that it emanates from the debtor, known in this context not as the drawee but as the *maker*, instead of the creditor, who becomes the *beneficiary*. A very simple form of promissory note, payable to bearer, is the ordinary banknote.

Aval

English law recognises the rights of no parties to a bill of exchange other than the drawer, payee, drawee and intermediate holders in due course or for value. Many other countries, however, allow for the intervention of a guarantor of payment. The existence of such a guarantee is indicated on the bill (or note) by the signature of the guarantors *por aval*. The system of avalisation has formed the basis for the growth of the specialised form of bill finance known as *forfaiting*, which will be discussed more fully in Chapter 18. It is of interest to note here, however, that (at the time of writing) London is the major centre for *à forfait* finance in the world, yet an aval could not be enforced in an English court.

Summary

To summarise the bill of exchange from the point of view of the drawers, or sellers, the bill must be complete and regular in that it must be dated and signed, the amount shown in words must agree with that in figures, it must be for a specific sum of money, must not include any conditions as regards payment, and there must be no doubt as to when it is payable, although where the bill is payable at a stated period after sight by the drawee such doubt will remain until it has been accepted. If the money the bill represents is to be received by any party other than the payees, it must be properly endorsed by those payees. If it is a usance bill it is probably desirable and may be essential for it to be presented first for acceptance by the drawees. Presentation for payment at maturity must be made in business hours on the correct date at the place named on the bill as the drawee's address or at the place named in the acceptance if it is a domiciled one. In practice, of course, such presentation will frequently be carried out by the holder's bankers, and the responsibilities of such agents will be discussed in the next chapter, dealing with collections.

From the buyers' point of view, it is important to remember that once the bill has been accepted, it acquires an existence independent from the contract to which it relates. It may be presented for eventual payment by a holder who was not a party to and has no knowledge of that contract and the rights of such a holder will be rigidly enforced by the law. Conversely, a flaw in a bill of exchange, or an irregularity in its presentation, does not mean that a buyer's obligations under the commercial contract may be evaded, but merely that the bill cannot be used to enforce those obligations.

8
Collections

In the majority of international trade transactions, the fact of the geographical distance which separates sellers from buyers means that, where a bill for collection is the agreed method of settlement, the physical collection of the debt must be entrusted to an agent. That agent may, of course, be the sellers' commercial representative in the buyers' country, but because of their worldwide networks of correspondents which involve the exchange of lists of authorised signatories and the agreement of test arrangements for telexes and other electronic communications systems, the role of collecting agent is almost invariably filled by a bank.

Clean collections

The action required of the sellers' bank may be merely to arrange for the presentation of the bill for payment or acceptance without any accompanying documents, in which case the item is known as a clean collection. Whether or not such an item is honoured depends very much upon the drawees' willingness to pay, and if they refuse there is very little that can be done other than to protest the bill if considered appropriate. Since no documentation accompanies the bill, it must be assumed that this has been sent direct to the drawees and that they are therefore in a position to obtain control of the relative goods, or that the bill is a usance one being presented for payment at maturity and that documents were previously released against acceptance.

Documentary collections

More often, the documents which the buyers require to obtain delivery of the goods and to clear them through import procedures in their own country are sent with the bill of exchange and the item becomes a documentary collection. By doing this, the sellers can make release of the documents conditional upon the honouring of the bill by the buyers. This is of little help if the buyers have lost interest in the goods altogether, but in normal circumstances provides a considerable incentive to them to pay or accept the bill.

It is very important that when handing the collection to their bankers the drawers provide full instructions as to how that item is to be handled. Where the bill is payable at sight the documents will normally be released only against payment, and the terms of the collection are said to be D/P. The sellers may, however, be prepared to make some concessions to the buyers, such as giving them the option to await arrival of the goods before taking up the documents. This is in fact the custom in many parts of the world, particularly in the East, and local banks will automatically allow it to happen unless they are specifically instructed to the contrary. The buyers may be able to inspect the goods before deciding whether or not to honour the bill, and may even be permitted to take away samples for testing. Neither of these privileges will be granted by any bank unless the instructions which it has received expressly authorise it to do so.

Where the bill is at usance, it is vital that the bank be informed by the drawers whether the documents are to be released to the drawees against acceptance (D/A terms) or payment (D/P terms). Buyers will normally ask for D/A terms since this will enable them to clear the goods quickly on arrival, but the granting of these terms means that reliance must thereafter be placed upon the acceptance on the bill, the promise to pay. If that promise is worthless there is little that can effectively be done other than to resort to law, and the exhortation to sellers which has been repeated often in this book, to know the buyers before entering into the contract, must be given yet again. Nonetheless, the vast majority of usance bills set for collection are handled on D/A terms, since, after all, few would grant a complete unknown a period of months to pay for goods which have already changed hands.

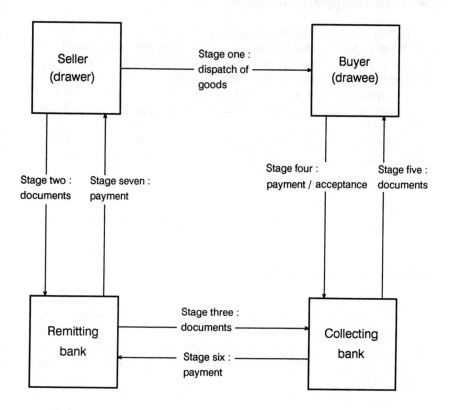

The collection process

Warehousing and insurance of goods

Despite this, D/P terms are fairly frequently encountered, and are often convenient where the buyers are merchants operating either with restricted storage space or with a very tight cash flow. They may not require to take possession of the goods until they have a firm contract for the onward sale of those goods, or until they are needed for a specific purpose. This arrangement means that the goods may well arrive before the buyers are in a position to pay for them, and as such will need protection for the intervening period. They remain, of course, the property of the sellers, who will need an agent to act on their behalf to clear the goods into a bonded warehouse, to supervise their storage and to attend to insurance while they remain in store. Often that agent is the collecting bank. In these circumstances it is even more important that full instructions are given at the outset as to how that bank is to proceed.

Goods on consignment

A similar situation arises where the goods are sent on a consignment basis. This means that no payment will be made until the buyers have firm contracts for their onward sale, which may constitute all or part of the total consignment. Sometimes a limit is placed on the time allowed for total disposal of the goods. This may involve the buyers in giving an undertaking to pay any remaining balance at the expiry of that period. Once again, it is important that full instructions are given by the sellers at the time of handing the collection to their bankers, since those instructions will determine the actions taken by the collecting bank over what may well be a considerable period of time.

Historically, many banks, particularly in important seaports around the world, maintained their own warehouses and employed their own staff to run them. They were thus well-placed to carry out this type of service on behalf of their correspondents. Although bank warehouses, or "godowns", are not entirely unknown at the present time, the modern tendency is to subcontract this type of work to a specialist company. What usually happens in practice is that when necessary a bank will release an original bill of lading to its warehousing agents with instructions to clear the goods and to place them in store in the bank's name until further notice. The instructions may also cover insurance of the goods, or the bank may have its own policy under which they may be declared.

It is desirable that periodically a bank bearing responsibility for the safe keeping of goods in this way makes physical checks on those goods to ascertain their continued presence and condition. When the time comes for the goods, or part of them, to be released to the first buyers or their nominees, the bank will, on receipt of payment, issue a delivery order addressed to the warehouse keepers authorising them to deliver the goods to a named party or to bearer. These documents are effectively title to the goods and in some countries have acquired almost the status of negotiable instruments. They fail to achieve this distinction, however, for a number of reasons but particularly because they can convey no better title to the goods than was possessed by the person giving them, unlike a marine bill of lading.

Such involvement of banks in the warehousing of goods is not as unusual as might at first be thought. There are a number of circumstances where goods may be warehoused in the bank's name, of which we have so far considered but two, goods on D/P usance terms and goods on consignment. Another is where acceptance or payment of the bill of exchange has been refused by the drawees and the goods have arrived. Again, the collecting bank in the buyers' country is best placed to ensure that the goods come to no harm, as the holder of the documents of title and as the sellers' already-appointed agent. As will be discussed later in this chapter, the last-mentioned circumstance is often important in determining the course of action which a bank will take in particular circumstances, but to be sure that the sellers' wishes are carried out in case of dishonour of the bill it is important that they include specific instructions at the outset as to what their requirements are.

It may also be necessary for the collecting bank to arrange for storage of the goods where the collection order authorises the drawees to inspect them, or to take away samples, before payment or acceptance of the drawing. In these circumstances, an inspection order or a sampling order will be issued by the bank to the warehouse keepers to enable this to happen.

Protest of dishonoured bill

Storage and insurance of goods are but two of the possible courses open to the sellers where those goods are not taken up following either acceptance or payment of the bill. Protest or noting of the bill, as described in the last chapter, is another, and again it is important in view of the statutory time limits on when this may be done that instructions be given at the outset, before anything has gone wrong. There is then no risk that a bill may be left unprotested and therefore invalid in a court of law merely because no-one was asked to carry out that protest. Great care should be taken, however, to ensure that protest is indeed a desirable remedy in the individual circumstances applying to each collection, since its effect in some countries can be little short of catastrophic for the buyers. On the other hand, the mere threat of its being carried out may be sufficient to induce the buyers to honour the drawing. Only the sellers can make this decision and it should be made before the documents leave their control.

Case of need

Another possibility is that the sellers have their own commercial agents in the buyers' country who may be in a position to represent them in negotiations with the buyers in an attempt to reach a settlement. No bank will divulge information regarding its customers' affairs to a third party without written authority to do so. Again, such authority should be given when the drawing is first sent for collection. Furthermore, this should state the precise extent of the powers which may be delegated to the agents, known as the *case of need*, since they are only brought into the transaction in case of the need arising for their services. Such powers may be advisory, in which case their action will be simply to try to use their influence to persuade the buyers to take up the goods. They may be absolute, enabling the agents if they see fit to take documents of title from the bank free of payment and seek to sell the goods elsewhere or even ship them back to the sellers. They may lie anywhere between these two extremes. Whatever they are, there must be no room for doubt on the part of the bank seeking to put the sellers' instructions into effect.

Collection charges

Before leaving the subject of instructions which should be given by the sellers to their bank with the collection, mention must be made of the often vexing question of bank charges. Naturally, banks who are providing the services which have been described above require adequate payment for those services. As was mentioned in Chapter 2, all too often no

provision is made at the contract stage regarding who should be responsible for the payment of such charges and it is therefore important that
the sellers state clearly in their instructions what, if anything, has been
agreed on the subject. If, in their perception, the buyers are responsible
for meeting all bank charges, or for perhaps only those levied by the
bank or banks handling the collection in the buyers' country, then
instructions should be given for the amount of such charges to be
collected in addition to the amount of the drawing. Instructions should
also give the banks clear guidance as to the action required of them
should the buyers' perception of the responsibility be different from that
of the sellers. This is usually achieved by stating that charges should be
collected but may be waived if refused, or may not be waived as the case
may be. Careful consideration should be given to the matter before the
latter alternative is used, however, since economically speaking, it is
often nonsense to sacrifice payment of the principal amount for the sake
of what are usually relatively insignificant amounts. Buyers, of course, are
well aware of this and many refuse bank charges as a matter of principle.
In such cases, the law of agency will apply, and as in a collection the
sellers are the principals, so they are the party with ultimate responsibility for reimbursement of expenses incurred on their behalf by their
agents.

Effect of the law of agency

It is perhaps time to examine this question of agency in more detail,
since in the still significant number of countries where the ICC's Uniform
Rules for Collections have not been adopted it is the law of agency
which exerts most influence on the actions of the various parties involved in the collection process. All the banks which may become involved in the collection are regarded as acting on behalf of the drawers,
though they may have played no part in the selection of those banks
other than the first in the chain. This rule applies even where the ultimate collecting bank is presenting the drawing to its own customer for
settlement.

The first duty of agents is, of course, to act in accordance with their
principals' instructions. There are one or two exceptions to this rule, such
as where to carry out such instructions would be detrimental to the interests of the principals, or to those of the agents themselves. But, generally
speaking, a bank which acts in a way which is plainly not according to

the instructions it has received is taking a very grave risk should its principals incur a loss as a result.

Another important responsibility applying to agents and one which is not so easily definable as the first, is to take any action appropriate to the protection of their principals' interests. This is likely to happen where a situation arises which is not covered by the principals' instructions, such as where goods have arrived and a collecting bank decides to take steps to protect those goods through storage and insurance even though it has no instructions to do so. Since it is plainly of considerable benefit to the owners of the goods that such action be taken, they would not be able to claim that the agents had acted outside the terms of their instructions and would be bound to reimburse the agents for any expenses incurred. Similarly, where a bill is unpaid and the collecting bank arranges for its protest without specific instructions to that effect, such action would be regarded as being in the interests of the drawers in preserving their rights to sue under the bill. The costs (and the consequences) would have to be borne by the drawers. This further underlines what has been said previously in this chapter, that it is important that complete and clear instructions be given at the outset regarding what action is to be taken in particular circumstances, especially in the event of dishonour of the bill.

The prime responsibilities of the drawers, as we have seen, are those of principals towards their agents. Other than these, their chief responsibility is to themselves, since imperfect documentation may well result in delayed payment, unnecessary expense, or even eventual dishonour of the drawing. It therefore makes good sense to ensure that all the documents called for under the contract have been supplied, that they are properly completed, signed and endorsed where necessary, and that any statement regarding the goods or any other aspect of the transaction which is required to be made on the invoice or elsewhere is present.

What of the responsibilities of the other parties in the collection process?

The remitting bank

The first of these parties is the bank to which the collection is entrusted by the drawers, known as the *remitting bank*. Most frequently, this will be the drawers' own bank, though this is not always the case. Too often, the remitting bank sees itself as nothing more than a post office, dispatching the collection to its overseas correspondents, charging its commission, but doing little more to bring the collection to a successful conclusion. However, it is a good idea to examine the documents, both for completeness and accuracy. It should be alert for such possibilities as missing endorsements or signatures, absence of documents known to be required for the country of destination of the goods or indicated as being required by the contract terms quoted on the invoice and so on. This examination need not be in minute detail, but it is to the benefit of all concerned if obvious discrepancies in the documents are identified and corrected at this stage rather than when those documents are perhaps ten thousand miles away. The remitting bank, however, is not expected to carry out the exporters' own checking procedures. No legal liability is likely to be incurred by the remitting bank if it fails to detect errors in the documents at this stage. However, if it does detect them its relations both with its customers and its correspondents are enhanced and much correspondence at a later stage is avoided, besides improving the chances of the collection being paid by the drawees.

Endorsement of bill

Since the essence of a collection is usually the bill of exchange and this document may at some later date be required as evidence in legal proceedings, particular attention should be paid to ensure that it fulfils all the requirements of a bill of exchange as laid down in the relevant legislation and described in Chapter 7. If it is made out payable to the order of the drawers, as is usually the case, it should be endorsed by them to enable the proceeds to be paid to a third party, the collecting bank. Such endorsement may be specifically to the remitting bank, which will in turn need to add its own endorsement in favour of the collecting bank. It may be restricted, making the bill payable to "any bank or trust company", or blank, in which case the remitting bank will often close the endorsement by adding words making the bill payable to itself or its correspondent. It is desirable that words such as "value for collection only" be added to the endorsement as an indication that the banks handling the collection are not parties to the financial aspect of the bill or they might find themselves liable to a later "holder in due course" of the bill. Such a qualification should obviously not be used where the bank is providing finance against the bill but will still apply to the endorsement in favour of the collecting bank.

The collection order

Having examined the documents, the remitting bank should next examine the drawers' instructions. If it is not satisfied that they are adequate or, if there are any apparent contradictions, or requirements which might be impossible to comply with or are even to the drawers' detriment should they be complied with, it should take such matters up with its principals immediately rather than slavishly repeating the instructions to its correspondent as is too often the case. Again, by doing so, it is avoiding much needless correspondence and expense at a later date when the bill is unpaid and the collecting bank is unclear as to the action required of it.

It is worth mentioning at this point that great care should be taken by banks when drawers include an instruction that money, usually representing agent's commission, be paid direct from the proceeds of the drawing to a third party. Considerable amounts have been obtained by fraudsters in this way in the past, simply by diversions of relatively insignificant percentages of drawings into their private accounts. Such amounts are easily assumed to have been deducted in the form of bank charges. It is much safer if such commission payments are made as a separate remittance after receipt of proceeds by the drawers. In any case, bill schedules are rarely signed in accordance with the mandate held by the bank for operation of the account, which, of course, they should be if they include payment instructions.

The remitting bank must then give its attention to the instructions which it in turn will give to the collecting bank. For the most part, these will mirror those it has received from the drawers, but it may wish to add its own contribution in such matters as the method by which proceeds of the drawing will eventually be remitted, including the nomination of a receiving bank if the bill is expressed in a foreign currency. It must then send the collection to its selected correspondent by the most expeditious means. Many banks make extensive use of courier services for their international mail and a careful record should be kept of the date on which the item was entrusted to the couriers along with the bag reference if any. If the documents are despatched by airmail they should be sent by registered post, not so much for the nominal compensation which is paid in case of non-delivery of such mail, as for the means of proof of dispatch which this affords. At least a Post Office registration receipt will be evidence that missing documents have not been accidentally shredded or dropped behind a filing cabinet before they have even left the premises of the remitting bank.

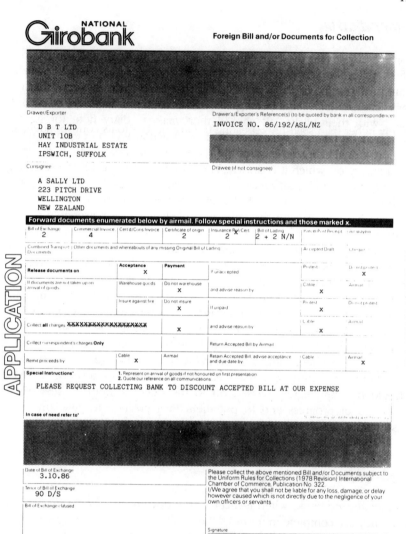

Giirobank NATIONAL

Foreign Bill and/or Documents for Collection

Drawer/Exporter

D B T LTD
UNIT 10B
HAY INDUSTRIAL ESTATE
IPSWICH, SUFFOLK

Drawer's/Exporter's Reference(s) (to be quoted by bank in all correspondence)

INVOICE NO. 86/192/ASL/NZ

Consignee

A SALLY LTD
223 PITCH DRIVE
WELLINGTON
NEW ZEALAND

Drawee (if not consignee)

Forward documents enumerated below by airmail. Follow special instructions and those marked x.

Bill of Exchange	Commercial Invoice	Cert d/Cons Invoice	Certificate of origin	Insurance Pol/Cert	Bill of Lading	Parcel Post Receipt	Air waybill
2	4		2 x	2	2 + 2 N/N		

Combined Transport / Other documents and whereabouts of any missing Original Bill of Lading

	Acceptance	Payment		Accepted Draft	Cheque
Release documents on	X		If unaccepted	Protest	Do not protest X
If documents are not taken up on arrival of goods	Warehouse goods	Do not warehouse X	and advise reason by	Cable X	Airmail
	Insure against fire	Do not insure X	If unpaid	Protest	Do not protest X
Collect **all** charges XXXXXXXXXXXXXXXXXXXXXX		X	and advise reason by	Cable X	Airmail
Collect correspondent's charges **Only**			Return Accepted Bill by Airmail		
Remit proceeds by	Cable X	Airmail	Retain Accepted Bill, advise acceptance and due date by	Cable	Airmail X

Special Instructions*
1. Represent on arrival of goods if not honoured on first presentation
2. Quote our reference on all communications

PLEASE REQUEST COLLECTING BANK TO DISCOUNT ACCEPTED BILL AT OUR EXPENSE

In case of need refer to*

Date of Bill of Exchange
3.10.86

Tenor of Bill of Exchange
90 D/S

Bill of Exchange refused

Please collect the above mentioned Bill and/or Documents subject to the Uniform Rules for Collections (1978 Revision) International Chamber of Commerce, Publication No. 322
I/We agree that you shall not be liable for any loss, damage, or delay however caused which is not directly due to the negligence of your own officers or servants

Signature
(for customer)

date 6.10.86

Bill of Exchange value A XXXXXXXXXXX

£15,231.60

A well-designed and properly completed collection order

Fate enquiries

Having dispatched the collection, the remitting bank should send a copy of its collection schedule to the drawers, both to act as an acknowledgement of receipt of the drawing and to enable them to verify that the instructions which have been given to the collecting bank are in accordance with their wishes. It should then make a diary note for further action to be taken if necessary. What that action will be depends upon the individual characteristics of the collection and more particularly upon the country on which it is drawn. The important thing is for the remitting bank to be aware at all times of the current status of the collection, and in this, of course, it must rely largely upon its correspondent. If it does not receive advice from the collecting bank within a reasonable time it should institute enquiries itself. These enquiries are usually referred to in the banking industry as "chasers", and are often carbon copies of the original collection schedule which accompanied the documents. It has to be admitted that the value of these chasers is questionable in the extreme, since they seldom have the appearance of being important communications and tend to be either ignored completely or given very low priority. A formal letter, or a telecommunication if it is considered that the additional expense is warranted, is far more likely to elicit a response than a routine chaser, and it is desirable that no more than one such be sent before resorting to other means of enquiry. Any advices received should be immediately passed on to the drawers, both to keep them informed of progress and to put them in a position to give any fresh instructions which they may consider appropriate.

The collecting bank

The collecting bank, when it receives the documents, should first ensure that they are complete in terms of the remitting bank's covering schedule, and should then carefully read the instructions which it has been given. If either of these operations reveals any cause for enquiry it should contact the remitting bank immediately. It should then check whether any of the documents requires its own endorsement to validate them and affix any stamps to the bill which may be required under the tax laws of its country. It is then faced with the problem of presentation of the collection to the drawees without prejudicing the interests of its principals, the drawers. There are a number of ways of achieving this, depending on local practice, on the standing of the drawees in the local community and their geographical location relative to the collecting bank.

Presentation

If the drawees' premises are nearby, it may be possible for their representative to call at the bank to inspect the documents, or for a bank messenger to take them to the drawees' premises for that purpose. If the documents are found to be in order, arrangements can then be made for payment, or a usance bill can be accepted and the documents released in exchange, unless of course the terms of the collection are D/P and the bill is at usance.

If, however, the drawees are at some distance from the bank, nonnegotiable copy documents can be mailed for examination, the documents of title only being released when the drawing is honoured. This can be unsatisfactory, however, since often it is essential to have sight of the original bill of lading in particular before a decision can be made on the acceptability of the documents. An alternative, but more expensive and troublesome method, is to send photocopies of the documents, or to transmit their images by facsimile machine if such is available.

The collecting bank is in a much better position where the drawees are their own customers, since they then have the information necessary to make a decision on whether the documents may be sent or released on trust for examination. If distance is a problem, they may be able to use the services of their local branch to make physical presentation of the collection to the drawees. Since, however, the collecting bank has been entrusted with the drawing because of its correspondent relationship with the remitting bank rather than any connection with or proximity to the drawees, it is quite common for the drawees to be customers of a different bank as well as being too far distant for physical presentation to be a possibility. In these circumstances it is common for the collecting bank to ascertain the identity of the drawees' bankers and to forward the drawing to them with all relevant instructions for collection. The decision as to the trustworthiness of the drawees is thus delegated to those best placed to make it. The disadvantages of this method are that payment is likely to be made slower by the extra processing in the third bank, a further set of collection charges will be incurred, and the possibility of a fruitful marketing contact with another bank's customer is lost.

Large numbers of collections are on sight D/P terms and are paid without problems. In this situation, the only responsibility of the collecting bank is to remit the proceeds as quickly as possible in the manner laid down by the remitting bank in its instructions, under advice to that bank if necessary. It is entitled to deduct its charges from the amount sent, if they have not been collected from the drawees, and further charges may accrue where the payment is made through the collecting bank's correspondent to a nominated bank in a third country.

Payment "pipelines"

In some countries, a shortage of hard currency with which to pay for imports has led to a system whereby, provided the collection order so authorises, documents are released to the buyers against payment in local currency. The collecting bank then makes application to the authorities for an allocation of foreign exchange to enable it to remit proceeds to the remitting bank. If none is immediately available, the application is placed in what is known as a "pipeline", which means that it joins a queue and that payment will not reach the sellers until the application arrives at the head of that queue. Usually the sellers will have been aware of this factor at the time of entering into the contract, but it remains important that notification of payment in local currency is sent to the remitting bank so that all are aware that the buyers have fulfilled their obligations. Remitting banks should note that from this point on there is little to be gained by continuing to send monthly chasers, since there is nothing which the collecting bank can usually do to expedite payment— the matter is out of their hands. The waiting period for items in pipelines is normally a known factor and may be anything up to three years or beyond in some cases.

Terms of payment

Where the terms are usance D/A, the acceptance on the bill should be checked for apparent correctness. It should be signed in the same name as is stated on the bill for the drawee and if the bill is payable at a given period after sight the acceptance must be dated in order that the maturity date may be ascertained. If the bill is domiciled for payment at the collecting bank by one of that bank's own customers, the acceptance amounts to an instruction to pay and should therefore be checked in accordance with the mandate held, and the signatures verified. There is no legislative requirement regarding the actual position of the acceptance, but the domestic regulations of many financial markets, including that of London, require the acceptance to be on the face of the bill and endorsements to be on the back.

What happens next will depend upon the instructions held. Sometimes it is requested that the bill be returned to the remitting bank after acceptance, and in these circumstances this should be done as soon as possible, any charges claimed and the item discharged. More often the instructions are to hold the bill until maturity and then to present it for payment, in which case it is essential to advise the remitting bank of acceptance and of the bill's maturity date as soon as possible. Particularly if a bill is to be protested for dishonour, it is vital that it is presented on its maturity date and so careful records must be kept in a diary specifically for that purpose. Although sight bills and unaccepted usance bills are virtually worthless, it should be remembered that an accepted usance bill is a promise of payment and a fully negotiable instrument. It is therefore potentially worth whatever amount is shown on its face. It should therefore be kept, unendorsed, in a secure place until the time comes for its presentation for payment. It must then be presented to the place for payment stipulated, if the acceptance is a domiciled one, or to the drawees' address as shown on the bill if it is not. On payment, proceeds are dealt with as described above for a sight bill.

Where the terms of the collection are usance D/P, the bill should be presented for acceptance and its maturity noted in a diary in the same way as for a D/A bill. In this case, however, the documents must be kept with the bill and, furthermore, the collecting bank must ascertain from the shipping company's agents the expected arrival date of the carrying vessel (a diary note should be made of this). This is because the goods may well arrive and therefore need protective measures before the bill is presented for payment. In practice, many acceptors will want to take up the documents on arrival of the goods and will therefore pay the bill before its maturity, a process known as *retiral*. In some trades it is customary to allow a rebate on the amount of a retired bill to reflect the interest advantage to the drawers arising from early receipt of proceeds. This should be covered in the instructions received from the remitting bank.

Sometimes the drawees may state that they wish to defer payment or acceptance of a bill until arrival of the goods and in many countries this is accepted as standard practice. If this occurs, the collecting bank should again ascertain the expected arrival date of the vessel and immediately advise the remitting bank of the position, following which a diary note should be made for re-presentation and the documents kept securely until that time.

Procedure on dishonour

Similar considerations apply where a bill is dishonoured for any other reason, since the protection of the goods is of paramount importance. As previously stated, such action may be in accordance with specific instructions received, or may voluntarily be undertaken by the collecting bank to protect the interests of its principals. With this aspect taken care of, it should be clear from the instructions held as to what other actions are to be taken. In any case, the remitting bank must be informed immediately, by telecommunication if possible, of the dishonour and of the reasons for it, if any have been given, the expected date of arrival of the carrying vessel and of what action has been or is being taken to obtain payment or acceptance of the bill.

If protest of the bill is required and it is an unaccepted usance bill payable at a stated period after sight, it must first be protested for non-acceptance. The only effect of this is to establish a date from which the bill's maturity can be calculated. When this date is reached it must be represented, this time for payment, and a fresh protest executed if payment is refused.

Where the remitting bank's instructions permit reference to a "case of need" where dishonour occurs, this must be done immediately, since any delay may make its intervention ineffective. Great care should be taken, however, to ensure that the bank does not exceed its powers, and if those powers are stated to be advisory it must not be allowed to intervene in the goods themselves. If the extent of the bank's powers is not clear from the instructions (and these instructions were not clarified on receipt, as they should have been), it must be assumed that its function is merely advisory. Where it is stated to have full powers, however, it would be in order for the collecting bank to release the documents to it against a simple receipt and possibly payment of any outstanding charges, and thereafter to discharge the item from its records. In these circumstances, of course, the remitting bank must be advised immediately of the action taken, and the receipt forwarded to it.

The drawees

It remains to consider the position of the drawees themselves, which of course is the strongest of any party involved in the collection process. When documents are presented for payment or acceptance it is essential that they be examined carefully to ensure that they are as called for in the contract, that they are in a form which will allow trouble-free import of the goods when they arrive, that those goods have not in fact already arrived and therefore are possibly incurring demurrage charges, that there is nothing in the documents to suggest that the goods are sub-standard or damaged in any way, and that the goods appear to be of the specification ordered.

In the absence of authority to inspect the goods or to take samples before paying or accepting the bill, there is little more that can be done to ensure that the merchandise will be in order and therefore much will rest upon the relationship between sellers and buyers, as has been said many times before. Should any dispute arise later it is outside the scope of the collection and must be settled under the contract itself. Where a bill has been accepted for payment at a future date, it is not unknown for buyers and sellers to notify the collecting bank, through the remitting bank, that a discount may be allowed when the bill is presented for payment to redress some discovered defect or shortage in the goods. It should be remembered, however, that this will not be possible if the bill has since been discounted and may be presented by a holder in due course who has no connection with and no knowledge of the underlying contract. For this reason, it is generally more satisfactory if such settlements are made outside the collection after the bill has been honoured.

9
Uniform Rules for Collections

In keeping with its twin objectives of the standardisation and simplification of international trade procedures, the International Chamber of Commerce (ICC) in 1956 introduced a set of rules for voluntary adoption by national banking associations or individual banks for the handling of collections, both clean and documentary. Subsequent revisions of these rules came into effect in 1968 and 1979, and it is the latter version which remains in force at the present time, under the title Uniform Rules for Collections (URC), and published by the ICC in its publication no. 322.

By comparison with the similar rules relating to documentary credits, the URC are a straightforward code, based largely upon common sense and reflecting already established methods of handling collections. This is not to say that Uniform Customs and Practice for Documentary Credits (UCP), to be discussed later in this book, are in any way not based on common sense principles, but collections by their nature are much simpler transactions than credits and this factor expresses itself in the relative simplicity of the rules required for their governance.

As with any set of rules, it is of paramount importance that all those who may be affected by them are fully aware of their contents. In countries where they have been adopted, all bank collection schedules will incorporate a clause stating that the collection is handled subject to the provisions of URC. It therefore makes sense for exporters and forwarders to familiarise themselves with the rules, since they will have a direct bearing on the way in which their documents, and the monetary proceeds arising from them, are handled, and, as we have seen, may even extend to the treatment of the goods themselves.

Many of the processes and situations covered by URC have already been dealt with in the preceding chapters. The purpose of this one is to examine each rule with reference to how it relates to the collection as we have described it in Chapter 8, with such additional comment as may be necessary. The Rules consist of 23 Articles preceded by three General Provisions and Definitions. It is these which will be looked at first.

General provisions and definitions

A   These provisions and definitions and the following articles apply to all collections as defined in (B) below and are binding upon all parties thereto unless otherwise expressly agreed or unless contrary to the provisions of a national, state or local law and/or regulation which cannot be departed from.

Comment

The adoption of URC has been by no means as widespread as that of UCP and there are thus potential problems where one or the other of the banks involved in a collection does not recognise them. Where this is the remitting bank and the collecting bank states on its acknowledgement of receipt of the item that it will handle it in accordance with the provisions of URC, it could be said that it has placed that condition upon its acceptance of the responsibilities of an agent. Where the reverse situation arises, the remitting bank will state on its covering schedule that the terms of URC apply to the collection, and unless the collecting bank expressly rejects that stipulation in its acknowledgement of receipt it would be held to have accepted the condition along with all the other instructions contained in the schedule. In practice, therefore, even where one bank has not adopted the Rules they may be applied by the courts anyway, provided that they do not contravene any existing law as provided for by General Provision A.

B   For the purpose of such provisions, definitions and articles:
   (i)   "Collection" means the handling by banks, on instructions received, of documents as defined in (ii) below, in order to
       (a)   obtain acceptance and/or, as the case may be, payment, or

      (b)   deliver commercial documents against acceptance and/or, as the case may be, against payment, or

      (c)   deliver documents against other terms and conditions

Comment

Item (c) above covers the situation which occasionally arises where documents are to be delivered free of payment against the provision of a simple receipt, or against the presentation of evidence that payment has been effected by other means, or against evidence of the issue of a standby letter of credit covering payment.

     (ii)   "Documents" means financial documents and/or commercial documents:

         (a)   "financial documents" means bills of exchange, promissory notes, cheques, payment receipts or other similar instruments used for obtaining the payment of money;

         (b)   "commercial documents" means invoices, shipping documents, documents of title or other similar documents, or any other documents whatsoever, not being financial documents.

    (iii)   "Clean collection" means collection of financial documents not accompanied by commercial documents.

    (iv)   "Documentary collection" means collection of

         (a)   financial documents accompanied by commercial documents;

         (b)   commercial documents not accompanied by financial documents.

  (2) The "parties thereto" are

      (i)   the "principal" who is the customer entrusting the operation of collection to his bank;

     (ii)   the "remitting bank" which is the bank to which the principal has entrusted the operation of collection;

    (iii)   the "collecting bank" which is any bank, other than the remitting bank, involved in processing the collection order;

    (iv)   the "presenting bank" which is the collecting bank making presentation to the drawee.

Comment

The use of the word "principal", 2(i), is interesting in that it is borrowed directly from the phraseology of the law of agency, of which much has been said in preceding chapters.

(3) The "drawee" is the one to whom presentation is to be made according to the collection order.

(C) All documents sent for collection must be accompanied by a collection order giving complete and precise instructions. Banks are only permitted to act upon the instructions given in such collection order, and in accordance with these Rules.

If any bank cannot, for any reason, comply with the instructions given in the collection order received by it, it must immediately advise the party from whom it received the collection order.

Comment

It is probably the case that no article of URC is flouted more frequently than this one, in that complete and precise instructions are unfortunately the exception rather than the rule. The apparent prohibition on banks taking independent action outside the terms of the collection order is mitigated by the provision that the rules themselves may be the source of authority for such action. As will be seen, certain articles provide for non-obligatory independent action by banks as agents protecting the principals' interests, notably Article 19 relating to goods.

Liabilities and responsibilities

ARTICLE 1
Banks will act in good faith and exercise reasonable care.

Comment

It should be noted that past legal decisions have indicated that the judiciary expect a high standard in both these commodities from banks which are charging for professional services and are expected to provide staff with the necessary expertise to handle collections effectively and efficiently. Any bank which does not do so could be liable for breach of contract and bound to cover any losses to its principals which result from such breach. This article merely underlines the already established principle of the law of agency.

ARTICLE 2
Banks must verify that the documents received appear to be as listed in the collection order and must immediately advise the party from whom the col-

lection order was received of any documents missing.

Banks have no further obligation to examine the documents.

Comment

Despite the final sentence of this article, there are in fact common sense reasons for at least a cursory examination of the documents, as outlined in Chapter 8.

ARTICLE 3

For the purpose of giving effect to the instructions of the principal, the remitting bank will utilise as the collecting bank:

   (i)   the collecting bank nominated by the principal, or, in the absence of such nomination,

   (ii)   any bank, of its own or another bank's choice, in the country of payment or acceptance, as the case may be.

The documents and the collection order may be sent to the collecting bank directly or through another bank as intermediary.

Banks utilising the services of other banks for the purpose of giving effect to the instructions of the principal do so for the account of and at the risk of the latter.

The principal shall be bound by and liable to indemnify the banks against all obligations and responsibilities imposed by foreign laws or usages.

Comment

Again, the URC are following the law of agency as already established.

ARTICLE 4

Banks concerned with a collection assume no liability or responsibility for the consequences arising out of delay and/or loss in transit of any messages, letters or documents, or for delay, mutilation or other errors arising in the transmission of cables, telegrams, telex, or communication by electronic systems, or for errors in translation in interpretation of technical terms.

ARTICLE 5

Banks concerned with a collection assume no liability or responsibility for consequences arising out of the interruption of their business by Acts of God, riots, civil commotions, insurrections, wars, or any other causes beyond their control or by strikes and lockouts.

Comment

Articles 4 and 5 provide a degree of protection which should make adoption of the URC attractive to banks. Bearing in mind what has been said about their responsibilities under the law of agency, they have everything to gain and little to lose by such adoption. It should not be thought by banks, however, that the protection afforded by Article 4 would absolve them of their responsibility to exercise reasonable care as required by Article 1.

ARTICLE 6

Goods should not be despatched direct to the address of a bank or consigned to a bank without prior agreement on the part of that bank.

In the event of goods being despatched direct to the address of a bank or consigned to a bank for delivery to a drawee against payment or acceptance or upon other terms without prior agreement on the part of that bank, the bank has no obligation to take delivery of the goods, which remain at the risk and responsibility of the party dispatching the goods.

Comment

The justice of this provision should be apparent on two counts. Firstly, the handling of goods is not a service which the banks offer in the normal run of their business and is outside the scope of their usual activities. Although, as has been seen, they do quite frequently become involved with the goods, this takes place in specific circumstances and in no way obliges them to assume the duties of a mercantile agent. Secondly, no-one can be expected to assume responsibility for a duty which they have not previously agreed to perform.

Presentation

ARTICLE 7

Documents are to be presented to the drawee in the form in which they are received, except that remitting and collecting banks are authorised to affix any necessary stamps, at the expense of the principal unless otherwise instructed, and to make any necessary endorsements or place any rubber stamps or other identifying marks or symbols customary to or required by the collection operation.

Comment

The authority to affix stamps is necessary because in countries where stamp duty is payable on bills of exchange such instruments would have no legal significance if duty were not paid and evidenced on the bill. In some countries, similar considerations apply to other documents such as bills of lading and insurance policies or certificates. The right to do this is probably conferred already by Article 3 in its reference to foreign laws and usages. Endorsements are likewise necessary to validate certain documents.

The addition of identifying marks refers to the practice of many banks of stamping their collection reference number on each document received to guard against the possibility of that document becoming detached from the rest and subsequently making it difficult or perhaps impossible to reunite it with its fellows, particularly where those fellows have passed out of the possession of the bank.

The practice in banks of marking accepted usance bills with the maturity date must be treated with caution. Although perhaps necessary to the collection operation, if a mistake is made and an alteration becomes necessary, such a change would constitute a material alteration to the instrument, and as such would require validation by all previous holders. It is therefore good practice to write the maturity date in pencil which can later be erased if necessary.

ARTICLE 8

Collection orders should bear the complete address of the drawee or of the domicile at which presentation is to be made. If the address is incomplete or incorrect, the collecting bank may, without obligation and responsibility on its part, endeavour to ascertain the proper address.

Comment

This article covers a frequent problem which occurs where the address given is limited to a post office box number. Since physical presentation of the documents is therefore impossible without relinquishing control of them, the collecting bank can do no more than to write to the drawees advising them of their arrival. This will mean that a delay, perhaps crucial, will occur in the documents being made available to the drawees. If no reply is received by the collecting bank it is helpless to proceed further. The prime responsibility for ensuring that this article is complied with rests with the drawers, but the remitting bank should ensure that full details of the drawees' address appear on the documents before they are sent to the collecting bank.

ARTICLE 9
In the case of documents payable at sight the presenting bank must make presentation for payment without delay.
In the case of documents payable at a tenor other than sight the presenting bank must, where acceptance is called for, make presentation for acceptance without delay, and where payment is called for, make presentation for payment not later than the appropriate maturity date.

ARTICLE 10
In respect of a documentary collection including a bill of exchange payable at a future date, the collection order should state whether the commercial documents are to be released to the drawee against acceptance (D/A) or against payment (D/P). In the absence of such statement, the commercial documents will be released only against payment.

Comment

Article 10 ensures that in the absence of proper instructions the collecting bank will take the safest of the alternatives open to it and retain documents until the goods have been paid for. Whilst this may sound fine in principle, it often places the collecting bank in an extremely awkward situation when the drawees claim that the terms of their agreement with the sellers are D/A. It should not happen and no usance drawing should ever leave the possession of the remitting bank without this most essential piece of information accompanying it.

Payment

ARTICLE 11
In the case of documents payable in the currency of the country of payment (local currency), the presenting bank must, unless otherwise instructed in the collection order, only release the documents to the drawee against payment in local currency which is immediately available for disposal in the manner specified in the collection order.

Comment

In a number of countries, particularly those with exchange control regulations, money must be designated "external" before it may be credited to the account of a non-resident. Funds not so designated are likely to be of little use to the sellers and are therefore not acceptable as payment in exchange for the release of documents.

ARTICLE 12
In the case of documents payable in a currency other than the country of payment (foreign currency), the presenting bank must, unless otherwise instructed in the collection order, only release documents to the drawee against payment in the relative foreign currency which can immediately be remitted in accordance with the instructions given in the collection order.

ARTICLE 13
In respect of clean collections partial payments may be accepted if and to the extent to which and on the conditions on which partial payments are authorised by the law in force at the place of payment. The documents will only be released to the drawee when full payment thereof has been received.

In respect of documentary collections partial payments will only be accepted if specifically authorised in the collection order. However, unless otherwise instructed, the presenting bank will only release the documents to the drawee after full payment has been received.

In all cases partial payments will only be accepted subject to compliance with the provisions of either Article 11 or Article 12 as appropriate.

Partial payment, if accepted, will be dealt with in accordance with the provisions of Article 14.

ARTICLE 14
Amounts collected (less charges and/or disbursements and/or expenses where applicable) must be made available without delay to the bank from which the collection order was received in accordance with the instructions contained in the collection order.

Comment

It should be remembered that the collecting bank is acting as the agent of the drawers and it follows that amounts collected in this capacity cannot be offset against debit balances of the remitting bank.

Acceptance

ARTICLE 15

The presenting bank is responsible for seeing that the form of the acceptance of a bill of exchange appears to be complete and correct, but is not responsible for the genuineness of any signature or for the authority of any signatory to sign the acceptance.

Comment

See Article 16.

Promissory notes, receipts and other similar instruments

ARTICLE 16

The presenting bank is not responsible for the genuineness of any signature or for the authority of any signatory to sign a promissory note, receipt or other similar instrument.

Comment

These two articles make distinction between bills accepted, and promissory notes made, by a bank's own customers and those accepted or made by the customers of other banks. In the former the bank has the means of checking on both the genuineness and the authority from the mandate it holds for operation of the account. In these circumstances it would be well-advised to check these aspects. In any case, if the acceptance or note is a domiciled one, the checks will have to be made at some stage as the acceptance or note constitutes an authority to pay at maturity.

Protest

ARTICLE 17

The collection order should give specific instructions regarding protest (or other legal process in lieu thereof), in the event of non-acceptance or non-payment.

In the absence of such specific instructions the banks concerned with the collection have no obligation to have the documents protested (or subjected to other legal process in lieu thereof) for non-payment or non-acceptance.

Any charges and/or expenses incurred by banks in connection with such protest or other legal process will be for the account of the principal.

Comment

The article says that the collection order should give specific instructions. Where protest is not required a specific instruction would be the words "do not protest" or the like on the collection order, not an absence of reference of any kind to protest. Note that the collecting bank is not obliged to protest in the absence of specific instructions, but neither is it precluded from doing so if it sees fit.

With regard to charges, as was stated in Chapter 7, the cost of the protest or noting of a bill is automatically added to its face amount and therefore if it is later paid these charges must be included in the payment made.

Case-of-need (principal's representative) and protection of goods

ARTICLE 18

If the principal nominates a representative to act as case-of-need in the event of non-acceptance and/or non-payment the collection order should clearly and fully indicate the powers of such case-of-need.

In the absence of such indication banks will not accept any instructions from the case-of-need.

Comment

In the latter circumstances the powers of the case-of-need will be advisory only, ie they will be informed of the position and left to intercede with the drawees in an attempt to induce payment or acceptance but will be unable to instruct the bank.

ARTICLE 19

Banks have no obligation to take any action in respect of the goods to which a documentary collection relates.

Nevertheless in the case that banks take action for the protection of goods, whether instructed or not, they assume no liability or responsibility with regard to the fate and/or condition of the goods and/or for any acts and/or omissions on the part of any third parties entrusted with the custody and/or protection of the goods. However, the collecting bank must immediately advise the bank from which the collection order was received of any such action taken.

Any charges and/or expenses incurred by banks in connection with any action taken by banks for the protection of the goods will be for the account of the principal.

Comment

In common with the statement made in the comment following Article 4, it is extremely doubtful whether a bank could rely on this article for protection where it had not exercised reasonable care as required by Article 1. A good example of failure to exercise reasonable care might be arranging for the storage of perishable goods in unrefrigerated accommodation.

Advice of fate, etc

ARTICLE 20
Collecting banks are to advise fate in accordance with the following rules:
(i) FORM OF ADVICE. All advices or information from the collecting bank to the bank from which the collection order was received, must bear appropriate detail including, in all cases, the latter bank's reference number of the collection order.
(ii) METHOD OF ADVICE. In the absence of specific instructions, the collecting bank must send all advices to the bank from which the collection order was received by quickest mail but, if the collecting bank considers the matter to be urgent, quicker methods such as cable, telegram, telex, or communication by electronic systems, etc may be used at the expense of the principal.
(iii) (a) ADVICE OF PAYMENT. The collecting bank must send without delay advice of payment to the bank from which the collection order was received, detailing the amount or amounts collected, charges and/or disbursements and/or expenses deducted, where appropriate, and method of disposal of the funds.
      (b) ADVICE OF ACCEPTANCE. The collecting bank must send without delay advice of acceptance to the bank from which the collection order was received.
      (c) ADVICE OF NON-PAYMENT OR NON-ACCEPTANCE. The collecting bank must send without delay advice of non-payment or advice

of non-acceptance to the bank from which the collection order was received.

The collecting bank should endeavour to ascertain the reasons for such non-payment or non-acceptance and advise accordingly the bank from which the collection order was received.

On receipt of such advice the remitting bank must, within a reasonable time, give appropriate instructions as to the further handling of the documents. If such instructions are not received by the presenting bank within 90 days from its advice of non-payment or non-acceptance, the documents may be returned to the bank from which the collection order was received.

Comment

Banks should note that the mere acknowledgement of receipt of chasers, or the constant repetition of assurances that the principals have been advised of the position and their instructions are awaited, do not constitute instructions as to the further handling of the documents in the context of this article. The period of three months which is allowed for the remitting bank to initiate some positive action is in any case extremely generous and there can really be little excuse for a continued failure to do so. This being so, it is surprising that so many collections fall into this category.

Interest, charges and expenses

ARTICLE 21

If the collection order includes an instruction to collect interest which is not embodied in the accompanying financial document(s), if any, and the drawee refuses to pay such interest, the presenting bank may deliver the document(s) against payment or acceptance as the case may be without collecting such interest, unless the collection order expressly states that such interest may not be waived. Where such interest is to be collected the collection order must bear an indication of the rate of interest and the period covered. When payment of interest has been refused the presenting bank must inform the bank from which the collection order was received accordingly.

If the documents include a financial document containing an unconditional and definitive interest clause the interest amount is deemed to form part of the amount of the documents to be collected. Accordingly, the interest amount is payable in addition to the principal amount shown in the financial document and may not be waived unless the collection order so authorises.

Comment

As was seen in Chapter 7, if an interest clause on a bill of exchange is not unconditional and definitive, the document will very likely fail to qualify as a bill of exchange within the terms of the legal definition.

ARTICLE 22

If the collection order includes an instruction that collection charges and/or expenses are to be for the account of the drawee and the drawee refuses to pay them, the presenting bank may deliver the document(s) against payment or acceptance as the case may be without collecting charges and/or expenses unless the collection order expressly states that such charges and/or expenses may not be waived. When payment of collection charges and/or expenses has been refused the presenting bank must inform the bank from which the collection order was received accordingly. Whenever collection charges and/or expenses are so waived they will be for the account of the principal, and may be deducted from the proceeds.

Should a collection order specifically prohibit the waiving of collection charges and/or expenses then neither the remitting nor collecting nor presenting bank shall be responsible for any costs or delays resulting from this prohibition.

Comment

The stand taken by the ICC in the final paragraph of this article can only be applauded. As has been said previously, the instruction not to waive charges if refused is possibly the most masochistic possible from the point of view of the banks. This is underlined by the frequent refusal of banks to accept the instructions where they are requested to provide finance for the bill. This aspect will be looked at again in Chapter 18.

ARTICLE 23

In all cases where in the express terms of a collection order, or under these Rules, disbursements and/or expenses and/or collection charges are to be borne by the principal, the collecting bank(s) shall be entitled promptly to recover outlays in respect of disbursements and expenses and charges from the bank from which the collection order was received and the remitting bank shall have the right promptly to recover from the principal any amount so paid out by it, together with its own disbursements, expenses and charges, regardless of the fate of the collection.

Comment

Yes, this does means that charges are payable by the drawers even though the banking system has failed to secure payment of the principal debt. Under the law of agency, this would in any case be the position, and justly so, since the time spent and expenses incurred by the banks have been at the instigation of the drawers, who are often not entirely blameless in the matter of the reasons for refusal of payment. In these circumstances, such charges are likely to be far higher than those which would have been incurred had the collection been paid on presentation, since factors such as the cost of telex advices, storage of goods and protest of bills may well have been added to the normal collection charges. Also, many banks now make additional charges for irregular items, often based on the actual work performed. It therefore makes economic sense to take immediate action when a collection is first reported to the sellers as unpaid or unaccepted.

10
Documentary letters of credit

The basic principles of a documentary letter of credit were outlined in Chapter 1 of this book, along with a discussion of the advantages and disadvantages to sellers and buyers arising from the use of this method of settlement. Because the credit is frequently a dauntingly complicated document, at least in its general appearance if not in the actuality, attempts at defining it frequently lead to equally complex and verbose descriptions. In reality it is very simple: it is a promise by a bank that sellers will receive payment for goods provided that they comply with all the conditions laid down in the credit.

This promise is as solemn as that made by the issuing bank when it signs a bank draft. Just as the dishonour of such a draft when presented for payment would be damaging in the extreme to the bank's reputation, so the promise made in its letter of credit is one which it breaks at its peril. It is a great pity at the present time that some banks hedge the promise with so many conditions as to render it virtually worthless. The piece of paper issued by such banks may look like a letter of credit, may call itself such, but in reality carries with it no assurance to the sellers that they will receive payment if they carry out their duties under the contract. It is one of the prime objectives of this book to provide sellers with the ability to judge for themselves whether a particular instrument is truly a credit or not. If it is not, in that it does not guarantee payment, then buyers who have agreed in the contract to arrange for the issue of a letter of credit are in breach of that contract. The only way to purge the financial world of these undesirables is to reject them. True, this may lead to frustration of the contract, but it should be remembered that a sale of goods for which payment is not made is a loss.

Issue

When applying for a letter of credit, the chief concern of the buyers is, as far as possible, to ensure that they receive the goods they require and the correct documentation relating to those goods, at the right time. The advantages, discussed in Chapter 1, which accrue to the sellers from its use, while significant, are incidental to this objective. Most banks will not issue letters of credit other than under a pre-arranged facility and the agreed limit of such facilities will be treated by the bank in exactly the same way as an application to borrow money. In effect, this is what is happening, since although no money actually changes hands at the time of issue of the credit, the bank is committing itself to making payment to the sellers at a later date, and of course will look to the buyers for repayment. A request to a bank for letter of credit facilities will therefore only be granted when the bank has satisfied itself that its customers meet all the criteria which they would normally apply to a potential borrower. Several years' accounts will be required for analysis of trends in the customer's profitability; the bank will consider the type of goods to be dealt in and the experience and competence of the customer's management team in the markets in which they are engaged; security may well be asked for. Sometimes the latter may be in the form of the deposit with the bank of cash cover for a percentage of the amount of each credit issued.

The promise made by the issuing bank to the sellers, who from henceforward will be referred to as the *beneficiaries*, constitutes the core of the credit and theoretically no other parties need be involved. Even should the buyers, who, in a credit transaction are called the *applicants*, go out of business, the core remains and the promise must be honoured.

Advising

In practical terms, however, other parties are brought into the process for various reasons, which will become apparent as we examine a typical transaction. Because of the distances, not to mention national frontiers, which separate sellers and buyers in international trade, the letter of

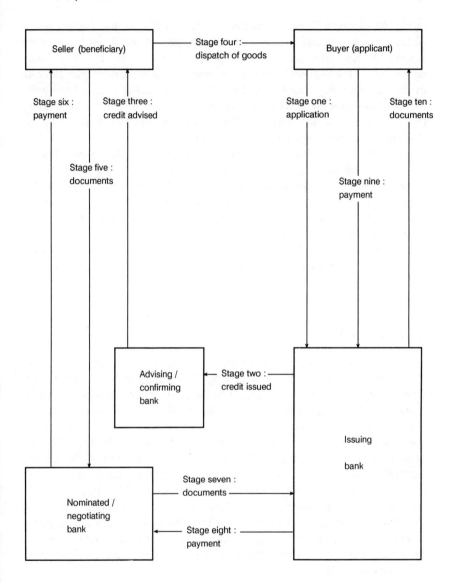

The documentary credit process

credit on issue will not normally be sent direct to the beneficiaries. Although it is not unknown for this to happen, when it does the credit almost always turns out to be a forgery (see Chapter 17). The usual procedure is for the issuing bank to make use of its correspondent bank in the beneficiaries' country, and it will send the credit to that bank with the request that it advises the beneficiaries of its issue. The correspondent thus becomes the *advising bank* and it is by that title that it will be referred to in the remainder of this book.

The advising bank incurs no liability under the credit by acceding to its correspondent's request, but in advising the credit to the beneficiaries it does warrant to them, and to any other party who may become involved at a later stage, that it has taken all appropriate steps to check that the credit is genuine. Beneficiaries who may be unfamiliar with the issuing bank may therefore take reassurance regarding that bank's actual existence, and know that it is sufficiently highly regarded to have established a correspondent relationship with a bank in their own country with which they are familiar.

Confirmation

Very often beneficiaries desire more than this, however, and ask that the advising bank join in the undertaking of the issuing bank. Where this occurs, and if the advising bank is willing to comply, it adds its confirmation to the credit, which in effect means that it adds its own promise that payment will be made provided that the terms and conditions of the credit are complied with. It is often thought, mistakenly, that this is a guarantee that the confirming bank will make payment if the issuing bank does not. The promise of the confirming bank stands alone, however, with the beneficiaries looking to that bank to make payment irrespective of the status of the issuing bank. Hence the occasional reluctance of banks to provide confirmation, for the promise that they are required to make is every bit as binding as that of the issuing bank and since they are geographically closer to the beneficiaries theirs is the liability which will materialise first.

Presentation

When the beneficiaries are ready to present their documents for settlement, they do so to the bank, if any, nominated in the credit. What happens next depends upon the credit's terms. If the nominated bank is authorised to pay, or is the confirming bank of a sight credit, and does so, the transaction is complete so far as the beneficiaries are concerned. If, in a usance credit, it is authorised to accept the beneficiaries' bill of exchange (draft), or, where no draft is called for, to give an undertaking that payment will be made at a future date, the beneficiaries have that undertaking to rely on. If it is authorised to negotiate, the beneficiaries will receive reimbursement but the negotiating bank will retain a right of recourse to them in case of its not receiving payment from the issuing bank. If there is no nominated bank, then any bank is free to negotiate the drawing if it so wishes, although in practice such negotiation would normally be undertaken only by the advising bank or, perhaps, by the beneficiaries' own bank.

Reimbursement

One further bank may be involved in the transaction where the credit is expressed in a currency which is neither that of the applicants' nor the beneficiaries' countries, or where there is no account relationship between the nominated and issuing banks. Settlement will be made by the bank which will then look to obtain reimbursement for the amount it has paid from a paying agent named by the issuing bank in the credit. This is the *reimbursing bank.*

All this is the way in which the system should work. Sadly, the reality is often far removed from the ideal. Frequently, so-called confirmation of a credit is regarded by the bank which enters into it as more a source of income than a liability of honour, such as where it refuses to pay the beneficiaries until it has received covering funds from the issuing bank or the reimbursing bank. Many credits are issued, in this age of hyperawareness of cost cutting possibilities, which are payable only upon receipt of documents by the issuing bank, or they are issued in a third country's currency without bearing any indication as to how a negotiating bank is to obtain reimbursement. Such instruments hardly deserve the title of credits at all, since they are tantamount to mere conditional guarantees of payment of collections.

It is, of course, the beneficiaries who are most concerned regarding the acceptability of a letter of credit. It is of vital importance, on receipt of a credit, to read it carefully without delay. The beneficiaries' concern is partly to ensure that the terms laid down for payment are acceptable to them in accordance with their own understanding of the commercial contract, and that unanticipated and onerous conditions have not been included, prices and specifications are as agreed, and so on. It is just as important, however, to examine the document from the point of view of how, where, when, and, indeed, if, it will give rise to payment. This will be looked at in more detail in Chapter 17.

Types of credit

Revocable/irrevocable

Credits may be revocable, in which case they may be amended or even cancelled without the beneficiaries' consent, or they may be irrevocable, in which case the beneficiaries have the right to refuse to accept any amendments. Since the greatest advantage to the sellers in utilising a letter of credit is security of payment, it might be thought that there would be no circumstances in which a revocable credit would be acceptable, but they do have one particular advantage over irrevocable credits: they are cheaper. This makes them attractive where the use of a credit is dictated not by commercial prudence but by government decree. This might be the case where trading partners have the kind of relationship which would normally foster an open account arrangement between them but to satisfy local legislation they are compelled to utilise letters of credit.

The reason for the banks charging less for the issue of this type of credit is that where a bank is concerned about its customers, the applicants, and if it feels that it may not be able to obtain repayment of any drawings which may be made under the credit, it can cancel it unilaterally, without seeking the agreement of any other party. The degree of risk to which it is exposed is therefore considerably reduced and the commission it charges should reflect this.

Sight/usance

A credit may provide for payment at sight, or it may be a usance credit providing for payment to be deferred for a specified period. The credit thus caters for instances where the sellers have allowed a period of credit to the buyers. Usually a usance credit will call for the beneficiaries to accompany their documents with a bill of exchange drawn at the specified tenor and drawn on a named party. This drawee may be the nominated bank, the issuing bank, or the applicants. The bill of exchange has no effect on the bank's promise to pay and where it is drawn on and accepted by the applicants and dishonoured on presentation for payment the issuing bank must honour it. From the point of view of the beneficiaries the most advantageous drawee is undoubtedly the nominated bank, for they will then have a first-class acceptance which can be discounted at prime rates in the local bill market (for more information on discounting, see Chapter 18). Where the beneficiaries require to raise finance in this way and the bill is drawn on the issuing bank or the applicant, they must request the bank to which they have presented the documents to negotiate the drawing, which will mean that, not only will they receive less money after allowance has been made for the transit times for documents and proceeds, but that the negotiating bank will retain recourse against them if it is unable to reimburse itself from the issuing bank.

Deferred payment

Not all credits which provide for payment other than at sight call for presentation of a bill of exchange. Where one or other of the countries involved applies heavy stamp duty to bills, they may be dispensed with by the replacement of the acceptance with an undertaking that payment will be made after expiry of the usance period. Such undertakings cannot be discounted, as can a bill, but the beneficiaries may be able to negotiate them, ie obtain an advance in anticipation of receipt of payment.

We have seen that a credit may be revocable or irrevocable, confirmed or unconfirmed, and provide for payment at sight or at usance. To further illustrate the flexibility of the letter of credit as a means of settlement, we will now look at various types of more specialised credits, designed to cater for specific circumstances affecting trade between the two parties to the commercial contract.

Revolving

Where buyers and sellers are trading with each other on a regular basis they may find it to their mutual advantage to utilise a revolving letter of credit. A normal non-revolving credit is issued for a specified amount and, provided it allows partial drawings, may be drawn against for fractions of that amount until it is exhausted, after which it is fully drawn and defunct. Furthermore, it will have an expiry date beyond which no further drawings may be made. Although a revolving credit will still have an expiry date, it is likely to be valid for a far longer period, being designed to cover the continuing trade between buyers and sellers.

There are two basic ways in which a revolving credit may operate, one relating to time and the other to payment. A time revolving credit will incorporate a clause providing for the reinstatement of the full amount of the credit at specified intervals, such as monthly. Thus, if it is estimated that the total annual value of imports from a particular supplier is US$ 600,000, with an average individual shipment worth US$ 10,000, this would either mean the issue over a year of about 60 letters of credit each covering a single consignment, or perhaps 12 credits allowing partial drawings and each covering one month's trade. Such a system would be wasteful of both time and money and, furthermore, would mean that the buyers' total outstanding liability under letters of credit issued on their behalf would be unnecessarily high. A revolving credit, however, would, say, allow the beneficiaries to draw up to US$ 50,000 in any one month, at the end of which the amount would be reinstated to cover the following month's shipments. In this instance, the issuing bank would probably regard its total liability under that credit as being US$ 100,000, since in theory the full value could be drawn on the last day of a month and again on the following day whilst the first set of documents were still in transit.

This consideration can be rendered unnecessary by the use of a revolving payment credit. Drawings can be made under this up to the amount of the credit and documents forwarded by the negotiating bank to the issuing bank in the normal way. As reimbursement for each drawing is obtained from the applicants the amount of that drawing is reinstated, by means of an advice by mail or telex from the issuing bank to the negotiating bank, and thus becomes available for further drawings. In this way the total outstanding liability never exceeds the value of the credit, though the credit is slightly less flexible as a result.

Whatever their format, revolving credits are extremely useful instruments where circumstances permit their use. Not only do they bring about a considerable saving in time and effort by replacing large numbers of applications and individual letters of credit with just one of each, but further time is saved by the familiarity of their terms to all parties concerned.

Red clause

It sometimes occurs that sellers of goods need finance to assist in the production or acquisition of those goods but do not have the necessary financial standing to obtain that finance in their own name locally. If the buyers are prepared to assist, the transaction can be greatly simplified by the use of a red clause credit. These instruments originated in the wool trade, where importers in England appointed buying agents in Australia whose task it was to travel round the outback farms at shearing time, or to the various official wool sales, to select and buy fleeces on behalf of their principals. They would then arrange with a local carrier for the fleeces to be transported to the nearest port for shipment.

The problem which these agents faced was that the farmers with whom they were dealing had little use for a piece of paper issued by a bank in Bradford and much preferred to be paid in hard cash. To enable the agent to accommodate this preference, the letter of credit would carry a clause authorising the advising bank to advance a stated percentage of the credit's value to the beneficiary against presentation of a simple receipt and an undertaking to present full documentation as each consignment of wool was shipped. Reimbursement for the amount of such advances would be claimed by the advancing bank, which would in turn debit the account of the applicants. Normally the advance would be for less than the full credit amount in order to ensure that the goods would be shipped and documents presented in accordance with the credit terms. When this occurred, any payment made would be nett of the amount of the relative advance.

The clause which made these advances possible was traditionally written in red ink to distinguish such credits from the normal kind. Red ink (and even red ribbons on typewriters) has disappeared into museums but the name remains with us to describe any credit which allows pre-shipment advances to be made to the beneficiary at the risk and expense of the applicant. The use of such credits tends to be restricted to trade in natural products such as that in which they had their origin. However, there is no reason why they should not be used where, for instance, manufacturers have to set up a new assembly line to produce goods to meet a particular order and require financial help to do so which is beyond the level which would normally be available to them. It will be evident that the buyers must hold a high degree of trust for the sellers where a red clause credit is contemplated.

Transferable

Similar considerations of finance for the purchase of goods by the party contracted to supply them brought about the introduction of another variant on the credit theme, the transferable letter of credit. In this case the beneficiaries may be buying agents but in many cases are merchants, whose task is to act as intermediaries between original suppliers and ultimate buyers of goods. They rely on commission or profit for their livelihood but never enter into physical possession of the goods. Their problem is the matching of a contract to supply goods with the natural reluctance of suppliers to relinquish control of those goods without the assurance of being paid for them.

The answer is to request the issue of a transferable credit in their favour. They can then ask the advising bank to transfer all or part of the value of that credit to a third party, the suppliers of the goods, who thus have the advantage of a promise by a bank that they will receive payment for their wares. The suppliers can then safely arrange for shipment of those goods to their ultimate destination, claiming payment under the transferred credit. The first beneficiaries can then exchange their own invoices for those of the suppliers and draw under the original credit for the balance, if any, between the amount of their invoices and the amount paid by the bank to the second beneficiaries. This amount represents their profit on the transaction, and the bank now has a full set of documents conforming to the terms of the original credit and can claim reimbursement from the issuing bank. Thus, again a particular set of circumstances has been met by the flexibility of the letter of credit as an instrument of settlement.

A word of warning to buyers at this point. It is not unusual to develop blind spots to such words as transferable, particularly when they are all but concealed in a string of adjectives, as in the phrase "settlement by means of a confirmed, irrevocable, transferable letter of credit" which might appear on the *proforma* invoice. The request for a transferable credit should always put buyers on notice that they are not dealing with the actual manufacturers of the goods. This has two major implications. One is that a strong possibility exists that the buyers could obtain the goods more cheaply by dealing directly with the manufacturers; the other is that, whatever enquiries they have made about the sellers, they have no means of knowing the status of the party who will ship the goods and must rely upon the judgement of the merchant with whom they are dealing.

The transferable credit is dealt with exhaustively by Uniform Customs and Practice for Documentary Credits and will be looked at again in that context in Chapter 13. The circumstances under which it is used can be similar to those giving rise to the back-to-back credit but this will be dealt with in its proper place in the chapter on bank finance for international trade.

Standby

An example of a letter of credit being utilised to remedy an imperfection in the usefulness of another bank undertaking is the standby credit. As a reaction to certain abuses of the system during the construction of the pioneer railroads in the nineteenth century, certain States in the USA passed legislation preventing banks registered in those States from is- suing bank guarantees. Such documents see frequent use in other parts of the world wherever someone requires reassurance that trading part- ners will fulfil their obligations under a contract, but their proscription in America forced the development of an alternative which would satisfy the law but serve the same purpose. That alternative was the standby credit.

Although there is not, and never has been, any restriction on the issue of guarantees by federally-registered US banks, the fact that they were continuously dealing with State-registered banks who were subject to the restrictions led to the universal adoption of the standby credit in America. It has in fact proved a very successful instrument, offering far more flex- ibility than the document it replaced. Especially since the extension of UCP in 1984 to cover standby letters of credit and also partly as a result of the heavy involvement of American banks in the financing of devel- opment projects all around the world, but particularly in the Middle East oil production industry, its use has now spread far beyond the shores of America, and its virtues have come to be appreciated on a more global basis.

A credit of the traditional variety provides for payment to take place following the occurrence of certain events, usually the shipment of the goods. With a standby credit, however, the opposite is the case. Just as a bank guarantee promises that the bank will recompense the benefi- ciaries if they claim payment of money due from contractors and they fail to pay, so a standby credit conveys a promise that if payment is not forthcoming from the processes provided for in the contract, the benefi- ciary may draw under the credit for the sum due.

A standby credit need not be a complex document; far less so than its documentary equivalent. Indeed, the only document that is really necessary is a statement by the beneficiary that payment has been claimed and has not been received. It can be used to replace most, if not all, of the more traditional types of guarantee, such as the tender bond, frequently called for when a major project is put out to tender. Here, the beneficiary requires assurance that if the tenderers are awarded the contract they have sufficient strength to be able to carry it through to its conclusion. The means by which they obtain such assurance is by receiving a bank guarantee, in their favour, under which, if work is not started on the project within a specified time of the contract being awarded, they can claim compensation under the guarantee. Substitute "standby credit" for "guarantee" and "draw" for "claim" in the last sentence and we have a description of the purpose and operation of a standby credit.

The standby credit can also take the place of the performance bond, which provides for compensation in the event of non-compliance with the terms of the contract and usually replaces the tender bond after the contract has been awarded. It can replace the retention bond, which provides for payment in full of the contract value, despite a clause therein to the effect that the buyers are entitled to retain a percentage of that value after completion against the eventuality of later discovery of defects in the work done. It can replace the facility guarantee, which provides the security for a bank to lend money to a subsidiary of a foreign company. It can replace the customs bond, which guarantees to the revenue authorities that duty will be paid on goods imported into storage against future use (this is the origin of the term "bonded warehouse").

There are few applications for a bank guarantee that cannot be alternatively served by a standby credit, often in a much simpler fashion. Whereas a guarantee is frequently a complex document drawn up by lawyers, the standby credit is often expressed in a standard format which clearly and in concise fashion states the terms under which drawings will be paid. Beware, however, when this is not the case. As with guarantees, attempts are made to make the standby credit so complex as to make a successful claim thereunder highly unlikely to succeed. As with ordinary credits, the only effective defence against this malpractice is to refuse the credit; again, as with ordinary credits, nothing is likely to be lost by such action since the credit will probably be of little or no value anyway. It is of interest that the sellers rather than the buyers are normally the applicants for a standby credit and the buyers the beneficiaries, exactly the reverse of the position under a documentary credit.

The format of a letter of credit

Having examined the variety of forms which the letter of credit may take, and the above list is by no means exhaustive, we will now return to the ordinary, everyday credit covering the sale of goods under a single contract. We are seeing the gradual adoption as a standard format of the design brought into being by the International Chamber of Commerce and illustrated on page 148. This process is far from complete, as is the situation regarding the introduction of a standard form of bill of lading, but slowly banks are recognising the advantages of abandoning their own distinctive but often defective designs and adopting the ICC format which groups particular aspects of the credit in the same position on the form, regardless of which bank has issued the credit. Since application forms are similarly designed, this greatly facilitates the transfer of the information from application to credit, and is also of enormous assistance to those banks which advise credits by transferring the data from the original instrument on to their own paper.

At the top of the form appear three important pieces of information: the name and address of the issuing bank; the title of the document indicating that it is either a revocable or an irrevocable letter of credit; and the credit number, usually accompanied by a statement that it must appear on all bills of exchange drawn under the credit. Although the vast majority of credits are irrevocable, it is worth a quick glance at this part of the form when a credit is received to ensure that such is the case.

Issue and expiry

Next, on the right hand side of the form, appear the date and place of issue and the date and place of expiry of the credit. The place of expiry is important, as has already been mentioned, since if the beneficiaries are to enjoy the full advantages of a letter of credit it should expire in their own country.

Applicant and beneficiary

Below this comes a series of boxes, the top two of which contain the applicants' name on the left and the beneficiaries' name and address on the right. It is particularly important that the name and address of the beneficiaries is given accurately and in full, since without this information the advising bank may be unable to fulfil its function.

NAME OF ISSUING BANK - NOM DE LA BANQUE EMETTRICE	**Irrevocable Documentary Credit** **Crédit documentaire irrévocable**	Number - Numéro

Place and date of issue - Lieu et date d'émission

Date and place of expiry - Date et lieu de validité

Applicant - Donneur d'ordre

Beneficiary - Bénéficiaire

Advising Bank - Banque notificatrice   Ref. nr. - No. Ref.

Amount - Montant

Credit available with - Crédit réalisable auprès de

☐ by sight payment / par paiement à vue   ☐ by acceptance / par acceptation   ☐ by negotiation / par negociation

☐ by deferred payment at / par paiement differe à

Partial shipments / Expeditions partielles

☐ allowed / autorisées   ☐ not allowed / non autorisées

Transhipment / Transbordement

☐ allowed / autorisé   ☐ not allowed / non autorisé

against the documents detailed herein / contre les documents précisés ci-après

Loading on board/dispatch/taking in charge at/from
Mise à bord/expédition/prise en charge à/de

☐ and beneficiary's draft at / et la traite du bénéficiaire au

for transportation to: / à destination de:

on / sur

Documents to be presented within
Documents à présenter dans les

[ ] days after the date of issuance of the transport document(s) but within the validity of the credit.
jours après la date d'émission du/des document(s) de transport mais dans la période de validité du crédit.

We hereby issue the Documentary Credit in your favour. It is subject to the Uniform Customs and Practice for Documentary Credits (1983 Revision, International Chamber of Commerce, Paris, France, Publication No. 400) and engages us in accordance with the terms thereof. The number and the date of the credit and the name of our bank must be quoted on all drafts required. If the credit is available by negotiation, each presentation must be noted on the reverse of this advice by the bank where the credit is available

Nous émettons par la présente ce crédit documentaire en votre faveur. Il est soumis aux Règles et Usances Uniformes relatives aux Crédits Documentaire (Révision 1983, Publication No. 400 de la Chambre de Commerce Internationale, Paris, France) et nous engage selon leurs termes. Le numéro et la date du crédit ainsi que le nom de notre banque devront être mentionnés sur toute traite requise. Si le crédit est utilisable par négociation chaque présentation devra être inscrite au verso de cet avis par la banque ou le crédit est utilisable.

This document consists of   [ ] signed page(s)
Ce document consiste en   page(s) signée(s)

Advice for the Beneficiary - Avis pour le bénéficiaire

© Copyright 1986. International Chamber of Commerce / Chambre de Commerce Internationale

International Chamber of Commerce standard format letter of credit

Amount

The next two boxes contain the name of the advising bank on the left and the amount of the credit in words and figures on the right. Obviously, the latter should agree with each other. If the amount is stated as "approximately", UCP state that it may be reduced or exceeded by up to ten per cent. This will be discussed further both later in this chapter and in Chapter 13.

Shipment

The lower box on the left-hand side is subdivided to accommodate the credit's requirements regarding the shipment of the goods. Separate sections state whether partial shipments are allowed, whether transhipment is permitted, and whether insurance will be covered by the applicants. The credit then gives details of the journey which is to be evidenced by the transport document and the latest date on which the goods may be shipped or taken in charge.

Drawings

The corresponding space on the right gives the name of the bank which is nominated to honour drawings and whether that honour is to be by way of payment, negotiation, acceptance or deferred payment undertaking. Details of the required bill of exchange, if any, are also given, including its tenor and on whom it is to be drawn.

Documents

What follows may vary according to which bank has issued the credit. The extremes are represented by a completely blank area, in which any documentary and other requirements may be inserted in precise terms, or preprinted requirements with boxes to be marked to show which documents are actually required and blank spaces left to allow for special requirements relating to those documents. It is the author's opinion that the former is the preferable option, since any attempt to standardise documentary requirements inevitably omits essential items and clutters the credit with irrelevant sections which only serve to confuse the reader. Furthermore, special requirements for a particular transaction must be squeezed into any unoccupied space on the credit, resulting in extensive use of continuation marks such as single, double and even triple asterisks, daggers and the like. The result is usually an incomprehensible mess.

The customary order in which the documents which are required under the credit are listed commences with the invoices and the packing list, stating how many copies of each are required, what information should appear on each and, in respect of the invoice, usually repeating the contract terms. The required transport document is customarily described next and if this is to be a bill of lading the number of originals which are needed will be stated. The credit will specify whether or not the transport document should or should not indicate prepayment of freight and whatever is stated should be compatible with the terms of the contract as evidenced elsewhere in the credit.

There follows reference to the requirements regarding insurance, which, depending on the contract, will be either details of the document required or a statement that insurance will be attended to by the applicants.

Goods

Any further documents which may be required will then be listed and there follows a description of the goods. UCP prohibit the inclusion of excessive detail in this respect and, provided that the description is sufficiently detailed to enable the banks to ascertain that the correct goods have been shipped, there is little to be gained and much to be lost by the inclusion of detailed specifications here. Far better to call for a certificate from the beneficiaries to the effect that the goods comply with the relative order or contract.

Also shown in this section are the contract terms applicable to the transaction. From this information can be determined whether or not the transport document should evidence that freight has been prepaid, and whether or not an insurance document should be called for. Special circumstances may occasionally give rise to an apparent discrepancy here, but any such variation from the norm should at least give grounds for query, as when an FOB contract calls for a transport document to show that freight has been paid.

Presentation

The credit now states the number of days after the date of issue of the transport document which are allowed for presentation of documents by the beneficiaries. If no stipulation is made, UCP specifies that 21 days will be the maximum period allowed. Where the voyage is sufficiently long, and it is essential that documents of title are received by a certain time in order to avoid demurrage or other extra charges being incurred, it may be possible by manipulation of this period to minimise the chances of late receipt. By estimating the period required for processing the documents in the banks and adding the time required for transit, then deducting the total from the estimated duration of the voyage of the carrying vessel, a figure will be reached which is a rough indication of the maximum period which may safely be allowed between the date of shipment and the date of presentation. This figure should, however, be realistic in being of sufficient length to allow the beneficiaries to meet it.

It is an encouraging sign, indicating that the credit has been prepared by professionals, when the number of days so allowed corresponds with the period between the latest date for shipment and the expiry date of the credit. To illustrate this, if a credit states that shipment must be not later than September 30, and expires on October 15, but allows only ten days for presentation of documents, then where goods are shipped on the last possible date the effective expiry of the credit falls on October 10, not October 15 as stated therein, because the ten day rule must be complied with. Beneficiaries who fall into this trap are understandably annoyed, but there is absolutely nothing which the nominated or negotiating bank can do to help.

Miscellaneous provisions

The credit will normally then state for whose account are bank charges and give any instructions intended for the negotiating bank, such as those relating to disposal of documents and the obtaining of reimbursement for amounts paid or negotiated under the credit.

Finally, there will be a statement that the credit is subject to Uniform Customs and Practice for Documentary Credits, identifying the appropriate revision of those rules which is applicable, probably an undertaking that payment will be made against conforming documents (although in view of the allusion to UCP this is not strictly necessary) and the signature(s) on behalf of the issuing bank.

Such, then, is the usual content of the documentary letter of credit. As stated, many banks have yet to adopt the ICC recommended format, but nonetheless all the above information should appear on the credit, however it is laid out. Further consideration of the detailed aspects of the credit will be given in the following chapters on UCP and in those with particular relevance to the various parties involved.

11
Uniform Customs and Practice for Documentary Credits (1)

Like the Uniform Rules for Collections, dealt with in Chapter 9, the UCP were drawn up by the International Chamber of Commerce (ICC) in order to regulate the practices and procedures relating to documentary credits as adopted by banks worldwide. The UCP are considerably senior to the URC, having been first formulated in 1933, and the current edition is the fifth, its official title being the 1983 Revision and published by the ICC in its publication no. 400. They are also far more widely adopted than URC and the likelihood of encountering a credit which is not subject to their provisions is remote.

It is perhaps even more important than was the case with URC that all parties involved in the documentary credit should have at least a working knowledge of the content of UCP, since its provisions are far more comprehensive than that of its younger cousin and may have a profound effect upon the rights and duties of each of those parties. Furthermore, in some cases the apparent effect of the 1983 Revision has since been clouded by opinions expressed by the ICC's Banking Commission. It should be mentioned here that the ICC is placed in a very difficult situation when doubts arise as to the correct interpretation of the rules as published. Amendment and republication in revised form is a lengthy and costly procedure, involving as it does the obtaining of consensus of opinion from its worldwide membership, and where its assistance is sought in cases of dispute it can only give its considered opinion on the facts of the case before it. Whether or not the disputants choose to accept that opinion is their own affair, and in any case the decision is not binding upon any parties who may later be in dispute from the same cause.

In the following detailed examination of UCP, reference will be made where appropriate to such opinions, but all concerned, particularly banks, are urged to keep themselves up to date with the situation as it develops. Opinions of the Commission are published periodically by the ICC, the most recent at the time of writing being its publication no. 434, which details decisions reached from 1984 until 1986, although publication of the volume for 1987/88 is imminent.

General provisions and definitions

ARTICLE 1
These articles apply to all documentary credits, including, to the extent to which they may be applicable, standby letters of credit, and are binding on all parties thereto unless otherwise expressly agreed. They shall be incorporated into each documentary credit by wording in the credit indicating that such credit is issued subject to Uniform Customs and Practice for Documentary Credits, 1983 Revision, ICC Publication No. 400.

ARTICLE 2
For the purposes of these articles, the expressions "documentary credit(s)" and "standby letter(s) of credit" used herein (hereinafter referred to as "credit(s)"), mean any arrangement, however named or described, whereby a bank (the issuing bank), acting at the request and on the instructions of a customer (the applicant for the credit),

    (i)   is to make payment to or to the order of a third party (the beneficiary), or is to pay or accept bills of exchange (drafts) drawn by the beneficiary,

    or

    (ii) authorises another bank to effect such payment, or to pay, accept, or negotiate such bills of exchange (drafts)
          against stipulated documents, provided that the terms and conditions of the credits are complied with.

Comment

Note that an instrument does not have to call itself a documentary credit in order for the rules to apply. It must merely comply with the requirements and include the incorporation clause as specified in Article 1. Presentation of documents in order to secure payment is an essential feature, though presentation of a bill of exchange is not. Generally speaking, a sight bill of exchange under a letter of credit is completely unnecessary and issuing banks should consider seriously the question of deleting this requirement from their letter of credit forms.

Specific instruments which have been considered to qualify for incorporation of UCP in their terms have been the "documentary payment orders" commonly issued by banks in Greece, which in fact differ from the common concept of a documentary credit only in their title, and letters of guarantee which, although they are similar in effect to a credit, the ICC would prefer were styled "standby letters of credit" in order to avoid any possible confusion.

ARTICLE 3

Credits, by their nature, are separate transactions from the sales or other contract(s) on which they may be based and banks are in no way concerned with or bound by such contract(s), even if any reference whatsoever to such contract(s) is included in the credit.

Comment

In practical terms, this article is one which cannot be repeated frequently enough. Banks are not party to the commercial contract between buyer and seller, have no wish to be, and formulate their charges accordingly. It is the buyers' responsibility to ensure that all relevant conditions of the contract are incorporated in the credit, and the sellers' responsibility upon receipt of that credit to ensure that such conditions have been so incorporated. Where the credit is irrevocable, the buyers' task is the more onerous, since if a mistake is made the credit is binding in its issued form unless the sellers agree to its amendment.

ARTICLE 4

In credit operations all parties concerned deal in documents, and not in goods, services and/or other performances to which the documents may relate.

Comment

This is another article which should be etched deep into the consciousness of all concerned with credits. Suspicion that the goods are defective, or even non-existent, cannot be used as grounds to prevent an issuing or confirming bank from discharging its solemn obligations under a credit, such matters being the concern solely of the buyers and sellers under the appropriate law of contract.

ARTICLE 5

Instructions for the issuance of credits, the credits themselves, instructions for any amendments thereto and the amendments themselves must be complete and precise.

In order to guard against confusion and misunderstanding, banks should discourage any attempt to include excessive detail in the credit or in any amendment thereto.

Comment

It was stated in Chapter 10 that the preferable alternative is to call for a signed declaration from the beneficiaries to the effect that they have supplied goods which conform with the requirements of the relative contract, which can be identified by reference to a pro-forma invoice and/or order number. Generally speaking, the more complex a credit is, the more chance there is that something will go wrong with it, but such is the mystique of the subject that many issuing banks seem to feel that the credit gains in stature in line with the increase in the number of pages required to express its terms and conditions. In pursuance of this mistaken belief they will blithely accept pages of detailed specification of the goods, lifted straight from the contract, as appendages to form part of the terms of the credit. As a result, all concerned are occasioned much unnecessary work in checking all this superfluous detail, the chances of a mistake being made are greatly increased and, most significantly, the applicants gain no additional security in the process.

Two interesting opinions have been expressed by the Banking Commission with relevance to this article.

The first concerns the frequent stipulation in the credit that the packages containing the goods be marked in a specific fashion. The Commission is of the opinion that unless the credit stipulates otherwise, banks should accept shipping documents showing the required marks as a minimum and not reject those showing additional markings.

The second relates to the equally frequent requirement that the letter of credit or export licence number appears on all documents. For legal reasons in certain countries it is undesirable from the point of view of the carriers for such detail to be included in the bill of lading and the ICC has indicated that such conditions in credits should be discouraged.

ARTICLE 6

A beneficiary can in no circumstances avail himself of the contractual relationships existing between the banks or between the applicant for the credit and the issuing bank.

(B) Form and notification of credits

ARTICLE 7

(a) credits may be either
  (i)   revocable, or
  (ii) irrevocable
(b) All credits, therefore, should clearly indicate whether they are revocable or irrevocable.
(c) In the absence of such indication the credit shall be deemed to be revocable.

Comment

This is a very good reason for beneficiaries to check carefully that the word "irrevocable" appears in the description of the credit when it is received. The reason for the stipulation in (c) is to provide a safety net for credit applicants in case of an error being made. If a credit should be revocable, but is issued without such specification and deemed irrevocable, nothing can be done about it; if, however, it is deemed revocable it can be amended without the beneficiaries' agreement, although in practice such agreement would be unlikely to be withheld, since the amendment would amount to an enhancement of the credit's value to the beneficiary.

ARTICLE 8

A credit may be advised to a beneficiary through another bank (the advising bank) without engagement on the part of the advising bank, but that bank shall take reasonable care to check the apparent authenticity of the credit which it advises.

Comment

This topic was mentioned in Chapter 10, and will be looked at again in the sections dealing with the advising bank and with fraud and forgery. From the beneficiaries' point of view, and from that of the negotiating bank if that bank is different from the advising bank, the article gives some relief from the worry about whether or not a credit is forged, since the responsibility of verification is placed squarely upon the advising bank. The latter should note that, in certain circumstances, "reasonable care" may mean more than the mere verification of signatures from specimens held.

ARTICLE 9

(a)   A revocable credit may be amended or cancelled by the issuing bank at any moment and without prior notice to the beneficiary.

(b)   However, the issuing bank is bound to:

    (i)   reimburse a branch or bank with which a revocable credit has been made available for sight payment, acceptance or negotiation, for any payment, acceptance or negotiation made by such branch or bank prior to receipt by it of notice of amendment or cancellation, against documents which appear on their face to be in accordance with the terms and conditions of the credit.

    (ii)   reimburse a branch or bank with which a revocable credit has been made available for deferred payment, if such branch or bank has, prior to receipt by it of notice of amendment or cancellation, taken up documents which appear on their face to be in accordance with the terms and conditions of the credit.

Comment

For security reasons it would be unwise for a bank to negotiate documents under a revocable credit which it has not advised, since that credit may have been subsequently amended or cancelled and such a bank would have no knowledge of this. Whether it would be able to claim protection under this article is questionable, since normal banking prudence ought to dictate that it should not negotiate. The ICC has in fact expressed the opinion that all revocable credits should nominate a bank to which documents must be presented for negotiation and, if adopted, such action would prevent this situation from arising.

ARTICLE 10(a)

An irrevocable credit constitutes a definite undertaking of the issuing bank, provided that the stipulated documents are presented and that the terms and conditions of the credit are complied with:

(i)   if the credit provides for sight payment – to pay, or that payment will be made;

(ii)   if the credit provides for deferred payment – to pay, or that payment will be made, on the date(s) determinable in accordance with the stipulations of the credit;

(iii) if the credit provides for acceptance – to accept drafts drawn by the beneficiary if the credit stipulates that they are to be drawn on the issuing bank, or to be responsible for their acceptance and payment at maturity if the credit stipulates that they are to be drawn on the applicant for the credit or any other drawee stipulated in the credit;

(iv) if the credit provides for negotiation – to pay without recourse to drawers and/or bona fide holders, draft(s) drawn by the beneficiary, at sight or at a tenor, on the applicant for the credit or on any other drawee stipulated in the credit other than the issuing bank itself, or to provide for negotiation by another bank and to pay, as above, if such negotiation is not effected.

Comment

This article, of course, defines the very heart of the principle of the irrevocable credit—the absolute liability of the issuing bank to honour its obligations thereunder, provided that the beneficiaries have honoured theirs.

Much confusion tends to arise as to the difference between payment and negotiation under a credit. With a sight credit the situation is really quite simple. If the credit nominates a bank in the sellers' country which is authorised to pay drawings and documents are presented to that bank in order, then payment takes place at that point, without recourse. If they are presented to any other bank, negotiation takes place, with the negotiating bank retaining recourse against the drawer (beneficiary) until it is reimbursed. Where the credit calls for drafts on either the issuing bank or the applicants, only negotiation can take place in the beneficiaries' country, payment being made by the issuing bank without recourse in both cases in view of its obligations under the credit.

ARTICLE 10(b)

Where an issuing bank authorises or requests another bank to confirm its irrevocable credit and the latter has added its confirmation, such confirmation constitutes a definite undertaking of such bank (the confirming bank) in addition to that of the issuing bank, provided that the stipulated documents are presented and that the terms and conditions of the credit are complied with:

(i) if the credit provides for sight payment – to pay, or that payment will be made;

(ii) if the credit provides for deferred payment – to pay, or that pay-

ment will be made, on the date(s) determinable in accordance with
the stipulations of the credit;

  (iii) if the credit provides for acceptance – to accept drafts drawn by the
beneficiary if the credit stipulates that they are to be drawn on the
confirming bank, or to be responsible for their acceptance and payment at maturity if the credit stipulates that they are to be drawn on
the applicant for the credit or on any other drawee stipulated in the
credit;

  (iv) if the credit provides for negotiation – to negotiate without recourse
to drawers and/or bona fide holders, draft(s) drawn by the beneficiary at sight or at a tenor, on the issuing bank or on the applicant
for the credit or on any other drawee stipulated in the credit other
than the confirming bank itself.

Comment

This section of Article 10 effectively places exactly the same burden of
responsibility on the confirming bank as the preceding section did on the
issuing bank, ie where documents are in order its liability is absolute and
without recourse.

ARTICLE 10(c)

If a bank is authorised or requested by the issuing bank to add its confirmation
to a credit but is not prepared to do so, it must inform the issuing bank without
delay. Unless the issuing bank specifies otherwise in its confirmation authorisation or request, the advising bank will advise the credit to the beneficiary without adding its confirmation.

Comment

Circumstances under which a bank might be unwilling to confirm
another bank's credit include the following:

  (a) where it is not the correspondent of the issuing bank;

  (b) where it is not happy with the terms of the credit, or with the
arrangements for reimbursement;

  (c) where its commitments on behalf of the issuing bank are already
at the limit of what it is prepared to undertake;

  (d) where its commitments on behalf of the issuing bank's country
have already reached a similar limit.

ARTICLE 10(d)

Such undertakings can neither be amended nor cancelled without the agreement of the issuing bank, the confirming bank (if any), and the beneficiary. Partial acceptance of amendments contained in one and the same advice of amendment is not effective without the agreement of all the above named parties.

Comment

It is perhaps strange that the agreement of the applicants is not required before partial acceptance of an amendment can be effective, but in practice the issuing bank would be unlikely to give its agreement without first referring to its customers for guidance.

ARTICLE 11

   (a)   All credits must clearly indicate whether they are available by sight payment, by deferred payment, by acceptance or by negotiation.

   (b)   All credits must nominate the bank (nominated bank) which is authorised to pay (paying bank), or to accept drafts (accepting bank) or to negotiate (negotiating bank), unless the credit allows negotiation by any bank (negotiating bank).

   (c)   Unless the nominated bank is the issuing bank or the confirming bank, its nomination by the issuing bank does not constitute any undertaking by the nominated bank to pay, to accept, or to negotiate.

   (d)   By nominating a bank other than itself, or by allowing for negotiation by any bank, or by authorising or requesting a bank to add its confirmation, the issuing bank authorises such bank to pay, accept, or negotiate, as the case may be, against documents which appear on their face to be in accordance with the terms and conditions of the credit, and undertakes to reimburse such bank in accordance with the provisions of these articles.

Comment

It is unfortunate that Article 11 is frequently disregarded by banks, which give no indication in their credits of how a negotiating bank is to obtain reimbursement. This has the effect of reducing the so-called credit to the status of a collection, albeit one for which payment is guaranteed by the issuing bank. Even worse are the banks which word their credits to call for drafts on the applicants and on receipt of documents send them, unexamined, to their customers for payment or acceptance. These are collections indeed, at least from the point of view of the time which must elapse before the beneficiaries can hope to receive payment. Exporters would do well to examine the payment terms of credits issued in their favour very carefully, and if they are in any doubt as to when they will be paid, to reject them out of hand.

Another frequent problem is where a credit restricts negotiation to a particular nominated bank and drawings are in fact negotiated by a third bank. Here, the ICC has given the opinion that the issuing bank is obliged to pay against documents presented in accordance with the credit terms, however those documents were received.

ARTICLE 12

(a) When an issuing bank instructs a bank (advising bank) by any teletransmission to advise a credit or an amendment to a credit, and intends the mail confirmation to be the operative credit instrument, or the operative amendment, the teletransmission must state "full details to follow" (or words of similar effect), or that the mail confirmation will be the operative credit instrument or the operative amendment. The issuing bank must forward the operative credit instrument or the operative amendment to such advising bank without delay.

(b) The teletransmission will be deemed to be the operative credit instrument or the operative amendment, and no mail confirmation should be sent, unless the teletransmission states "full details to follow" (or words of similar effect), or states that the mail confirmation is to be the operative credit instrument or the operative amendment.

(c) A teletransmission intended by the issuing bank to be the operative credit instrument should clearly indicate that the credit is issued subject to Uniform Customs and Practice for Documentary Credits, 1983 revision, ICC Publication no. 400.

(d) If a bank uses the services of another bank or banks (the advising bank) to have the credit advised to the beneficiary, it must also use the services of the same bank(s) for advising any amendments.

(e) Banks shall be responsible for any consequences arising from their failure to follow the procedures set out in the preceding paragraphs.

Comment

Although the meaning of this article should be reasonably clear, there remains the question of what action should be taken when although a telex, say, gave no indication that a mail confirmation was to follow, one is in fact received. Attitudes vary between banks in these circumstances, with some completely disregarding the mail advice as superfluous. Indeed, where the telex advice has been passed to the beneficiaries as an irrevocable letter of credit, nothing can be altered without their consent. The practical approach, however, is to check the confirmation against the telex and if there are discrepancies advise the issuing bank immediately of the situation by telex, at the same time approaching the beneficiaries to enquire whether they are prepared to accept an amendment. In this way the issuing bank is put on notice that it is in breach of UCP and can take steps to alter its procedures on future occasions, while the advising bank is seen to be doing all in its power to remedy the situation. The ICC has acknowledged that in a future revision of UCP it might be preferable to call for the telecommunication to state specifically whether it is the operative instrument and if it does not so state, it should be automatically regarded as being subject to mail confirmation, ie precisely the opposite attitude to that currently prevailing.

Another problem which arises is where the telecommunication is a message passed through SWIFT (Society for Worldwide Interbank Financial Telecommunications). Here is a case where the rules of an outside organisation can conflict with the rules of UCP. Article 12(c) states that a telecommunication which is intended to be the operative instrument must specifically refer to UCP. The SWIFT rules, however, state that in any communication the UCP are deemed to apply automatically unless the contrary is expressly stated. Membership of SWIFT is currently restricted to banks and therefore when messages are passed on as received to beneficiaries this information can be left out, and frequently is. Another conflict arises over the sending by SWIFT of a pre-advice of the issue of a credit or amendment, which by the SWIFT rules obliges the issuing bank to follow this with the actual instrument. UCP imposes no such obligation and the ICC has in fact expressed the opinion that a bank is uncommitted until the operative instrument is in the hands of the beneficiaries. This is potentially a far more dangerous situation which has yet to be tested in the courts, but it is suggested that the SWIFT view would prevail since it is based on a written rule accepted by all members, whereas the opposing ICC view is but a considered opinion.

ARTICLE 13
When a bank is instructed to issue, confirm, or advise a credit similar in terms to one previously issued, confirmed, or advised (similar credit) and the

previous credit has been the subject of amendment(s), it shall be understood that the similar credit shall not include such amendment(s) which is/are to apply to the similar credit. Banks should discourage instructions to issue, confirm, or advise a credit in this manner.

ARTICLE 14

If incomplete or unclear instructions are received to issue, confirm, advise or amend a credit, the bank requested to act on such instructions may give preliminary notification to the beneficiary for information only and without responsibility. The credit will be issued, confirmed, advised or amended only when the necessary information has been received and if the bank is then prepared to act on the instructions. Banks should provide the necessary information without delay.

(C) Liabilities and responsibilities

ARTICLE 15

Banks must examine all documents with reasonable care to ascertain that they appear on their face to be in accordance with the terms and conditions of the credit. Documents which appear on their face to be inconsistent with one another will be considered as not appearing on their face to be in accordance with the terms and conditions of the credit.

Comment

Article 15 is a relatively short article with a disproportionately high degree of significance. It really is two articles, since the two constituent sentences have little connection with each other. The first refers to "reasonable care" and this catch-all expression will mean totally different things depending on whether it is being interpreted by the prosecution or the defence. What constitutes reasonable care will vary according to the circumstances of the case. In one example a bank was held not to have applied reasonable care when it accepted a certificate of origin which, although on an official form and properly signed, failed to state from where the goods had come. On the other hand, the ICC has ruled that the requirement does not extend to the detailed checking of arithmetical calculations on documents, unless the error is an obvious one; they do not suggest, however, what should be considered as obvious and what should not.

The second sentence gives a requirement which provides a dangerous trap for beneficiaries who are unfamiliar with the rules. As we shall see when we come to discuss the checking of documents under credits, there are a number of checks which must be made other than the obvious one against the terms of the credit; this is one of them. Of particular significance here are the shipping marks, regarding which all documents should agree with the bill of lading.

ARTICLE 16(a)

If a bank so authorised effects payment, or incurs a deferred payment undertaking, or accepts, or negotiates against documents which appear on their face to be in accordance with the terms and conditions of a credit, the party giving such authority shall be bound to reimburse the bank which has effected payment, or incurred a deferred payment undertaking, or has accepted, or negotiated, and to take up the documents.

Comment

Effectively, this is re-stating the liability of the issuing bank laid down in Article 10.

ARTICLE 16(b)

If, upon receipt of the documents, the issuing bank considers that they appear on their face not to be in accordance with the terms and conditions of the credit, it must determine, on the basis of the documents alone, whether to take up such documents, or to refuse them and claim that they appear on their face not to be in accordance with the terms and conditions of the credit.

Comment

This is an important article which is regularly flouted by issuing banks. Banks which have adopted the practice of sending documents to the applicants for examination without checking them themselves should take careful note of the first six words of this article. Furthermore, where goods are sent by air or are otherwise available for inspection before documents have arrived, and are found to be sub-standard, issuing banks frequently bow to pressure from their customers to find some pretext for the rejection of the documents when they are received. This is obviously contrary to the spirit of the requirement that the issuing bank decides on the basis of the documents alone whether or not they should be rejected.

ARTICLE 16(c)

The issuing bank shall have a reasonable time in which to examine the documents and to determine as above whether to take up or to refuse the documents.

Comment

Here we have the word "reasonable" again, with no indication as to what might be considered reasonable. At present, all we have for guidance is a ruling by a London court that a period of 14 days was *not* reasonable, but the court made no attempt to define what was. The ICC has stated that when it sought opinions from its member organisations the replies varied between extremes of 36 hours and 30 days! It therefore felt unable to make any recommendations on the subject.

It is of passing interest that although the negotiating bank receives some protection from UCP by means of this requirement of the issuing bank, the beneficiaries receive no such protection from delay in processing of documents by the negotiating bank, which is not even required to make a decision within a "reasonable time".

ARTICLE 16(d)

If the issuing bank decides to refuse the documents, it must give notice to that effect without delay by telecommunication or, if that is not possible, by other expeditious means, to the bank from which it received the documents (the remitting bank), or to the beneficiary, if it received the documents directly from him. Such notice must state the discrepancies in respect of which the issuing bank refuses the documents and must also state whether it is holding the documents at the disposal of, or is returning them to, the presentors (remitting bank or the beneficiary as the case may be). The issuing bank shall then be entitled to claim from the remitting bank refund of any reimbursement which may have been made to that bank.

Comment

The wording of this article gives sweeping powers to the issuing bank which, unfortunately, are frequently abused. Disregard of the requirements of Article 16(b) means that often 16(d) is invoked for what can only be described as petty discrepancies, to the understandable fury of negotiating banks and beneficiaries alike. In the author's view it is to be hoped that a future revision of UCP will attempt to remedy this, perhaps by requiring the issuing bank not only to state the discrepancies for which it is refusing the documents, but also the way in which the contract is frustrated as a result.

It is often amusing to note how the "Chinese Wall", thought of as a recent development in the field of securities trading, has been in existence for a very long time in the credits area. A bank which may complain bitterly of the treatment it has received as a negotiating bank will be blithely handing out exactly the same treatment when it is acting as the issuing bank.

ARTICLE 16(e)

If the issuing bank fails to act in accordance with the provisions of paragraphs (c) and (d) of this article and/or fails to hold the documents at the disposal of, or to return them to, the presentor, the issuing bank shall be precluded from claiming that the documents are not in accordance with the terms and conditions of the credit.

Comment

See (c) and (d) above.

ARTICLE 16(f)

If the remitting bank draws the attention of the issuing bank to any discrepancies in the documents or advises the issuing bank that it has paid, incurred a deferred payment undertaking, accepted or negotiated under reserve or against an indemnity in respect of such discrepancies, the issuing bank shall not be thereby relieved from any of its obligations under any provision of this article. Such reserve or indemnity concerns only the relations between the remitting bank and the party towards whom the reserve was made, or from whom, or on whose behalf, the indemnity was obtained.

Comment

What frequently happens in practice in these circumstances is that the remitting bank extends its own indemnity to the issuing bank in respect of the discrepancies, in which case the issuing bank does become involved. In most cases the issuing bank will still seek instructions from its principles, but in doing so must nevertheless notify the remitting bank of its actions if it wishes to preserve its right to later reject the documents. If the applicants agree to take up the documents in reliance on the indemnity, it is vital that when advising the remitting bank of payment the issuing bank makes it absolutely clear that payment is being made under the protection of the indemnity offered. Such indemnities are normally valid for a restricted period only—traditionally six months but often less—to allow the buyers time to inspect the goods on arrival and then to decide whether or not they are acceptable. If they are accepted, the remitting bank should be released from its indemnity or reserve immediately in order that it may in turn release the beneficiaries, since they will, if proper records are being kept, be showing the indemnity or reserve in their books as a contingent liability.

ARTICLE 17

Banks assume no liability or responsibility for the form, sufficiency, accuracy, genuineness, falsification or legal effect of any documents, or for the general and/or particular conditions stipulated in the documents or superimposed thereon; nor do they assume any liability or responsibility for the description, quantity, weight, quality, condition, packing, delivery, value or existence of the goods represented by any documents, or for the good faith or acts and/or omissions, solvency, performance or standing of the consignor, the carriers, or the insurers of the goods, or any other person whomsoever.

Comment

This article emphasises and expands upon what has already been said in relation to Articles 4 and 15.

ARTICLE 18

Banks assume no liability or responsibility for the consequences arising out of delay and/or loss in transit of any messages, letters or documents, or for delay, mutilation or other errors arising in the transmission of any telecommunication. Banks assume no liability or responsibility for errors in translation or interpretation of technical terms and reserve the right to transmit credit terms without translating them.

Comment

With regard to translation, except in the relatively rare cases where staff in both the advising bank and the beneficiaries are bilingual, the credit will have to be translated at some stage in order that documents may be checked when presented for negotiation. It is therefore a good idea if at an early stage both the beneficiaries and the prospective negotiating bank are working from the same translation. It is suggested, therefore, that even though the advising bank has no duty to provide a translation, it does so and requests the beneficiaries to confirm that their own translation agrees with the bank's. If exporters receive an untranslated credit, they should take the initiative and provide the advising bank with their own translation accompanied by a similar request.

It is unwise to attempt any translation of technical terms, particularly in the description of the goods, since not only an absolute fluency in both languages but also an intimate knowledge of the particular product and its manufacture is required in order to do so. Even given this unlikely combination (particularly in a bank), some terms simply do not readily translate from one language into another and the result may be shipment of the wrong goods.

ARTICLE 19
Banks assume no liability or responsibility for consequences arising out of the interruption of their business by Acts of God, riots, civil commotions, insurrections, wars or any other causes beyond their control, or by any strikes or lockouts. Unless specifically authorised, banks will not, upon resumption of their business, incur a deferred payment undertaking, or effect payment, acceptance or negotiation under credits which expired during such interruption of their business.

ARTICLE 20
(a)   Banks utilising the services of another bank or other banks for the purpose of giving effect to the instructions of the applicant for the credit do so for the account and at the risk of such applicant.

(b)   Banks assume no liability or responsibility should the instructions they transmit not be carried out, even if they have themselves taken the initiative in the choice of such other bank(s).

(c)   The applicant for the credit shall be bound by and liable to indemnify the banks against all obligations and responsibilities imposed by foreign laws and usages.

Comment

Article 20 applies the principles of agency, which we have already discussed in some detail in relation to collections, to letters of credit. The difference, of course, is that here the chain of agency runs in the opposite direction to that of a collection, since in the case of the latter all banks are acting on behalf of the sellers whereas with a credit they act on behalf of the buyers.

ARTICLE 21
(a)   If an issuing bank intends that the reimbursement to which a paying, accepting or negotiating bank is entitled shall be obtained

by such bank claiming on another branch or office of the issuing bank or on a third bank (all hereinafter referred to as the reimbursing bank) it shall provide such reimbursing bank in good time with the proper instructions or authorisation to honour such reimbursement claims and without making it a condition that the bank entitled to claim reimbursement must certify compliance with the terms and conditions of the credit to the reimbursing bank.

(b) An issuing bank will not be relieved from any of its obligations to provide reimbursement itself if and when reimbursement is not effected by the reimbursing bank.

(c) The issuing bank will be responsible to the paying, accepting or negotiating bank for any loss of interest if reimbursement is not provided on first demand made to the reimbursing bank, or as otherwise specified in the credit, or mutually agreed, as the case may be.

Comment

Despite the provisions of this article, some banks persist in calling for a certificate stating that the terms of the credit have been complied with, to be included with any reimbursement claim made under that credit. This does not, of course, affect the beneficiary or the applicant, but is a problem which must be sorted out between the banks concerned. Since the advising bank is under no obligation to advise the credit unless it is satisfied with its terms, including the arrangements for reimbursement, it would be perfectly justified in refusing to advise until the offending requirement had been deleted. The reimbursing bank is acting merely as a paying agent and is in no way concerned with the credit itself and therefore has no interest in whether or not the terms have been complied with. This is solely a matter between the negotiating and issuing banks.

The question of interest accrued on delayed payment of claims for reimbursement continues to be a problem. Sometimes it is the beneficiaries who must bear the cost of this (where their drawing is presented for negotiation), and sometimes the negotiating bank (where they are acting as a paying bank), but whoever has lost, the article puts the responsibility for payment of interest squarely on the shoulders of the issuing bank. Prevarication over such claims is rife, but in reality such disputes should be between the issuing bank and its paying agent and, if they are frequent, then perhaps it is time for the issuing bank to seek a new paying agent.

12
Uniform Customs and Practice for Documentary Credits (2)

(D) Documents

ARTICLE 22

    (a)   All instructions for the issuance of credits and the credits themselves and, where applicable, all instructions for amendments thereto and the amendments themselves, must state precisely the document(s) against which payment, acceptance or negotiation is to be made.

    (b)   Terms such as "first class", "well known", "qualified", "independent", "official" and the like shall not be used to describe the issuers of any documents to be presented under a credit. If such terms are incorporated in the credit term, banks will accept the relative documents as presented, provided that they appear on their face to be in accordance with the other terms and conditions of the credit.

    (c)   Unless otherwise stipulated in the credit, banks will accept as originals documents produced or appearing to have been produced;
        (i)   by reprographic systems;
        (ii)   by, or as the result of, automated or computerised systems;
        (iii)   as carbon copies,
    if marked as originals, always provided that, where necessary, such documents appear to have been authenticated.

Comment

The relevance of section (b) is fairly evident. It is unfair to leave the negotiating bank to judge whether the issuer of a document is first class (a term often encountered in credits in connection with the insurers of the goods) and impractical to demand evidence of an issuer's qualifications (a veterinary surgeon, for instance). It is the responsibility of the applicants to identify the party who should issue each document and to nominate them in the credit, having made prior arrangements for them to carry out the required work or service.

Section (c) sets out the basic position of the banks and is intended to accommodate modern cost-saving methods of production of documents. Many countries will not accept such short cuts and insist, for instance, on at least one originally-typed invoice being presented. Where this is the case, the applicants and the issuing bank should be aware of the requirement and ensure that the credit makes it clear that Article 22 is not to apply in its entirety.

It is unfortunate that the article states that these documents must be marked as originals, since this is not the normal practice with such documents as commercial invoices. Beneficiaries should note that where they are using one of these systems of production of documents they should be so marked to avoid any possibility of rejection of the drawing on these grounds.

The position remains unclear as to whether the signature to a document should be an original or whether it too may be reproduced by the same system as the rest of that document. Practice in this varies so widely that the ICC has been unable to make a ruling on the subject. Bills of lading, for instance, are often signed with a facsimile of an authorised signature and seem to be generally accepted. Frequently, however, invoices are rejected for this reason; where there is doubt beneficiaries are advised to provide at least one invoice bearing an original signature. The problem is really a legal one, since there is doubt as to whether parties can be committed by signatures not actually applied by them. Since, however, under most legal codes no-one can be committed by a forged signature, original or otherwise, the question is largely academic, but still the disputes continue.

ARTICLE 23
When documents other than transport documents, insurance documents and commercial invoices are called for, the credit should stipulate by whom such documents are to be issued and their wording or data content. If the credit does not so stipulate, banks will accept such documents as presented, provided that their data content makes it possible to relate the goods and/or ser-

vices referred to therein to those referred to in the commercial invoice(s) presented, or to those referred to in the credit if the credit does not stipulate presentation of a commercial invoice.

Comment

As with Article 22(b), the responsibility of ensuring that the credit's requirements are clearly and unambiguously stated lies with the applicants. An example might be a requirement for presentation of a certificate of origin, where, in the absence of any further stipulation the beneficiaries' own certificate would be perfectly acceptable and the applicants could not refuse the drawing because they had actually needed a certificate issued by a chamber of commerce.

ARTICLE 24

Unless otherwise stipulated in the credit, banks will accept a document bearing a date of issuance prior to that of the credit, subject to such document being presented within the time limits set out in the credit and in these articles.

Comment

Some countries will not accept such documents as bills of lading which are dated prior to the issue of the credit or, alternatively, the relative import licence. Again, where this is the case the applicants and the issuing bank are expected to be aware of the situation and must add a clause to the credit accordingly.

(D1) Transport documents (documents indicating loading on board or dispatch or taking in charge)

Comment

When the current revision of UCP was drawn up, it was the intention of ICC to draw firm lines of demarcation between articles intended to deal with post receipts (Article 30), marine bills of lading (Article 26) and all other transport documents (Article 25). The result has unfortunately been that Articles 25 and 26 have become extremely lengthy and their wording so convoluted as to make them very difficult to understand and to apply, even for experienced people. Much of the content of Article 25 is duplicated in Article 26 and it becomes very much a case of "spot the difference". It should be noted that the preamble to each of these articles (25 and 26) is intended to establish exactly to which documents the respective articles are to apply, and in each case applies grammatically only to section (a) of the article.

ARTICLE 25

Unless a credit calling for a transport document stipulates as such document a marine bill of lading (ocean bill of lading or a bill of lading covering carriage by sea), or a post receipt or certificate of posting:

(a) banks will, unless otherwise stipulated in the credit, accept a transport document which:
   (i)   appears on its face to have been issued by a named carrier, or his agent, and
   (ii) indicates dispatch or taking in charge of the goods, or loading on board, as the case may be, and
   (iii) consists of the full set of originals issued to the consignor if issued in more than one original, and
   (iv) meets all other stipulations of the credit.

Comment

Many of the problems stemming from the operation of Articles 25 and 26 result from the habit of banks of including in their credit forms and in the relative application forms, a preprinted requirement for presentation of a marine or ocean bill of lading. Too often this is allowed to stand without any consideration being given to the method of transport which will actually be used. Both the buyers, when completing their application, and the sellers, on receipt of the credit, should give careful consideration to this question in the light of these articles and ensure that the wording of the credit is adequate to the situation.

Section (a), then, defines the minimum requirements of a transport document other than a marine bill of lading or post receipt in order that it may be acceptable under a credit. In particular sub-section (ii) codifies the bill of lading's function as the carriers' receipt for the goods, and (iii) recognises its importance as a negotiable instrument. Sub-section (i) appears to preclude presentation of bills which are signed by the master of the vessel but which do not bear any carrier's name and the ICC has confirmed that this is the case. However valid such documents may be in practice, they are not acceptable under a credit. An exception has been made by the ICC in the case of charter party bills of lading, where the credit authorises their use but remains silent on the subject of whether or not they should be issued by a named carrier. This is in deference to the common practice in the charter trade of using vessels owned by the captain as an individual. These opinions of the ICC have been reached since the present revision of UCP was brought into operation and possibly an attempt will be made to incorporate them in a future revision.

ARTICLE 25(b)

Subject to the above, and unless otherwise stipulated in the credit, banks will not reject a transport document which:

(i)   bears a title such as "Combined transport bill of lading", "Combined transport document", "Combined transport bill of lading or port-to-port bill of lading", or a title or a combination of titles of similar intent and effect, and/or

(ii) indicates some or all of the conditions of carriage by reference to a source or document other than the transport document itself (short form/blank back transport document), and/or

(iii) indicates a place of taking in charge different from the port of loading and/or a place of final destination different from the port of discharge, and/or

(iv) relates to cargoes such as those in containers or on pallets, and the like, and/or

(v)   contains the indication "intended" or similar qualification, in relation to the vessel or other means of transport, and/or the port of loading and/or the port of discharge.

Comment

Sub-section (i), the content of which is perhaps more important when it is repeated in Article 26, is intended to convey the message that what is important is not what a document calls itself but what it actually is, as evidenced from the data contained in the document itself.

Sub-section (ii) has been in UCP for many years now, yet still some banks incorporate in their preprinted credit forms a stipulation that short-form bills of lading are not acceptable, this without any legal justification whatever. Whether through laziness or ignorance on the part of those banks, this practice, like that previously mentioned of asking for certificates of compliance, should be discouraged. A refusal on the part of advising banks and beneficiaries to accept such anachronistic restrictions would be greatly beneficial in furtherance of this aim.

The remaining sub-sections relate to the modern methods of cargo-handling whereby goods are accepted by the carriers at places which may be remote from the actual port of loading, usually container bases, and their similar delivery at the destination. Such methods are essential in order that valuable space at the dockside may be kept free from goods other than those currently being loaded or discharged from vessels along-side, thus ensuring the speedy turnround of those ships.

ARTICLE 25(c)

Unless otherwise stipulated in the credit in the case of carriage by sea or by more than one mode of transport but including carriage by sea, banks will reject a transport document which:

(i)   indicates that it is subject to a charter party, and/or

(ii)   indicates that the carrying vessel is propelled by sail only.

Comment

The defects of charter party bills of lading were discussed in Chapter 3. To sum up these defects, charter party bills do not necessarily indicate the true conditions of carriage since they are issued subject to the provisions of another document, the charter party itself; they do not cover liner voyages which means that the date of arrival of the goods cannot be accurately forecast; the status of the issuers is sometimes in doubt; they may cover shipment by substandard vessels; and they often feature in cases of fraud, either maritime or documentary. They must therefore be specifically permitted under a credit. Applicants should bear this in mind when applying for the issue of the credit if it is known that, because of the nature of the goods or voyage, or because of specific arrangements with the sellers under the contract, the goods will or may be shipped on a chartered vessel. From the above, they will also be aware of the dangers inherent in allowing their presentation.

For the position regarding shipment by chartered aircraft, see the comments under Article 25(d) below.

ARTICLE 25(d)

Unless otherwise stipulated in the credit, banks will reject a transport document issued by a freight forwarder unless it is the FIATA Combined Transport Bill of Lading approved by the International Chamber of Commerce or otherwise indicates that it is issued by a freight forwarder acting as a carrier or agent of a named carrier.

Comment

House bills of lading and the FIATA Combined Transport Bill of Lading (FBL), were discussed at length in Chapter 4. The position under this article, where the credit is not calling for presentation of a marine bill of lading, is fairly clear. Where the document presented is not a FIATA FBL, a great deal will depend upon the manner in which it is signed. Where the signature states "as carriers", or words of similar effect, there is no doubt that the document is acceptable. The words "for the carriers" or similar, however, are not acceptable unless those carriers are named and, furthermore, identifiable as the actual carriers and not merely an associate company of the forwarders. The provisions of Articles 15 and 17 mean that, provided the transport document presented appears to comply with Article 25(d), banks need make no further enquiry. Again, it is advisable for sellers to make it clear to the buyers when they intend using the services of a freight forwarder and request that presentation of a house bill of lading is specifically authorised in the credit.

Many problems arise when the goods are to be sent by air. Although intended to be all-embracing as regards transport documents other than marine bills of lading and post receipts, it is evident from the wording of Article 25 that sea transport was nonetheless uppermost in the minds of its compilers. The chaos which arises when banks attempt to apply the terms of sub-sections (c)(i) and (d) to air waybills without recognition of the realities of air transport seem to make it highly desirable that a future revision of UCP reinstates the principle of separate treatment for this document. In air transport, aircraft are frequently chartered and the way-bills (in fact air consignment notes) are far more frequently issued by forwarding agents than by the airlines themselves. Experience tells that these factors in no way prejudice the value of the transport document, which is in any case low since it is not a document of title to the goods. Furthermore, the speed of air transport and of modern communications makes it relatively easy, in cases of doubt, to verify the arrival of the goods. Much more flexibility is needed, but is denied by the provisions of this article, which in all fairness banks must apply even though they may be aware that in doing so they are incurring the wrath of the beneficiaries, who cannot understand why they cannot be paid when they know that the buyers have already received and possibly even disposed of the goods. Again, the only solution is to ensure that the credit specifically allows for the presentation of a house air waybill or air consignment note, and allows for shipment by chartered aircraft if this is thought to be a possibility.

ARTICLE 26

If a credit calling for a transport document stipulates as such document a marine bill of lading:

(a) banks will, unless otherwise stipulated in the credit, accept a document which:

   (i)   appears on its face to have been issued by a named carrier, or his agent, and

   (ii) indicates that the goods have been loaded on board or shipped on a named vessel, and

   (iii) consists of the full set of originals issued to the consignor if issued in more than one original, and

   (iv) meets all other stipulations of the credit.

Comment

As did Article 25, this article commences with a description of the minimum requirements of a document before it can be acceptable under a credit. The one, significant, difference is that here, unless stipulated otherwise, the document must evidence that the goods are actually on board the named carrying vessel.

ARTICLE 26(b)

Subject to the above, and unless otherwise stipulated in the credit, banks will not reject a document which:

   (i)   bears a title such as "Combined transport bill of lading", "Combined transport document", "Combined transport bill of lading or port-to-port bill of lading", or a title or a combination of titles of similar intent and effect, and/or

   (ii) indicates some or all of the conditions of carriage by reference to a source or document other than the transport document itself (short form/blank back transport document), and/or

   (iii) indicates a place of taking in charge different from the port of loading and/or a place of final destination different from the port of discharge, and/or

   (iv) relates to cargoes such as those in containers or on pallets, and the like.

Comment

Identical to Article 25 (b), save for the omission of the fifth sub-section relating to use of the word "intended". With a marine bill of lading, this word cannot be permitted except where it is later superseded by a clause (see Article 27b) indicating actual loading of the goods on a named vessel.

ARTICLE 26(c)
Unless otherwise stipulated in the credit, banks will reject a document which:
  (i)   indicates that it is subject to a charter party, and/or
  (ii) indicates that the carrying vessel is propelled by sail only, and/or
  (iii) contains the indication "intended" or similar qualification in relation to
        – the vessel and/or the port of loading – unless such document bears an on board notation in accordance with Article 27(b) and also indicates the actual port of loading, and/or
        – the port of discharge – unless the place of final destination indicated on the document is other than the port of discharge, and/or
  (iv) is issued by a freight forwarder, unless it indicates that it is issued by such freight forwarder acting as a carrier, or as the agent of a named carrier.

Comment

Sub-sections (i) and (ii) are identical to those in Article 25(c) (refer back). Sub-section (iii) relates to use of the word "intended" and is merely transferred from the "permitted" sub-section in Article 25 to the "prohibited" sub-section here. Comment has already been made on this in Article 26(b) above. Sub-section (iv) is similar in its provisions to Article 25(d), save that no exception is made in the case of the FIATA FBL. As noted in Chapter 4, however, the ICC has ruled that the FBL is acceptable as a marine bill of lading under this article and by now most banks should be aware of, and be applying, this ruling. Disputes will probably continue to arise on occasions, however, until the next revision of UCP incorporates this doctrine into the published rules.

ARTICLE 27
  (a) Unless a credit specifically calls for an on board transport document, or unless inconsistent with other stipulation(s) in the credit, or with Article 26, banks will accept a transport document which indicates that the goods have been taken in charge or received for shipment.
  (b) Loading on board or shipment on a vessel may be evidenced either

by a transport document bearing wording indicating loading on board a named vessel or shipment on a named vessel, or, in the case of a transport document stating "received for shipment", by means of a notation of loading on board on the transport document signed or initialled and dated by the carrier or his agent, and the date of this notation shall be regarded as the date of loading on board the named vessel or shipment on the named vessel.

Comment

Sub-section (a), by reference to Article 26, excludes any credit which calls for marine or ocean bills of lading, since by implication these must indicate that the goods are on board a named vessel. Sub-section (b) should not require any clarification but regrettably some banks do not seem able to cope with the idea that if a bill of lading states in its printed preamble that the goods have been shipped, rather than "received for shipment" or merely "accepted", then no further notation is required. The words "shipped", "loaded" and "on board" are synonymous from this point of view of UCP, and are freely interchangeable.

The requirements of Article 27 cannot be deviated from, as has been made clear in repeated opinions given by ICC where dispute has arisen. In many cases, the words "shipped on board" or "clean on board" are typed on the bill of lading by the shippers before the document is lodged with the carriers for signature. Where the printed preamble to the bill of lading states that the goods are "received for shipment" the "on board" clause still requires to be separately signed and dated by the carriers, even though the words were present at the time when the bill was signed. In this respect, these rules, which are international in nature and application, are at variance with English law, since in what must rank as one of the most questionable decisions they have ever made the Judicial Committee of the Privy Council recently ruled that a bill of lading which bore the words "clean on board" at the time it was signed could not be rejected by a bank under a letter of credit. Apart from making the law of England divergent from that of the rest of the world and from the requirements of UCP, this decision fails to take into account the under-lying reason for the existence of the article, that a bank can have no means of verifying when and by whom the words were placed on the bill. With all due respect to their Lordships, therefore, banks have no choice but to disregard this ruling.

Although it will be mentioned again under Article 50, it is worth mentioning here that in the case of a "received for shipment" bill of lading the operative date for determining when the goods have been shipped is the date of the "on board" endorsement and not that of the document itself.

ARTICLE 28

(a) In the case of carriage by sea or by more than one mode of transport but including carriage by sea, banks will refuse a transport document stating that the goods are or will be loaded on deck, unless specifically authorised in the credit.

(b) Banks will not refuse a transport document which contains a provision that the goods may be carried on deck, provided it does not state specifically that they are or will be loaded on deck.

Comment

It is generally undesirable that goods be loaded on the deck of a ship rather than in the hold for two main reasons. Obviously, goods so stowed are more liable to damage from the elements or from being washed overboard in a storm; in addition, such goods are likely to be the first to go when it becomes necessary to jettison cargo in order to lighten the ship and thus save it from foundering. When the goods are of a nature which indicates that they will probably be stowed on deck, such as where they are hazardous or inflammable, or where they are too bulky for hold stowage, due provision should be made in the credit for acceptance of bills of lading indicating stowage on deck.

ARTICLE 29(a)

For the purpose of this article transhipment means a transfer and reloading during the course of carriage from the port of loading or place of dispatch or taking in charge to the port of discharge or place of destination, either from one conveyance or vessel to another conveyance or vessel within the same mode of transport or from one mode of transport to another.

Comment

This first sub-section is intended to define the meaning of the word "transhipment" in order that it may not be misunderstood in the remainder of the article.

ARTICLE 29(b)

Unless transhipment is prohibited by the terms of the credit, banks will accept transport documents which indicate that the goods will be transhipped, provided the entire carriage is covered by one and the same transport document.

ARTICLE 29(c)

Even if transhipment is prohibited by the terms of the credit, banks will accept transport documents which:

    (i)   incorporate printed clauses stating that the carrier has the right to tranship, or

    (ii)   state or indicate that transhipment will or may take place, when the credit stipulates a combined transport document, or indicates carriage from a place of taking in charge to a place of final destination by different modes of transport including a carriage by sea, provided that the entire carriage is covered by one and the same transport document, or

    (iii) state or indicate that the goods are in a container(s), trailer(s), "LASH" barge(s) and the like and will be carried from the place of taking in charge to the place of final destination in the same container(s), trailer(s), "LASH" barge(s), and the like under one and the same transport document.

    (iv) state or indicate the place of receipt and/or of final destination as "C.F.S." (container freight station) or "C.Y." (container yard) at, or associated with, the port of loading and/or the port of final destination.

Comment

As has been stated previously, modern methods of cargo handling dictate that goods, particularly those in containers, are taken in charge and delivered by the carriers at places which are remote from the dockside where the carrying vessel loads and discharges her cargo. The article recognises that, given the definition of transhipment in sub-section (a), it would be nonsense for a credit covering goods so shipped to prohibit transhipment. It was never the intention of the ICC, and it has so stated, to allow the transhipment of goods in the traditional sense, ie carriage by sea to one port, there to be discharged to await arrival of a second vessel on which to be carried to their final destination, merely by virtue of those goods being in a container, or by the extremities of the journey provided for in the credit being different from the ports of loading and destination. No doubt this anomaly will be rectified in a later version of UCP.

The reasons for the unpopularity of transhipment are the dangers which threaten goods during the period between discharge and reloading at the port of transhipment, including exposure to the weather, inappropriate storage facilities being available, pilferage, accidental damage and undue delay.

For those who are in any doubt, a "LASH" barge is a floating container, either towed by a tug or proceeding under its own power to a port where it is either loaded on board the ocean vessel or is accommodated between the hulls of a catamaran type of vessel.

Careful consideration should be given by applicants to the facts of each case before asking that transhipment be prohibited in a credit and this aspect should be checked by beneficiaries on receipt of the credit. Some voyages are simply not possible, or are rarely possible, without transhipment taking place, and this statement applies even more where shipment is by air. In the latter case it is not always immediately evident from the waybill that transhipment has occurred but the use of code letters denoting the airports which will handle the consignment *en route* is a useful clue. More than two sets of three letters normally indicates transhipment.

ARTICLE 30

If the credit stipulates dispatch of goods by post and calls for a post receipt or certificate of posting, banks will accept such post receipt or certificate of posting if it appears to have been stamped or otherwise authenticated and dated in the place from which the credit stipulates the goods are to be dispatched.

ARTICLE 31

(a) Unless otherwise stipulated in the credit, or inconsistent with any of the documents presented under the credit, banks will accept transport documents stating that freight or transportation charges (hereinafter referred to as "freight") have still to be paid.

(b) If a credit stipulates that the transport document has to indicate that freight has been paid or prepaid, banks will accept a transport document on which words clearly indicating payment or prepayment of freight appear by stamp or otherwise, or on which payment of freight is indicated by other means.

(c) The words "freight prepayable" or "freight to be prepaid" or words of similar effect, if appearing on transport documents, will not be accepted as constituting evidence of the payment of freight.

(d) Banks will accept transport documents bearing reference by stamp or otherwise to costs additional to the freight charges, such as costs of, or disbursements incurred in connection with, loading, unloading or similar operations, unless the conditions of the credit specifically prohibit such reference.

Comment

Note that, unlike the "on board" endorsement, the endorsement "freight paid" does not need to be separately signed by the carriers. In practice, bills of lading are not normally released to the shippers until freight has been paid or unless they operate an open account system for payment of freight by those shippers.

ARTICLE 32
Unless otherwise stipulated in the credit, banks will accept transport documents which bear a clause on the face thereof such as "shippers load and count" or "said by shipper to contain" or words of similar effect.

ARTICLE 33
Unless otherwise stipulated in the credit, banks will accept transport documents indicating as the consignor of the goods a party other than the beneficiary of the credit.

Comment

Yet again, it is incumbent upon the applicants and the issuing bank to ensure that, if the laws of their country prohibit the name of a third party to be shown on the bill of lading as shipper, the credit so states.

This particularly applies where it is known that the beneficiary is not the supplier of the goods, or that the bill of lading is likely to be a carrier's bill issued to a forwarding agent.

ARTICLE 34
(a)   A clean transport document is one which bears no superimposed clause or notation which expressly declares a defective condition of the goods and/or the packaging.
(b)   Banks will refuse transport documents bearing such clauses or notations unless the credit expressly stipulates the clauses or notations which may be accepted.
(c)   Banks will regard a requirement in a credit for a transport document to bear the clause "clean on board" as complied with if such transport document meets the requirements of this article and of Article 27(b).

Comment

Though ostensibly among the simpler articles in UCP, this one seems to be one of the most regularly misunderstood or disregarded. If the bill is a "shipped" one and bears nothing which indicates that there is anything wrong with the goods or the packing, then whatever it says in the credit the words "clean on board" are completely superfluous and, in fact, as indicated in the comments on Article 27 can cause more problems than they solve.

Disputes also arise as to what constitutes a clause indicating a defect in the goods and/or the packing, and the attitude of banks varies wildly in this respect. Banks have been known to reject a bill of lading as dirty when it bears a clause stating that surcharges may be payable at the destination if the ship is delayed in entering harbour by factors beyond the captain's control, a matter which is not even covered by this article but by Article 31. "Wrapping on bales torn and stained" should undoubtedly be regarded as detrimental and the document be rejected, but "In the opinion of the carrier the packing of these goods is insufficient, etc." should not. Where it is felt that because of the nature of the cargo a claused bill of lading may well be issued but the clause will be acceptable to the buyers, it is as well to provide for its acceptance in the credit. As always, it is also in the beneficiaries' interests if they consider this aspect when the credit is received and if necessary call for an amendment. The alternative may well be a severe delay in payment or worse.

(D2) Insurance documents

ARTICLE 35
(a) Insurance documents must be as stipulated in the credit, and must be issued and/or signed by insurance companies or underwriters, or their agents.
(b) Cover notes issued by brokers will not be accepted, unless specifically authorised by the credit.

Comment

The drawbacks of brokers' cover notes were dealt with in Chapter 5. Sellers should note that if they intend obtaining insurance cover from Europe, a brokers' cover note may well be the document provided, since it is well-established in that insurance market. They should therefore either request that the credit be framed so as to authorise presentation of such a document, or specifically request the brokers to provide the insurers' own policy or certificate.

All concerned, but especially the banks, should remember that a document is not always what it seems to be at first glance and it has been known for an insurance document bearing the heading of a broker to transpire to be the actual document signed by the various syndicates of underwriters which have subscribed to the cover provided.

ARTICLE 36
Unless otherwise stipulated in the credit, or unless it appears from the insurance document(s) that the cover is effective at the latest from the date of loading on board or dispatch or taking in charge of the goods, banks will refuse insurance documents presented which bear a date later than the date of loading on board or dispatch or taking in charge of the goods as indicated by the transport document(s).

Comment

Broadly speaking, this means that where the insurance document is a policy it must not be dated later than the relevant transport document. However, where it is a certificate issued under an open or a floating policy, the agreement between the insurers and the insured is that all shipments will be held covered and the cover is therefore in force from the time the goods leave the sellers' warehouse, even though the certificate is not issued until a later date.

ARTICLE 37
(a) Unless otherwise stipulated in the credit, the insurance document must be expressed in the same currency as the credit.

(b) Unless otherwise stipulated in the credit, the minimum amount for which the insurance document must indicate the insurance cover to have been effected is the CIF (cost, insurance and freight . . . "named port of destination") or CIP (freight/carriage and insurance paid to "named point of destination") value of the goods, as the case may be, plus 10%. However, if banks cannot determine the CIF or CIP value, as the case may be, from the documents on their face, they will accept as such minimum amount the amount for which payment, acceptance or negotiation is requested under the credit, or the amount of the commercial invoice, whichever is the greater.

Comment

Surprisingly, the ICC has given the opinion that where a credit specifies that insurance cover be effected for, say, CIF value plus 10%, where this percentage is exceeded even by a small amount the document should be rejected. It would seem, bearing in mind the low cost of insurance premiums relative to the value of the goods and the fact that the total amount of drawings will in any case be restricted by the amount of the credit, that this is taking too rigid a view of the kind which, if strictly enforced, gets banks a bad name among exporters. However, this is a personal view and the ICC's opinion should be respected.

ARTICLE 38
   (a)   Credits should stipulate the type of insurance required and, if any, the additional risks which are to be covered. Imprecise terms such as "usual risks" or "customary risks" should not be used; if they are used, banks will accept insurance documents as presented, without responsibility for any risks not being covered.
   (b)   Failing specific stipulations in the credit, banks will accept insurance documents as presented, without responsibility for any risks not being covered.

ARTICLE 39
Where a credit stipulates "insurance against all risks", banks will accept an insurance document which contains any "all risks" notation or clause, whether or not bearing the heading "all risks", even if indicating that certain risks are excluded, without responsibility for any risk(s) not being covered.

Comment

As mentioned in Chapter 5, the old "all risks" clauses drawn up by the Institute of London Underwriters have been superseded by a new set simply designated "Clauses A". The purpose of Article 39 is to cater for the surprising number of banks which have not yet realised this and continue to call for cover as per Institute "all risks" clauses in their credits.

ARTICLE 40
Banks will accept an insurance document which indicates that the cover is

subject to a franchise or an excess (deductible), unless it is specifically stipulated in the credit that the insurance must be issued irrespective of percentage.

Comment

Although a common practice in other areas of insurance, it is unusual for a percentage to be applied to marine cargo insurance, requiring the claimant to bear a stated percentage of any loss.

(D3) Commercial invoice

ARTICLE 41
(a)   Unless otherwise stipulated in the credit, commercial invoices must be made out in the name of the applicant for the credit.

(b)   Unless otherwise stipulated in the credit, banks may refuse commercial invoices issued for amounts in excess of the amount permitted by the credit. Nevertheless, if a bank authorised to pay, incur a deferred payment undertaking, accept, or negotiate under a credit accepts such invoices, its decision will be binding upon all parties, provided such bank has not paid, incurred a deferred payment undertaking, accepted or effected negotiation for an amount in excess of that permitted by the credit.

(c)   The description of the goods in the commercial invoice must correspond with the description in the credit. In all other documents, the goods may be described in general terms not inconsistent with the description of the goods in the credit.

Comment

Sub-section (b) covers the situation where, because of unforeseen increases in costs or because of a miscalculation of the amount of freight payable, the sellers invoice the full cost to the buyers but draw under the credit only for the amount payable thereunder. The negotiating bank is given the option of accepting or rejecting such invoices. Often there is no danger in accepting and the bank may be prepared to treat the difference between the amounts of the draft and the invoice as a separate clean collection. Sometimes, however, the bank will know from its experience that the discrepancy in amount will cause problems in the buyers' country; this frequently applies where that country exercises strict exchange controls. In these circumstances the bank may well exercise its option to refuse the invoice.

Sub-section (c) is one of the instances where UCP must be obeyed quite literally to the letter. Even if the credit description of the goods includes a spelling mistake this should be faithfully reproduced in the invoice description. This is because the detailed description is likely to be of a technical nature and banks cannot be expected to make judgements on whether or not a discrepancy is crucial. As an example, a Swiss bank rejected a drawing negotiated through a bank in New York because the invoice included the word "polyethilene" in the goods description, whereas the credit gave the word as "polyethylene". These are respectively the American and English spellings of the same word but it would have been unfair to expect the Swiss bank to make a judgement on this. One-letter differences can be crucial, as in "bisulphate" and "bisulphite", which indicate entirely different chemicals.

Unless specifically required by the credit or by the regulations of the importing country, a detailed description on the bill of lading is unnecessary and is discouraged by most carriers. There is a tendency among shippers, however, to describe the goods in such a way as to attract the lowest possible freight rate without (it is to be hoped) resorting to actual deception. This is a matter concerning only the contract of carriage but where the saving on the freight may possibly be vastly exceeded by the loss when payment under a credit is refused, this becomes a false economy.

(D4) Other documents

ARTICLE 42

If a credit calls for an attestation or certification of weight in the case of transport other than by sea, banks will accept a weight stamp or declaration of weight which appears to have been superimposed on the transport document by the carrier or his agent unless the credit specifically stipulates that the attestation or certification of weight must be by means of a separate document.

13
Uniform Customs and Practice for Documentary Credits (3)

(E) Miscellaneous provisions

Quantity and amount

ARTICLE 43

(a) The words "about", "circa" or similar expressions used in connection with the amount of the credit or the quantity or the unit price stated in the credit are to be construed as allowing a difference not to exceed 10% more or 10% less than the amount or the quantity or the unit price to which they refer.

(b) Unless a credit stipulates that the quantity of goods must not be exceeded or reduced, a tolerance of 5% more or 5% less will be permissible, even if partial shipments are not permitted, always provided that the amount of the drawings does not exceed the amount of the credit. This tolerance does not apply when the credit stipulates the quantity in terms of a stated number of packing units or individual items.

Comment

Sub-section (a) is fairly clear in its meaning. The difficulty arises when the words "about" or "approximately" are used in relation to the quantity or the unit price without being also applied to the credit amount. The resulting contradiction inevitably means that the beneficiary cannot be paid under the credit and all concerned should be alert for examples of this trap.

Sub-section (b) was originally intended to apply to bulk cargoes, allowing for such potential sources of discrepancy as absorption of moisture, residue in tanks, etc, but nowadays tends to be applied indiscriminately. It can be particularly useful in the many cases where the credit is stated to be for a specific amount, partial drawings are prohibited, but for whatever reason the drawing is for less than the credit amount. This attitude is understandable but dubious as to its validity, since the article refers specifically to the quantity and not to the amount. Where, for instance, a credit specifies the total weight of goods to be shipped and that total is actually shipped, this article would give no protection against documents being rejected for "short drawing" if such was the case. Where no unit price is given in the credit the immediate assumption by the banks is that inferior goods have been supplied, even though the real problem is usually that the freight amount differs from that estimated in the pro forma invoice. It will be remembered from Chapter 2 that the usual basis for commercial quotations is the FOB price, since this is a constant. In estimating other costs, such as freight and insurance, sellers naturally tend to err on the high side in order that they are not left with a shortfall which cannot be drawn under the credit. However, where those costs are less than estimated and they are honest enough to pass the saving on to their customers they may find themselves penalised by having their documents rejected as described above. Where doubt exists, the problem can be guarded against by asking for the amount of the credit to be expressed as a maximum which may be drawn ("up to . . ."), or by asking for it to be expressed as "approximately" or "about". Where no quantity is stated in the credit the problem may be avoided by the negotiating bank regarding the drawing as a partial one, provided that the credit allows these.

Partial drawings and/or shipments

ARTICLE 44
   (a)   Partial drawings and/or shipments are allowed, unless the credit stipulates otherwise.
   (b)   Shipments by sea, or by more than one mode of transport but including carriage by sea, made on the same vessel and for the same voyage, will not be regarded as partial shipments, even if the transport documents indicating loading on board bear different dates of issuance and/or indicate different ports of loading on board.

(c)   Shipments made by post will not be regarded as partial shipments if the post receipts or certificates of posting appear to have been stamped or otherwise authenticated in the place from which the credit stipulates the goods are to be dispatched, and on the same date.

(d)   Shipments made by modes of transport other than those referred to in paragraphs (b) and (c) of this article will not be regarded as partial shipments, provided the transport documents are issued by one and the same carrier or his agent and indicate the same place of issuance, the same place of dispatch or taking in charge of the goods, and the same destination.

Comment

Sub-section (a) is designed to cover situations such as where part only of a consignment is ready for shipment by the advertised dates for the vessel receiving cargo at a particular port but the balance is able to be shipped on the same vessel when it calls at another port. Reason suggests that provided that all the goods arrive together on the same vessel it is of little relevance that they may have been shipped at different ports on different dates.

Sub-section (d) is interesting when it is applied to shipments by air, although the matter is probably largely academic. Although it does not give the option to load goods on to the aircraft at different places, as is the case with the sea equivalent, it appears to allow for goods flown on the same day and by the same carrier to travel on different aircraft.

Drawings and/or shipments by instalments

ARTICLE 45

If drawings and/or shipments by instalments within given periods are stipulated in the credit and any instalment is not drawn and/or shipped within the period allowed for that instalment, the credit ceases to be available for that or any subsequent instalments, unless otherwise stipulated in the credit.

Comment

This article provides a dangerous trap of which all exporters should be aware. It is designed to protect buyers who have planned their business on the basis of receiving consignments of imports at certain times, an example being a contractor ordering raw materials for delivery at the appropriate stage of a construction project. If a particular shipment is late, the contract may be lost or the contractors may wish to seek alternative and more reliable sources of supply. Therefore, Article 45 automatically cancels the credit where any instalment is shipped or any drawing made later than the date specified in the credit. Normal procedure when this happens is for the bank handling the discrepant drawing to seek confirmation from the issuing bank that the credit will continue to be valid. The issuing bank will refer to its customer and either reinstate or confirm the cancellation of the credit. This is the only case where the irrevocability of a credit is threatened by UCP. Beneficiaries should take great care when they are shipping goods under such a credit, firstly that bills of lading are dated in accordance with the shipment dates specified for each instalment and secondly that documents for each shipment are presented within the specified time after shipment.

Expiry date and presentation

ARTICLE 46

(a)   All credits must stipulate an expiry date for presentation of documents for payment, acceptance or negotiation.

(b)   Except as provided in Article 48(a), documents must be presented on or before such expiry date.

(c)   If an issuing bank states that a credit is to be available "for one month", "for six months" or the like, but does not specify the date from which the time is to run, the date of issuance of the credit by the issuing bank will be deemed to be the first day from which such time is to run. Banks should discourage indication of the expiry date of the credit in this manner.

ARTICLE 47(a)

In addition to stipulating an expiry date for presentation of documents, every credit which calls for a transport document(s) should also stipulate a specified period of time after the date of issuance of the transport document(s) during which presentation of documents for payment, acceptance or negotiation must be made. If no such period of time is stipulated, banks will refuse documents presented to them later than 21 days after the date of issuance of the transport document(s). In every case, however, documents must be presented not later than the expiry date of the credit.

Comment

The 21 day rule should be deeply embedded in the consciousness of anyone involved with credits at the negotiation stage, whether they be the beneficiaries or the negotiating bank. The rule was introduced in the 1974 Revision of UCP to take the question of stale bills of lading out of the documentary credits field completely. Up until that time it was incumbent upon the negotiating bank to determine in each case whether the bill of lading had been presented in sufficient time for it to be able to reach the destination of the goods before their arrival. In many cases the only way in which this could be done was to enquire of the shipowners as to the arrival date of the carrying vessel.

This onerous duty is no longer necessary and it is left to the applicants to calculate how long they can afford to allow the beneficiaries for presentation of documents without running the risk of receiving stale bills of lading. This appears in the credit as the number of days after shipment within which the documents must be presented. In some cases this can be impractically short. Beneficiaries are advised to consider this point when the credit is received and to request an amendment if it is considered that they will be unable to comply with the requirements. Such an amendment may not be forthcoming, of course, if the applicants have done their calculations correctly. The greatest danger arises when the credit is silent on the topic and Article 47(a) is applied, or when negotiation is delayed because of other discrepancies to the point where the crucial date is passed.

ARTICLE 47(b)

For the purpose of these articles, the date of issuance of a transport document(s) will be deemed to be:

 (i) in the case of a transport document evidencing dispatch, or taking in charge, or receipt of goods for shipment by a mode of transport other than by air—the date of issuance indicated on the transport document or the date of the reception stamp thereon whichever is the later.

 (ii) in the case of a transport document evidencing carriage by air—the date of issuance indicated on the transport document or, if the credit stipulates that the transport document shall indicate an actual flight date, the actual flight date as indicated on the transport document.

 (iii) in the case of a transport document indicating loading on board a named vessel—the date of issuance of the transport document or, in the case of an on board notation in accordance with Article 27(b), the date of such notation.

(iv) in cases to which Article 44(b) applies, the date determined as above of the latest transport document issued.

Comment

This article is quite straightforward, with the exception of the provision in sub-section (ii) that the date evidenced by the flight stamp on the air waybill should only be taken as the date of issue of the document where the credit actually calls for the flight stamp to appear. Although they have not said as much in print, it is thought that the ICC has included this provision, which seems directly at variance with the position where the transport document is a bill of lading, because an air waybill, not being a negotiable document, has little value and will normally be issued on receipt of the goods by the carrier. If the credit calls for a flight stamp, this means that its issue will be delayed until after the goods have actually left, with consequent late arrival of documents at the place of destination. This may cause difficulties in the clearance of the goods but must be considered as a self-inflicted handicap on the part of the applicants. It would be manifestly unfair in such circumstances to allow the period for presentation of documents to run from the date of the document, since it may not be obtainable in its final form until after that period has elapsed.

Negotiating and issuing banks should note that, by implication in this article, it is unnecessary for an air waybill to bear a flight stamp unless the credit calls for one. Many acrimonious and unnecessary disputes have arisen in the past over this so-called discrepancy.

ARTICLE 48(a)

If the expiry date of the credit and/or the last day of the period of time after the date of issuance of the transport document(s) for presentation of documents stipulated by the credit or applicable by virtue of Article 47 falls on a day on which the bank to which presentation has to be made is closed for reasons other than those referred to in Article 19, the stipulated expiry date and/or the last day of the period of time after the date of issuance of the transport document(s) for presentation of documents, as the case may be, shall be extended to the first following business day on which such bank is open.

Comment

Article 19 covered closure of banks for reasons outside their control and stated that the dates referred to were not extended as a result of that closure. This article covers the weekend and public holiday types of closure and effectively applies the same rules to letters of credit as apply to maturing bills of exchange.

ARTICLE 48(b)

The latest date for loading on board, or dispatch, or taking in charge shall not be extended by reason of the extension of the expiry date and/or the period of time after the date of issuance of the transport document(s) for presentation of documents in accordance with this article. If no such latest date for shipment is stipulated in the credit or amendments thereto, banks will reject transport documents indicating a date of issuance later than the expiry date stipulated in the credit or amendments thereto.

Comment

It should be stressed that in the final sentence the expiry date referred to is the stated expiry date in the credit, not the extended one.

ARTICLE 48(c)

The bank to which presentation is made on such first following business day must add to the documents its certificate that the documents were presented within the time limits extended in accordance with Article 48(a) of the Uniform Customs and Practice for Documentary Credits, 1983 Revision, ICC Publication No. 400.

Comment

This certification is necessary because it is unlikely that the issuing bank will be aware of the dates of weekends and public holidays in every country where beneficiaries of its credits may reside.

ARTICLE 49

Banks are under no obligation to accept presentation of documents outside their banking hours.

Comment

But they are not precluded from doing so.

Loading on board, dispatch and taking in charge (shipment)

ARTICLE 50

    (a)   Unless otherwise stipulated in the credit, the expression "shipment" used in stipulating an earliest and/or a latest shipment date will be understood to include the expressions "loading on board", "dispatch" and "taking in charge".

    (b)   The date of issuance of the transport document determined in accordance with Article 47(b) will be taken to be the date of shipment.

    (c)   Expressions such as "prompt", "immediately", "as soon as possible", and the like should not be used. If they are used, banks will interpret them as a stipulation that shipment is to be made within thirty days from the date of issuance of the credit by the issuing bank.

    (d)   If the expression "on or about" or similar expressions are used, banks will interpret them as a stipulation that shipment is to be made during the period from five days before to five days after the specified date, both end days included.

Comment

    (a)   This sub-section removes the possibility of petty arguments developing over what constitutes shipment where, for instance, a combined transport document is called for.

    (b)   A possible problem for applicants exists here arising from the slightly peculiar position of the air waybill as established in Article 47(b). That article stated that the date of issue of the waybill was to override the actual flight date as evidenced on the flight stamp unless the credit called for the flight stamp to appear. Thus an air waybill may comply with the credit terms even though shipment in the sense of the actual movement of the goods has taken place after the specified latest date.

    (c)   It is a great pity that this sub-section appears here and not in a more general context, since its wording makes it clear that it relates only to the shipment of the goods. The greatest problems arising from words such as "immediately" occur when the credit uses them in connection with such requirements as the sending of a set of non-negotiable documents to the applicants, or the telexing of details of the shipment to an insurance company "immediately after shipment". Given that such details as reference numbers of transport documents, definitive shipping marks and details of freight charges, are not known until the transport document is received, and until such time it is impossible to draw up the commercial invoice and other documents which require such information to be incorporated in them; also given that it can very often take a week or more for the shipping company to process all the bills of lading relating to a particular sailing, the use of such words in a credit often creates an instant recipe for rejection of the drawing. When asked for help with this problem, the Banking Commission of the ICC was able to do no more than to look up the definition of the word "immediately" in the *Concise Oxford Dictionary*. Beneficiaries are therefore recommended to be on the alert for such requirements and to reject credits which include them, on the grounds that they incorporate a "built-in discrepancy".

ARTICLE 51

The words "to", "until", "till", "from", and words of similar import applying to any date term in the credit will be understood to include the date mentioned. The word "after" will be understood to exclude the date mentioned.

Comment

Much discussion has taken place since the introduction of this article in its present form on the subject of its effect upon the date on which payment is due where the terms are expressed as "X days after bill of lading date" as opposed to "X days from bill of lading date". Strict application of the article would mean a one day difference between the maturity dates of these alternatives (and the ICC, in emulation of the disregard for reality displayed by the Privy Council in their decision relating to the "on board" notation on a "received" bill of lading, have confirmed this to be the case), whereas they were formerly taken as synonymous. In practice the problem would only arise in the instance of a deferred payment credit, since where a bill of exchange is used the relevant legislation will override UCP and it is suggested that, under such legislation, in either case day one of the period would be the day after the date of the bill of lading.

ARTICLE 52

The terms "first half", "second half" of a month shall be construed respectively as from the 1st to the 15th, and the 16th to the last day of each month, inclusive.

ARTICLE 53

The terms "beginning", "middle", or "end" of a month shall be construed respectively as from the 1st to the 10th, the 11th to the 20th, and the 21st to the last day of each month, inclusive.

(F) Transfer

ARTICLE 54(a)

A transferable credit is a credit under which the beneficiary has the right to request the bank called upon to effect payment or acceptance or any bank entitled to effect negotiation to make the credit available in whole or in part to one or more other parties (second beneficiaries).

Comment

Note that the beneficiary has the right to request, not to compel. There might be circumstances, such as where the bank suspects fraud, where it would decline to transfer the credit. The facility to transfer to more than one second beneficiary is later qualified in sub-section (e). It is important to note that transfer can only be effected by a bank which is authorised to pay, accept or negotiate drawings under the original credit. This is not invariably the advising bank.

ARTICLE 54(b)

A credit can be transferred only if it is expressly designated as "transferable" by the issuing bank. Terms such as "divisible", "fractionable", "assignable", and "transmissible" add nothing to the meaning of the word "transferable" and shall not be used.

Comment

As was stated in Chapter 10, when asked for a transferable credit, the applicants should immediately be aware that they are not dealing with the suppliers of the goods and this sub-section ensures that this fact cannot be concealed from them.

ARTICLE 54(c)

The bank requested to effect the transfer (transferring bank), whether it has confirmed the credit or not, shall be under no obligation to effect such transfer except to the extent and in the manner expressly consented to by such bank.

Comment

Sub-section (a) gave the bank the right to stand aside from the transaction if it was in any way unhappy with it: this sub-section extends that protection to allow the bank to strictly control the manner of the transfer even when it has agreed to put it into effect. The reason for such delicacy on the part of the banks is that, although the vast majority of users of transferable credits are perfectly legitimate, the first beneficiary is in fact obtaining goods not on his or her own creditworthiness but on that of the applicants for the credit. This factor can attract the casual trader, the undercapitalised and even the criminal element into this aspect of documentary credits; the higher risks to which they are thereby exposed makes the issue of a transferred credit a much less attractive proposition to the banks.

ARTICLE 54(d)

Bank charges in respect of transfers are payable by the first beneficiary unless otherwise specified. The transferring bank shall be under no obligation to effect the transfer until such charges are paid.

ARTICLE 54(e)

A transferable credit can be transferred once only. Fractions of a transferable credit (not exceeding in the aggregate the amount of the credit) can be transferred separately, provided partial shipments are not prohibited, and the aggregate of such transfers will be considered as constituting only one transfer of the credit. The credit can be transferred only on the terms and conditions specified in the original credit, with the exception of the amount of the credit, of any unit prices stated therein, of the period of validity, of the last date for presentation of documents in accordance with Article 47 and the period for shipment, any or all of which may be reduced or curtailed, or the percentage for which insurance cover must be effected, which may be increased in such a way as to provide the amount of cover stipulated in the original credit, or these articles. Additionally, the name of the first beneficiary can be substituted for that of the applicant for the credit, but if the name of the applicant for the credit is specifically required by the original credit to appear in any document other than the invoice, such requirement must be fulfilled.

Comment

What the first part of this sub-section means is that a credit which has already been transferred cannot be transferred again, ie by the second beneficiary to a third beneficiary. Where the goods are to emanate from more than one supplier and the credit is therefore transferred to more than one second beneficiary, separate shipments will be made and separate sets of documents presented, so it is obviously essential that the original credit permits partial shipments/drawings.

The restrictions upon the aspects of a credit which may be varied on transfer reflect once again the reluctance of the banks to deal with certain elements of the trading community in respect of transferable credits. It is often of major concern to the first beneficiary that the identity of the second beneficiaries is not revealed to the applicants, and *vice versa*, thereby making it possible for them to be eliminated from future transactions. Consequently, the first beneficiary will often bring pressure upon the transferring bank to omit any requirements of the original credit which may bring about this undesirable result. Banks would do well to resist such requests, since they are afforded considerable protection by Article 54 and by setting it aside in part may well find that they have altogether lost that protection.

The amount of the credit and the unit prices must be alterable to allow for the first beneficiaries' profit margin. The dates of shipment and negotiation and the period allowed for presentation of documents, often need to be brought forward in order to protect the applicants against receiving stale documents. This will be discussed further under sub-section (g). The insurance percentage must be alterable because the cover taken out by the second beneficiary will be based on a lower CIF value than that quoted in the original contract. The name of the first beneficiary will appear as the applicant but it should always be made clear that the credit is a transferred one, since by remaining silent on this point the credit would give a false impression of the first beneficiary's creditworthiness to the second beneficiaries.

Finally, Article 54(g) allows for the place of payment to be changed to accommodate negotiation in the second beneficiaries' country where it is different from that of the first beneficiary. All other terms of the credit must remain unaltered.

ARTICLE 54(f)

The first beneficiary has the right to substitute his own invoices (and drafts if the credit stipulates that drafts are to be drawn on the applicant for the credit) in exchange for those of the second beneficiary, for amounts not in excess of the amount stipulated by the original credit and for the original unit prices if stipulated in the credit, and upon such substitution of invoices (and drafts) the first beneficiary can draw under the credit for the difference, if any, between his invoices and the second beneficiary's invoices. When a credit has been transferred and the first beneficiary is to supply his own invoices (and drafts) in exchange for the second beneficiary's invoices (and drafts) but fails to do so on first demand, the paying, accepting or negotiating bank has the right to deliver to the issuing bank the documents received under the credit, including the second beneficiary's invoices (and drafts) without further responsibility to the first beneficiary.

Comment

This sub-section affords a considerable degree of protection to the transferring bank. Where the first beneficiaries do not produce their substitute invoices the transferring bank is left with a set of documents against which it has paid in accordance with its obligations under the transferred credit but which are not in conformity with the original credit. By invocation of this article, it can obtain reimbursement from the issuing bank of the amount which it has paid. It will become clear, however, why emphasis was placed in the comments on sub-section (e) on the inadvisability of allowing any variations in the transferred credit other than those specifically authorised by this article, since in such circumstances it would be impossible to present a conforming set of documents to the issuing bank and therefore impossible to claim reimbursement.

ARTICLE 54(g)

Unless otherwise stipulated in the credit, the first beneficiary of a transferable credit may request that the credit be transferred to a second beneficiary in the same country, or in another country. Further, unless otherwise stipulated in the credit, the first beneficiary shall have the right to request that payment or negotiation be effected to the second beneficiary at the place to which the credit has been transferred, up to and including the expiry date of the original credit and without prejudice to the first beneficiary's right subsequently to substitute his own invoices and drafts (if any) for those of the second beneficiary and to claim any difference due to him.

Comment

The implications of this sub-section can be far-reaching for the applicants for the original credit. Firstly, although ordering goods in a particular country of their choosing, they may find that the goods supplied emanate from a completely different country with which they might not wish to deal in normal circumstances. Secondly, because the dates may be transferred with the rest of the credit which then becomes available within those dates in the second country, by the time that documents have been processed by the negotiating bank, sent to the transferring bank, processed by them including the substitution of invoices and then sent to the issuing bank, there is a very strong possibility that the documents will be stale on receipt. In one extreme case, where a transferable credit was issued in Jersey on behalf of English applicants in favour of a first beneficiary in France and then transferred to a second beneficiary in Taiwan, the demurrage charges which were payable in order to obtain delivery of the goods exceeded the value of the goods themselves, which were in any case substandard. When asked to issue a transferable credit it is a good idea for the issuing bank to draw the attention of the applicants to this danger and to suggest suitable restrictions which may be incorporated in the credit to reduce it.

ARTICLE 55

The fact that a credit is not stated to be transferable shall not affect the beneficiary's right to assign any proceeds to which he may be, or may become, entitled under such credit, in accordance with the provisions of the applicable law.

Comment

Very much the sting in the tail of UCP, this is one of the shortest articles and at the same time one of those which can cause the most trouble. Many believe that UCP should not mention it at all but leave disputes to be settled under the applicable law.

The usual circumstances where an assignment is made are where merchants are the beneficiaries of a credit which they have not asked to be transferable because they do not wish their buyers to be aware that they are not the source suppliers of the goods. They do not themselves have the wherewithal to buy the goods from the source suppliers, however, and those suppliers will not release the goods without some guarantee that they will receive payment. A credit is not possible because the merchants do not have the requisite standing to persuade a bank to issue one on their behalf. The letter of assignment is the answer. It usually takes the form of an "irrevocable" instruction to the bank requesting that it pay the suppliers out of the proceeds which will become due when documents are presented in compliance with the terms of the credit.

Understandably, banks do not like this type of transaction. It is fraught with danger for them, for a number of reasons. First, there is the inescapable fact that they are dealing with people who have little substance or they would have access to facilities from their own bankers. Second, there is the difficulty of authenticating such instructions, since even verification of signatures by the beneficiary's bankers would not necessarily mean that the signatories had authority to sign this type of document, and they would in any case be enforceable only in respect of the bank account to which the mandate relates. Third, there is the difficulty in enforcing the "irrevocability" of the assignment when faced with subsequent countermanding instructions. Fourth, there is the possibility that documents will never be presented under the credit but will be sent on a collection basis through another bank. Fifth, though probably not last, there is the fact that such assignments do not dovetail easily into the banks' normal methods of operation. To make matters worse, it is dubious whether the banks can legitimately charge for acceptance of such assignments. They are therefore expected to provide what is intended to be the equivalent of a letter of credit on behalf of persons who they would not normally consider worthy of such a service and to shoulder all the risks that that entails, for little or no reward.

It cannot be overstated that these instruments are dangerous, both for the party receiving the benefit of them (the assignees) and for the bank accepting them. The only effective answer is for each of these parties to refuse to have anything to do with them. In the case of the banks, this may mean denying to someone what is a basic legal right and there is a very slight risk that legal action may follow. However, this risk really is very slight, for an organisation which is forced to resort to this type of instrument in order to carry out its business is unlikely to possess the means to take on expensive litigation merely to prove a point, however much it may threaten to do so.

14
The avoidance of loss under documentary credits: the applicants

From the foregoing chapters, readers should have a thorough basic understanding of the way in which credits work and the rules which govern their use. It is time to put that knowledge to use by applying it, in turn, to the differing interests of the four main parties involved: the applicants, the issuing bank, the advising/confirming bank and the beneficiaries. Where the documentary credit is used properly, those interests, while differing, need not necessarily be conflicting and, given good faith coupled with the controls built into the system, the number of disputes should be minimal.

From the applicants' point of view, the chief benefits to be derived from the use of a documentary credit are that it answers any doubts their suppliers may have about their ability to pay, thus enabling the transaction to take place, whilst providing themselves with the means of ensuring that they receive both the goods (by stipulation of the latest date for shipment) and the correct documents (where possible, by stipulation of the period after the date of the relative transport document within which documents must be presented) at the right time. In order that this may be achieved, great care must be taken when making out the application form for the issue of the credit, since where it is irrevocable it cannot later be changed without the agreement of the beneficiaries.

As has been said many times in this book, it is of vital importance that before reaching this stage, the applicants have done all in their power to establish the *bona fides* of the suppliers, by means of bank enquiries, credit rating agencies and any other sources which may be available. This is because the credit will convey no assurance that the goods shipped will be in accordance with their description in the documents which relate to them. At the other extreme, government regulations aside, there is little point in using the more expensive letter of credit where a cheaper form of payment system would be acceptable to both parties and, as confidence builds up, suppliers may well be prepared to reconsider their payment terms.

It is advisable to give prior notification to the sellers of all requirements relating to the goods or the documents by including mention of them in the order. As we have seen, this forms part of the contract on which the credit will be based and if that credit, when it is issued, contains requirements of which the suppliers were formerly unaware and which they consider onerous, and which may, had they had foreknowledge, have affected their quotation, they may be able to avoid the contract altogether. In fact, the more consultation which takes place between buyers and sellers prior to the issue of the credit, the less chance there is of misunderstandings and disputes at a later stage. To reduce these chances still further, it is a good idea to agree that the appropriate Incoterms will govern the contract. This brings the advantage of both parties knowing exactly what their responsibilities are and the costs for which they are liable under the contract. One thing which will not be covered by Incoterms is responsibility for payment of bank charges, which in the absence of any agreement are the applicants' responsibility as principals even though the credit may have been opened at the insistence of the sellers; prior agreement should be reached on this matter also.

The contract terms which have been agreed will dictate the basic documentary requirements and the demands of the credit should reflect this. For instance, an FOB contract will normally produce bills of lading which are marked "freight payable at destination" and no insurance document, insurance being the responsibility of the applicants. The importing country's regulations will dictate others, perhaps certificates of origin, customs invoices and so on. The type of goods and their proposed method of conveyance will impose yet more constraints. Where dangerous or bulky goods are concerned, it may be necessary for the credit to allow for stowage on deck. Where they are of a nature which is liable to produce clauses on the bill of lading which are acceptable to the applicants, the credit should state the clauses which are acceptable. If the journey is to be by more than one form of transport, or if the services of forwarding agents are to be employed, the credit should state that an "on board" bill of lading is not essential, or that house bills of lading are acceptable, as the case may be. Prior consultation between sellers and buyers will provide answers to all these questions and make completion of the application form a far simpler process.

The exact requirements of the sellers regarding the letter of credit should be noted. It is assumed that any credit requested by sellers will in normal circumstances be irrevocable, but if they wish it to be confirmed in their own country this fact must be advised to the issuing bank; it should be remembered that this will entail additional charges. If they wish it confirmed by, or advised through a specific bank, charges may be increased even more, since the issuing bank may have no correspondent relationship with that bank and therefore yet another bank will be brought into the transaction.

If a transferable credit is called for, it is almost certain that the sellers are not the actual producers of the goods. Many buyers are prepared to accept this, relying on the sellers' expertise to locate a suitable supplier and save them the expense of maintaining their own buyers or agents in overseas locations. Otherwise it is almost certain that the goods could be obtained more cheaply by buying direct from the manufacturers. Also, it should be borne in mind that unless transfer of the credit is suitably restricted, there is no control over the origin of the goods and a strong possibility that documents will be stale by the time that they are received.

If the sellers request a red clause credit, the applicants will find themselves liable to reimburse the bank for pre-shipment advances made to the beneficiaries. It is unlikely that such a request would be made in the absence of prior agreement but it is as well to be aware of the meaning of the term just in case. Similar considerations apply to a revolving credit, in which the amount available for utilisation will be reinstated at preordained times or on payment by the applicants of previous drawings.

The application form

Most banks' credit application forms are preprinted, giving a range of options from which the applicants must choose and calling for specific pieces of information which the bank requires in order to complete the credit. Applicants should remember that the appearance of a printed option or document on the application form does not mean that they are obliged to exercise that option or call for that document, although some are of course essential.

Documentary Credit Application / Demande d'émission de crédit documentaire

Applicant / Donneur d'ordre	Issuing Bank / Banque émettrice
	Date and place of expiry of the credit / Date et lieu d'expiration du crédit
Date of this application / Date de cette demande	Beneficiary / Bénéficiaire

☐ Issue by (air) mail / Emettre par courrier avion   ☐ With brief advice by teletransmission / Avec bref avis par télétransmission

☐ Issue by teletransmission (which shall be the operative credit instrument) / Emettre par télétransmission (qui sera l'instrument permettant l'utilisation du crédit)

☐ Transferable credit / Crédit transférable

Confirmation of credit to the beneficiary / Confirmation du crédit au bénéficiaire
☐ not requested / non requise   ☐ requested / requise

Partial shipments / Expéditions partielles   Transhipment / Transbordement
☐ allowed / autorisées   ☐ not allowed / non autorisées   ☐ allowed / autorisé   ☐ not allowed / non autorisé

☐ Insurance will be covered by us / L'assurance sera prise en charge par nous

Loading on board/dispatch/taking in charge at/from
Mise à bord/expédition/prise en charge à/de

not later than / au plus tard le   for transportation to / à destination de

Amount / Montant

Credit available with / Crédit réalisable auprès de
☐ by sight payment / par paiement à vue   ☐ by acceptance / par acceptation   ☐ by negotiation / par négociation
☐ deferred payment at / par paiement différé à

against the documents detailed herein / contre les documents précisés ci-après

☐ and beneficiary's draft at / et la traite du bénéficiaire à

on / sur

Goods (brief description without excessive detail) / Marchandise (brève description sans detail excessif)	☐ FOB ☐ C&F ☐ CIF/CAF
	Other terms / Autres termes

Documents to be presented within [   ] days after the date of issuance of the transport document(s) but within the validity of the credit
Documents à présenter dans les [   ] jours après la date d'émission du/des document(s) de transport mais dans la période de validité du crédit

Additional instructions / Instructions supplémentaires

We request you to issue your **irrevocable** documentary credit for our account in accordance with the above instructions (marked with an x where appropriate). The credit will be subject to the Uniform Customs and Practice for Documentary Credits (1983 Revision, Publication No. 400 of the International Chamber of Commerce, Paris, France), insofar as these are applicable. We authorize you to debit our account

Nous vous demandons d'émettre pour notre compte un crédit documentaire **irrevocable** conformément aux instructions ci-dessus (cochées d'une croix dans les cases choisies). Le crédit sera soumis aux Règles et Usances Uniformes relatives aux Crédits Documentaires (révision 1983, Publication n° 400 de la Chambre de Commerce Internationale, Paris, France) dans la mesure où celles-ci sont applicables. Nous vous autorisons à débiter notre compte.

Name stamp and authorized signature(s) of the applicant
Cachet et signature(s) autorisée(s) du donneur d'ordre

Consult the Issuing Bank for guidance if the completion of this form should raise to questions / Demandez conseil à la banque émettrice si vous vous posez des questions en remplissant la formule

Documentary credit application form

The ICC has designed a standard application form for optional adoption by banks, which is designed so that the information given thereon by the applicants appears as nearly as possible in the same position as it eventually will upon the credit when issued, thus greatly facilitating the transportation and checking of that data. It removes any possibility of confusion or doubt by specifically referring to the issue of an irrevocable credit, and does not give the applicants the opportunity of nominating a bank through which the credit is to be advised. Both of these factors are considerable improvements on many older, non-standard, forms, which, in addition to giving the option of application for a revocable credit, invited nomination of the advising bank. This latter is undesirable since only in exceptional circumstances, such as at the specific request of the sellers, is it an advantage for the credit to be advised through a particular bank, which may in any case not be in correspondent relationships with the issuing bank.

Date and place of expiry

Near to the top right-hand side of the form the applicants are required to state the expiry date of the credit and its place of expiry. Some applicants base their calculation of the expiry date upon the sellers' stated ex-works delivery date, adding suitable periods to allow for the arrangements for shipment and the obtaining and presentation of documents to the negotiating bank. However, to avoid the possible need for amendment of the credit at a later date it is probably preferable to base it on the applicants' own needs. The normal time taken in transit by goods between the two countries by the agreed means of transport can be ascertained and thus a latest date for shipment can be established. Similarly the average time for processing of documents by the banks and postal transit periods can be calculated and deducted from the goods transit period to give the maximum period which can be allowed for negotiation. Adding this period to the latest shipment date automatically produces the expiry date of the credit. The place of expiry should always be in the beneficiaries' country if the full advantages of the credit system are to be enjoyed. However, applicants should bear in mind that this may involve them in reimbursing the issuing bank in respect of interest on the amount of the drawing between the time when the beneficiaries are paid and the time the applicants' own account is debited.

Method of transmission

The applicants are next asked to indicate by what means the credit is to be transmitted to the advising bank, the alternatives being teletransmission or airmail, the latter with or without prior teletransmitted advice of brief details. Which alternative is chosen will depend upon circumstances in individual cases, but it should be remembered that there is little point in the expenditure of what may amount to a considerable sum on teletransmission when the time scale involved allows the possibility of a timely arrival if airmail is used. Conversely, such a saving is a false economy if the arrival of the credit leaves the beneficiaries with too little time to arrange dispatch of the goods, thereby giving rise to delay and to additional charges in extending the credit.

Beneficiary

The beneficiaries' name and address should be shown completely and accurately — completely to enable the advising bank to carry out its prime function of advising the credit; accurately because any discrepancy may cause problems with payment at a later stage.

Transferable credit
Confirmation of credit

To be completed as appropriate.

Amount

The amount of the credit, in words and in figures, follows; obviously, these should agree. If the quotation has been an approximate one, either because of uncertainty as to the exact quantities which will be shipped or as to the freight which will be payable, then the stated amount should provide for this, either by use of the word "about" or "approximately" in which case the bank will allow a ten percent either way variation in the amount drawn, or by expressing the amount as a maximum by the use of the words "up to" or similar.

Partial shipment/transhipment

Shipping details appear next on the application, with options for partial shipments and transhipments to be allowed or prohibited. Unless there are compelling reasons for the contrary, partial shipments should always be allowed to provide the utmost flexibility. Transhipment is a variable regarding which a decision can only be based upon the facts of each case. Such decision will take into account the frequency of direct sailings or flights between the two countries, the nature of the goods and the method of transportation which is to be used. Whether or not transhipment is to be allowed should emphatically be based upon a decision rather than the mental toss of a coin, as is so often the case. It should also be remembered that the definition of transhipment given in Article 29 of UCP is rather different from the traditional concept.

Insurance

The statement that insurance will be attended to by the applicants would normally only be appropriate where the terms of the contract are such as make those arrangements the buyers' responsibility, eg FOB.

Journey

The voyage details stated should take into account the known plans for carriage of the goods, and specific ports of loading and discharge should only be inserted if they are truly relevant. Where goods are to be taken in charge and delivered at inland container bases there is seldom any point in hampering the carriers with unnecessary stipulations about the routing of the cargo.

Drafts

Next on the application comes the way in which the beneficiaries will be paid. UCP requires each credit to nominate a bank with whom it is to be available for settlement, either by payment, acceptance, deferred payment undertaking, or negotiation. In the last named case availability may be with any bank. Because of disputes which have occurred in the past regarding payment of interest on amounts paid to beneficiaries, some banks no longer give the option of making a credit available by payment in the beneficiaries' country and this is rather sad since it has led to the virtual withdrawal by those banks from responsibility for checking documents. A bank which is negotiating does so with recourse to the beneficiaries, and this results in many of them being quite happy to take their commission and leave detailed checking to the issuing bank; however, some issuing banks consider, quite wrongly, that where drafts are drawn on the applicants that bank also has no responsibility for checking documents.

This need not be so. If the applicants make it clear to the issuing bank that they wish the credit to be available for payment in the beneficiaries' own country and that they appreciate that this will involve payment of interest for the time during which the bank is out of funds, then the bank must comply.

The question of drafts needs to be considered carefully. In the vast majority of cases, a sight draft under a credit, whomsoever it is drawn on, is a totally functionless piece of paper and can quite easily be dispensed with. Where the terms of payment are at usance, the draft becomes rather more significant, but only if it is to be used for financing purposes. Where one of the countries involved applies heavy stamp duties on bills of exchange (currently, India, Italy and Germany are examples) they are quite regularly abandoned in favour of deferred payment credits. If a usance draft is to be used, the credit should be made available for acceptance in the country of the beneficiaries, since this will provide them with a first class acceptance which they can have discounted in their local market if required. The question of interest need not arise with a usance credit, since the maturity date of the bill will be known in advance and the bank can be paid by the applicants on the same date as their account overseas is debited.

Goods

Next, the description of the goods is invited. As has already been said, both in the text and in UCP, this should be in just sufficient detail to ensure that the right goods have been shipped. The sellers should be required to certify that the goods supplied are in accordance with the specification given in the appropriate order or pro forma invoice, which should be identified by its reference number. If unit prices are given, they should agree arithmetically with the credit amount, and if they or the quantity of goods are approximate it should be ensured that the credit amount is also stated as being approximate. The stated contract terms should correspond with the documents which are called for, or if they do not, the reason for such divergence should be made apparent.

Documents

Next, the documentary requirements must be considered. Again, many banks have preprinted lists of the documents which they consider will be necessary. As in other parts of the form, the inclusion by the bank of a particular document does not mean that it must be called for. A good example of a document which is frequently demanded without any justification is the packing list and applicants should ask themselves whether it is really necessary before placing an "X" in the box on the application. For instance, where a single unit, or a consignment of goods all of the same description and specification, is the subject of the credit, a packing list is likely to add nothing to the value of the documents and should not be called for. Another example, which has been mentioned more than once already in this book, is the frequent requirement for "complete set of not less than three original clean on board ocean bills of lading". As we have seen, modern methods of goods handling often make this a handicap rather than an asset and it should only be called for if it is absolutely necessary. Even if it is necessary, only one original is required to be given in exchange for the goods, any other purposes served by the bill being just as easily covered by photocopies. It should be remembered that the insurance terms "all risks", "with average" and "free of particular average" have now gone out of use, yet many banks still incorporate printed references to them in their application forms. The applicable clauses are respectively A, B, and C, and these should be substituted.

Where any documents are required other than transport and insurance documents, the application should state by whom they are to be issued and what information they should convey, whether they should be legalised and so on; otherwise the banks will accept them as tendered. Applicants should take care not to call for any documents which will either be completely unobtainable by the beneficiaries or unobtainable within the time constraints imposed by the credit. Also, they should take care that the documentary requirements are not inconsistent with the contract terms as stated following the credit amount or, if they are, that a clear explanation of the apparent discrepancy is given.

Presentation

By restricting the number of days after dispatch of the goods which are available to the beneficiaries for presentation of documents, applicants are able to influence the likely time of arrival of the documents in their hands. This can be useful where documents of title are required in order to obtain release of goods, though usually only where the voyage is of a significant length. Where the time of arrival of documents is not significant in this way there is usually little point in placing any restriction on presentation — UCP will in any case regard 21 days as the maximum period allowable. Where the period allowed for presentation is restricted by the applicants, they should take care to see that it does not contradict what the credit says about the expiry date of the credit. For example, if the period allowed for presentation is 15 days and the latest shipment date is on the last day of the month, then the expiry date should be on the 15th of the succeeding month. Finally, the period allowed for presentation should be realistic, allowing the beneficiaries adequate time to obtain, prepare and present their documents, otherwise the credit may prove to be unworkable.

Forward cover

If the credit is in a foreign currency, either that of the sellers' country or of a third country, a liability will arise in the future to reimburse the issuing bank for drawings made in that currency. Since in free currency markets there is no way in which the applicants' liability in their own currency can be forecast, unless they have accounts denominated in the required currency, they should carefully consider the desirability of buying the currency in the forward exchange market, thus fixing the amount in local currency which they will be required to pay for the goods. Since the exact date on which payment will be demanded will be uncertain, such cover will necessarily be of the option variety, allowing the deal to be struck at the agreed rate at any time within stated limits.

Summary

Applicants should be aware that the success or failure of the credit will depend largely upon the expertise and consideration which they give to the completion of the application, and that failing the co-operation of the beneficiaries they will have to live with any incorrect or incomplete documentation which may result from errors in its completion.

Having gone to so much trouble to ensure the smooth operation of the credit, it may seem rather harsh that from the time of its issue the applicants take a largely passive role in future as regards the credit. As was stressed at the beginning of the section of this book dealing with credits, the instrument is an undertaking given by the bank to the beneficiaries and this undertaking forms the core of the transaction. When documents are received, the bank will, or should, make its own decision as to whether they are acceptable in terms of its undertaking and, if they are, the applicants' account will be debited without further reference. This does not, of course, mean that if real discrepancies exist in those documents which the issuing bank has failed to notice the applicants will have no remedy against the bank, but the latter is likely to give scant consideration to objections based on what it considers to be trivia. The spirit of the documentary credit is a benign yet demanding one—the instrument exists to oil the wheels of commerce, not to lock them solid.

Discrepant documents

Undoubtedly, despite all precautions, documents will sometimes be presented which are not in accordance with the credit terms. If discrepancies have been noticed by the negotiating bank they will often telex for authority to pay despite those problems. The applicants should consider their position carefully when asked by the issuing bank for such authority. The rules relating to credits being what they are, often the discrepancies will be trivial and may be dismissed out of hand but if they cast any doubt upon the condition of the goods or their ease of clearance through import formalities when they arrive, it is probably preferable to ask that the documents be sent forward on a collection basis, perhaps with authority to inspect the goods before a decision is reached on their acceptability. Careful consideration should be given before agreeing to pay under the protection of a bank indemnity. The validity of such indemnities is often strictly limited, the problem being that they tend to relate specifically to the discrepancy mentioned therein, without regard to its wider implications. For instance, an indemnity may promise that the amount of the drawing will be refunded should any loss be incurred by reason of late presentation of documents, but the intention behind the issue of the indemnity may be merely to cover demurrage charges incurred by the goods: payment may be disputed if the cause of loss is forfeit of an onward sales contract by reason of the absence of documents of title to the goods. When giving notice of acceptance of discrepancies to the issuing bank, applicants should make it clear to that bank that they are doing so in reliance upon the indemnity held by the bank, if such is the case.

Wherever possible, however, every effort should be made to assist the beneficiaries in obtaining payment for the goods which they have supplied, even if this means reaching a separate agreement outside the letter of credit to compensate for any loss incurred by the buyers. "Do as you would be done by" is a good maxim for anyone involved in international trade, despite what may be said to the contrary in certain circles. A co-operative attitude now regarding someone else's difficulties will probably pay dividends in the future. Whatever happens, the credit must never, ever, be used as a flimsy excuse for the buyers' avoidance of their responsibilities under the contract in the absence of genuine reasons for refusal of payment.

Sadly, once in a while and despite all precautions, the applicants will discover that they have been dealing with dishonest sellers. In such circumstances it will be very difficult to attach any responsibility to the banks involved for any loss incurred as a result, those banks being well protected by UCP against such charges. Where documents are obvious forgeries but are nonetheless accepted by banks, a case may exist. However, by far the commonest cause of loss is where genuine documents are presented which cover goods which, when received, turn out to be either substandard or simply "case fillers", such as the substitution of common salt for pharmaceutical chemicals or drugs, or of bricks for machinery spares. Against such frauds there is no protection other than the exhortation, oft repeated in this book, to "know your trading partner".

15
The avoidance of loss under documentary credits: the issuing bank

The issuing bank is one of the two principal parties to the documentary letter of credit and its role is commensurately important in ensuring that, not only the individual credit, but also the whole credits system continues to serve the trading community in the way in which it was designed to do. That system has been subject in recent times to a variety of abuses, most of which stem from attempts by issuing banks to limit their liability under their letters of credit without reducing their income from that source. While this attitude may be supportable from the accounting aspect, it is certainly indefensible from a banking viewpoint and in many cases a choice must be made as to whether an organisation exists in order to operate as a bank or as a mere vehicle for the generation of short term profits. These may seem harsh words but the choice is a simple one.

However, this chapter is intended to examine the documentary credit from the point of view of the issuing bank and to recommend courses of action to ensure that it protects its interests as far as possible when dealing in documentary credits. At the point of issue of the credit, the chief concern of the issuing bank is that its credit should present an image of competency and professionalism to all who subsequently read it. This involves many considerations; not least among these is the basic design of the letter of credit itself. The International Chamber of Commerce has designed a standard letter of credit form which, for simplicity, coherency and practicality, would be difficult to surpass; any banks which have not yet adopted it should do so without delay. Such adoption on a universal scale would greatly simplify the checking of documents against credits and any chauvinistic bias in favour of individual bank forms would quickly evaporate following even a superficial consideration of the advantages to be gained from adoption of a standard format.

Given that the letter of credit itself is presented in an easily read form, the next important consideration is its content. This will depend upon a critical evaluation of the application form received. The overriding concern of the issuing bank should be to ensure that, when the credit in its final form is sent to the advising bank, it will not be a source of irritation or, worse, amusement, to either that bank or the beneficiaries. It should reflect the expertise of the bank which has issued it in a way which will engender respect for the name of the bank.

Applications for the opening of letters of credit would normally be received only from customers who have pre-arranged facilities with the bank for the issue of such instruments. Other applications of an *ad hoc* nature will occasionally be received, perhaps with full cash cover tendered as security for the credit. Experience shows that generally speaking the more reliance a bank has to place on such security the more chance there is of something going seriously wrong with the transaction and issuing banks are strongly recommended to have nothing to do with it.

Given that the application is from an acceptable source, that it is correctly signed in accordance with the mandate held and that the proposed credit can be accommodated within the customers' agreed facilities, the bank should then carefully check the customers requirements, in the light of the aim stated above of producing a credit which is concise, straightforward and technically excellent. The application will normally be for an irrevocable credit and any departure from this is worth querying with the customers in case a mistake has been made, unless of course they are in the habit of initiating revocable credits. Past experience of the customers' normal requirements helps considerably in the checking of the form and if any specialised form of credit is requested, such as red clause, revolving, or transferable, it may be advisable to check that they are fully aware of the implications of what they are asking for. This applies particularly to transferable credits: the customers should be aware that they are not dealing with the manufacturers of the goods and that in consequence they may find that they could obtain those goods more cheaply elsewhere. They should also be aware that unless safeguards are built into the credit the goods could emanate from any country in the world, subject to the voyage details included in the credit, and that documents could well be stale when received, without any remedy against the sellers being available.

The beneficiaries' name and address should appear in full, since this will be needed by the advising bank in order to advise the credit. If the applicants have nominated an advising bank, such nomination must be complied with, although if the nominated bank is not a correspondent of the issuing bank the credit will have to be forwarded to them through a bank which is. Because such involvement of an extra bank in the process is inefficient both in terms of time and cost, applicants should not be encouraged to make such nominations and it is questionable whether the opportunity to do so should be incorporated in the application form.

Amount

The amount in words should agree with the amount in figures, if both are given, and the currency in which the amount is expressed should be clearly identifiable. The contract terms should be appended to the amount to make it quite clear exactly what that amount represents.

Expiry, latest shipment and presentation

The dates should be examined for their correlation with each other and for whether they appear realistic in view of the arrangements which the beneficiaries may have to make for shipment and documentation. In particular, the difference between the latest date for shipment and the expiry date should exactly equal any period after shipment which is stipulated in the credit for negotiation of documents. If the expiry date is not far distant, it is probably advisable that full details of the credit are sent by telex or similar means of communication, and if the applicants have not asked for this to be done their authority should be sought, since they are the ones who will have to pay for it.

Shipment

The shipment details should make sense in the light of the information available elsewhere in the credit. If places of dispatch and delivery are airports, a call for presentation of a bill of lading in the documentary requirements is obviously nonsense. If they are inland cities then probably a combined transport document will be presented and the documentary requirements should allow for presentation of this, or of a forwarding agent's house bill of lading. The journey which the goods are to undertake should also be considered from the point of view of whether it is feasible without transhipment, if this is prohibited. If the quantity of goods is a large one similar questions should be asked about partial shipments.

Payment

The manner of payment requested by the applicants should be considered and if they wish the credit to be available to the beneficiaries in their own country by means of either payment or acceptance, then drafts should be on a bank in that country. In the case of the former the applicants should clearly understand that they will be liable for payment of interest for the time which elapses between payment of the beneficiaries and reimbursement of the issuing bank by themselves. Where drafts are to be drawn on either the issuing bank or the applicants themselves, the credit can only be available to the beneficiaries by negotiation. In the author's view credits should not be issued which state that they are available only at the issuing bank's own counters, since such instruments are scarcely worthy of being called credits, damage the issuing bank's reputation and bring the whole documentary credits system into disrepute.

Documents

The documentary requirements should be examined carefully for consistency with the contract terms (ie FOB, CIF, etc) and for compliance with current import regulations relating to the type of goods or to the exporting country. Applicants should be discouraged from asking for an excessive number of copies of documents such as invoices, packing lists and so on, since they are seldom really required and, even if they are, photocopies are perfectly acceptable for many purposes. Some documents may be unnecessary altogether, such as packing lists where only one specification of goods is ordered or where the goods form a single unit.

If documents other than those normally supplied by the sellers, and transport and insurance documents, are called for, the credit should make it clear who is to issue them and what they should contain. The issuing bank should also be alert for requirements for documents which will be impossible for the beneficiaries to supply—the so-called "built-in discrepancy". The credit should not prohibit short-form bills of lading, unless these are proscribed by regulations in the importing country, nor should it refer to such terms as "all risks", "with average" or "free of particular average" with reference to the insurance requirements; these expressions have long been superseded by the Institute of London Underwriters' "A", "B" and "C" clauses respectively.

Goods

The description of the goods should be sufficient to enable identification but should not contain excessive detail. Instead, the applicants should be encouraged to call for the beneficiaries' certificates that all conditions of the contract (identified by its reference number) have been complied with. Under no circumstances should attachments such as pro forma invoices, detailed specifications, etc, be accepted for attachment to, or to form part of, the credit. Multi-paged credits are costly to process, greatly increase the chances of mistakes being made, do nothing to enhance the issuing bank's reputation and, above all, are almost always unnecessary.

A credit should not include vague terms in descriptions of issuers of documents such as "qualified", "first class", etc, but should name a previously-identified party in the beneficiaries' country who has consented to issue them. It should also not contain unsubstantiable requirements such as "shipment by conference line vessel", but instead should call for a certificate to this effect to be presented with the other documents. Certificates issued by carriers or uncustomary declarations on transport documents, should be called for sparingly, if at all. Carriers understandably do not like issuing them and will refuse if at all possible; in fact such certificates are seldom truly necessary. An example of such a document is the so-called blacklist certificate which, contrary to popular belief, is an official requirement only in Iraq and Qatar.

If any unit prices are stated in the credit, multiplication by the quantity of goods, if known, should give the credit amount, or there should be a good explanation for any discrepancy. The application should state for whose account are bank charges, and any request for negotiable documents to be sent direct to any party other than the issuing bank should be considered very carefully, since this will mean that the bank has lost the security provided by its lien over the goods. Where goods are to be sent by post or air, the bank may wish to preserve its security by having the goods consigned to it, but such a course usually involves the bank in much unnecessary work on arrival of the goods, and is also undesirable because the bank becomes involved with those goods, thus negating one of the underlying principles of documentary credits.

Amendments

Any subsequent amendments should receive the same careful consideration, bearing in mind their effect upon the already-existing terms of the credit. It should not be assumed that, because the issuing bank's file copy of the credit has been amended, that the amendment is in force and operative. If the credit is irrevocable, the beneficiaries are under no obligation to accept amendments and under no legal obligation even to give notice of their rejection.

Procedure after issue

When the issuing bank has satisfied itself on the above points, and on any others that may concern it (the list is by no means exhaustive), the credit should be prepared, checked, signed and forwarded to the selected advising bank. It should contain a clear indication to the beneficiaries regarding where, when and from whom they will receive payment, and a clear indication to the negotiating bank as to how it is to obtain reimbursement. If the advising bank is required to add its confirmation to the credit, this instruction should be given, along with any other requirements such as telegraphic advice of drawings.

Where the credit is transmitted by full details telex, that must contain all the information normally appearing on a credit, including the undertakings regarding payment and the statement that the credit is subject to UCP which normally appear in the small print. Great care should be taken if less than full details are telexed to state clearly that full details are to follow. Otherwise the telex as sent will stand as the operative instrument and cannot be added to or altered without the consent of the beneficiaries. Where the credit is transmitted by airmail, it should be clearly typed in an easily-read format. In this connection, where a bank habitually uses preprinted credit forms it is a good idea to keep a small stock of forms which are blank, at least as regards the documentary requirements. Nothing is more confusing than a credit which consists mainly of deletions of preprinted requirements, with the actual terms inserted wherever there happens to be a little space on the form and interlinked by various reference marks such as asterisks. A standby credit is a good example of a credit which usually is better typed on a blank form.

It is not unknown for credits to be issued as "confirmed, irrevocable letters of credit". When this happens, it is a clear indication that the issuing bank has no understanding of the principles of confirmation and the probability is that this level of expertise has been applied to other aspects of the credit as well. The basis of confirmation is the addition by another bank of a promise which ranks alongside that of the issuing bank. Clearly, the addition of a second promise by the issuing bank conveys no further protection to the beneficiaries than they already had. Similarly, there is very little point in one branch of a bank adding its "confirmation" to that of another. Again, nothing is gained by the beneficiaries, although they sometimes insist on this happening in order that they may satisfy a clause in their export credit insurance policy which requires that all their exports be covered by confirmed, irrevocable letters of credit.

The credit having been sent, a copy should be sent to the applicants and another placed in the issuing bank's own files; its value should be recorded against the applicants' facility. Drawings received and settled by the applicants should be recredited to that facility, as should credits which have expired unutilised, but only when a suitable period has elapsed after expiry to allow for processing and transit of drawings negotiated up to its expiry date.

Discrepant drawings

On receipt of drawings, it is the issuing bank's duty, within a reasonable time, to check the documents against the credit and to decide on the basis of those documents whether or not they comply with the terms of the credit. If it considers that they do not it must immediately advise the negotiating bank by teletransmission of its refusal, with reasons, and state that it is either returning the documents (seldom a viable option) or holding them at the negotiating bank's disposal. It is perhaps at this stage that the reputation of the issuing bank is most at stake, since it has made a solemn promise to pay the beneficiaries provided that they comply with all the conditions of the credit. If it now seeks to avoid the honouring of that promise on the pretext of trivial "discrepancies", it will quickly find that its credits are despised and rejected in the commercial world.

Frequently, the course of action taken is to refer the discrepancies to the applicants for authority to pay, but this does not absolve the issuing bank of its duty to inform the negotiating bank. Care should be taken not to give the applicants the opportunity of evading their contractual responsibilities by taking advantage of trivial discrepancies noticed by the issuing bank. In some cases it is probably better to ignore such discrepancies. This, however, presupposes that the issuing bank is using staff with sufficient experience and expertise to make decisions upon what constitutes a "real" discrepancy and what may safely be ignored. Unfortunately, this is not always the case. Where applicants do try to avoid payment without just cause, it should be remembered that it will not be their reputation which will suffer most, but the issuing bank's. Fortunately, an explanation of the bank's position will usually suffice to persuade most applicants to take up the documents: where it fails, a simple threat of withdrawal of facilities will often succeed.

Sometimes a negotiating bank's covering letter will state that it has negotiated under reserve or under the beneficiaries' or their bankers' indemnity for discrepancies which it has noted. This does not affect the position of the issuing bank in any way and it must still carry out the procedures outlined above. If the negotiating bank has in turn offered its own indemnity to the issuing bank, this fact may be advised to the applicants and may affect their decision as to whether or not to take up the documents. However, great care should be exercised in ascertaining that the wording of the indemnity is acceptable, that it is valid for a suitable period and that payment of claims under the indemnity are not likely to be prejudiced by, for example, adverse exchange control regulations.

On some occasions, goods will arrive before the relative documents. This may mean that the documents were presented late, which will enable refusal under the credit, but this cannot be relied upon as the delay may have occurred after negotiation, either in the negotiating bank or in transit. In these circumstances, the applicants, if they are aware of the goods' arrival, may ask the issuing bank to issue an indemnity to the carriers to enable them to take delivery of the goods without production of the relative bill of lading. Again, goods which are consigned to the bank may arrive before the relative drawing and, rather than take them into store in its own name, the bank may elect to issue a delivery order in favour of the applicants. In either of these circumstances it should be made absolutely clear to the applicants that, having taken delivery of the goods, they will be obliged to pay for the documents when they eventually arrive, regardless of any defect in those documents or in the goods. Such matters must be taken up direct with the beneficiaries under the sales contract.

Drawings which the issuing bank decides are in accordance with the credit terms may be paid or reimbursed immediately and the applicants' account debited without further reference other than forwarding the documents to them without delay. Suitable arrangements must be made to match up any duplicate documents with the originals when received and where documents which have been refused are held at the disposal of the negotiating bank every effort must be made to obtain their instructions.

Acceptances under usance credits, whether by the applicants or the issuing bank, must be entered into a diary for payment at maturity, and kept in a safe place until that time, when proceeds must be disposed of in accordance with the instructions held. Very occasionally it happens that an issuing bank is restrained by an order of the courts from paying such an acceptance, often because the applicants have found the goods to be defective. Whilst this affects the issuing bank's power to debit the applicants' account, it in no way releases it from its obligations under the credit and it must pay in the normal way from its own resources. This inequitable situation should be pointed out to the court if possible and the bank should always be represented at any such court hearing of which it is aware. It should protest most strongly if the court takes a decision affecting it when it has not been notified of the hearing.

Such, then, are the responsibilities of the issuing bank. They are without doubt the heaviest of any involved in the credit process:

(a) heavier than those of the advising bank, which has merely to verify the apparent authenticity of the credit;
(b) heavier than those of the confirming bank, because that bank does not have to draw up the credit;
(c) heavier than those of the negotiating bank, because that bank has freedom of choice as to whether it negotiates or not;
(d) heavier than those of the applicants, because its promise is not conditional upon their agreement, or even their survival, in order for it to crystallise; and

(e)   heavier than the sum of all these because it is upon the willingness of the issuing bank to make the unequivocable promise so
essential to the documentary credit process, and its willingness to
stand by it, that the whole future of that process depends.

16
The avoidance of loss under documentary credits: the advising/confirming/ negotiating bank

It is convenient to deal with the responsibilities of these three banks in one chapter since they are often the same bank and the actions which they take at one stage may have a profound effect upon those necessary at a later time.

The advising bank

The advising bank is perhaps the party with the least responsibilities under a letter of credit. Only where it is asked to confirm the credit does its responsibility increase dramatically, both in its commitment to others and in its duty to itself to avoid loss, either of money or reputation.

The sole requirement of UCP, which is specifically aimed at the advising bank, is to check upon the apparent genuineness of the credit which the bank advises. It follows that under no circumstances should a bank advise a credit which it has received from another bank with which it does not have a correspondent relationship. In such circumstances it should return the credit, or identify the issuing bank's correspondents in that country and pass it to them without responsibility, advising the issuing bank of its action.

Checking is normally taken to mean verification of signatures and in many cases this is sufficient. Signatures imply transmission of the credit by airmail and such credits are usually fairly modest in value, the tendency being for the higher value credits to be transmitted by telex or similar means. Where this happens, the banks concerned will have testing arrangements between them and so can be reasonably secure in assuming that a message has emanated from the source from which it purports to have done. With airmailed credits, however, the only immediate check is upon the signatures. As is well-known, there are many who possess the talent of the accurate and virtually undetectable forging of signatures and there is no shortage of ways of obtaining specimens of the authorised signatures within banks. Suspicion should therefore be aroused when a credit for a substantial amount is received by airmail, particularly where that credit is in favour of beneficiaries who are unknown to the bank and about whom no information can be obtained. When this happens, it is advisable to telex the issuing bank, asking it to affirm, by tested telex message, that the credit is a genuine one.

Although in no way the advising bank's duty, it is a good idea, on receipt of a credit, to give its contents a quick glance to ensure that nothing is obviously wrong with it. This is suggested for two reasons. First, the bank may not wish to advise the credit in the form in which it has been received, either because it is technically incorrect or because it is likely to cause problems at a later date when documents are presented for negotiation, perhaps because it contains excessive detail. Second, because, like all the banks involved, the advising bank is the agent of the applicants and this is the last stage at which the credit will be alterable without the consent of the beneficiaries. The advising bank is perfectly entitled to refuse to advise until it is satisfied with the terms of the credit and in many ways it is desirable that it should do so, since such action frequently ensures that the issuing bank alters its procedures to avoid a repetition of the cause for rejection in the future. The same considerations apply to amendments.

Telexed credits

A credit which is received by telex may be assumed to be the operative credit instrument unless it specifically states that it is subject to a mail confirmation to follow. The question sometimes arises as to what action should be taken when a telex does not so state but a mail confirmation is nonetheless later received. This question was dealt with in Chapter 11, when it was suggested that the most practical approach was to check the confirmation against the original telex and if any discrepancies exist to telex immediately the issuing bank advising them of the position, whilst contacting the beneficiaries to ascertain whether they are prepared to accept an amendment to the credit. This, of course, they are not obliged to do; if they refuse there is no more action which the advising bank can effectively take.

The confirming bank

The position is rather different where the advising bank is asked to add its confirmation to a credit. It is now required to take on a responsibility similar in extent to that of the issuing bank, in that, if it consents to confirm, it makes a promise to the beneficiaries that they will receive payment provided that they comply with all the terms of the credit. This promise is just that; a prime liability and not a guarantee that the confirming bank will pay if the issuing bank does not, as is often thought. It is tantamount, therefore, to the issue of the confirming bank's own credit, with the same implications for its reputation, but since the credit was drawn up by another bank it is in the confirming bank's interest to check the terms of the credit very carefully, applying the same criteria as were recommended for the issuing bank in Chapter 15. In particular, the method of obtaining reimbursement should be absolutely clear, since the confirming bank will be the bank which is called upon to pay.

Confirmation may be requested by the issuing bank or by the beneficiaries. If it emanates from the latter and no authority is held from the issuing bank, that bank's authority should be sought before complying with the request. So-called "silent confirmation" is to be discouraged, since the issuing bank is unaware that the advising bank has accepted any additional responsibility and will therefore not feel obliged to take any action to protect its interests. Even more dangerous is the practice adopted by some banks of giving silent confirmation at the request of the beneficiaries to credits which have not even been advised by them. Such a bank has given a commitment to the beneficiaries under which, whilst it will be obliged to pay the beneficiaries against conforming documents, in cases of dispute it will have no enforceable claim against the issuing bank. The beneficiaries may even have accepted amendments to the credit of which the confirming bank is unaware and then failed to take those amendments into consideration in the documents which they have presented.

Confirmation having been added, the obligations of the bank which has done so are just as severe as are those of the issuing bank and confirmation should by no means be undertaken lightly or viewed as an easy source of revenue. Indeed, the reputation of the confirming bank is more at risk than that of the issuing bank, since that risk occurs in its home market and repercussions will be more immediately and keenly felt. The confirming bank does, however, acquire additional rights under the credit, and any amendments cannot be effective without its agreement. This may be particularly useful where the credit is to be increased or extended beyond the desired limits of the bank's exposure to either the issuing bank or the importing country.

The negotiating bank

The term "negotiating bank" is used here in its wider sense of any bank in the beneficiaries' country which makes payment to, or accepts or negotiates drafts drawn by the beneficiaries under a credit. The stricter meaning of the word "negotiating" was discussed in Chapter 11.

Unless it has confirmed the credit, no bank is under any obligation to negotiate documents, although in practice banks seldom refuse where documents are in order, since to do so could cast doubt upon their competence. The position of the negotiating bank is, however, a difficult one. On the one hand it has a mandate to pay provided that certain well-defined conditions are met; if this is not so that mandate ceases to exist. It must therefore be certain that the issuing bank will have no cause to refuse the documents because of alleged discrepancies, a factor which militates in favour of extreme caution. On the other hand, the credit is intended to facilitate and not to hinder international trade; rejection of otherwise complying documents for trivial matters will damage the bank's reputation in its home environment by gaining it a reputation for pettiness and obstruction. If neither of these is attractive to it, the negotiating bank is forced to tread a dangerous path between the twin precipices and, to continue the mountaineering analogy, unless its staff are adequately trained, experienced, and confident in their proficiency, it is moreover treading that path in thick mist.

"What constitutes a discrepancy?" This question has been asked on countless occasions but has never been satisfactorily answered. One bank's view will differ radically from that of the bank next door, ranging from the organisation which will negotiate anything with barely a glance at the documents, to the one which will reject a drawing because the word "Limited" has been abbreviated to "Ltd". A list of the more commonly encountered discrepancies is given shortly, but this should be regarded as a sample only and not taken as a definitive checklist.

Frequently encountered discrepancies in documents

Letter of credit:
    expired
    exceeded
    short drawn
    late presentation
    partial shipment

Invoice:
    amount differs from drawing
    contract terms not as stated in credit
    description of goods differs
    does not certify . . .
    unsigned
    insufficient copies
    shipping marks differ from bill of lading
    unit prices not as stated in credit
    additional charges claimed

Bill of lading:
    late shipment
    not issued by carrier specified
    issued by forwarding agent
    claused . . .
    not marked "freight paid"
    unauthenticated alteration
    evidences transhipment
    not endorsed
    subject to charter party
    insufficient originals/non-negotiable copies
    goods not consigned as specified
    evidences shipment on deck
    does not show goods shipped from . . .
    does not show goods shipped to . . .
    not marked "shipped"

Insurance certificate/policy:
>   open cover expired (certificates only)
>   shipment not covered (certificates only)
>   hull limit exceeded (certificates only)
>   location limit exceeded (certificates only)
>   not countersigned by assured (certificates only)
>   goods underinsured
>   . . . risks not covered
>   not endorsed
>   shipping marks differ from bill of lading
>   not in currency of credit
>   dated later than bill of lading (policy only)

Draft:
>   words and figures differ
>   not endorsed
>   tenor not as per credit
>   not signed

It is a common misconception that documents are checked against the credit and negotiated if they are in order. In fact they are checked in at least three other respects, although an experienced checker may well perform some or even all of these operations simultaneously.

Besides complying with the credit terms, documents must comply with the requirements of UCP and, as has been seen, many of these requirements will have no mention in the credit itself. An example of this would be where a set of documents, perfectly correct in terms of the credit, cover the second instalmental shipment under a credit, where the first shipment was made late and the credit therefore became invalid in terms of Article 45. A thorough knowledge of, and the ability to apply, the UCP is therefore essential in any document checker.

The documents must agree with each other, an aspect covered in UCP but nonetheless worthy of a separate mention here. As an example of this, where the shipping marks on an insurance document failed to correspond with those on the bill of lading, the document would be rejected.

Finally, they must stand alone as documents capable of fulfilling the purpose for which they were designed. Many documents carry their own requirements which must be adhered to before they may be considered as valid, such as the necessity for the countersignature of the insured party to appear on an insurance certificate.

Fraud and forgery

Although disclaimant clauses are incorporated into UCP to protect all banks against liability for the consequences of fraud and forgery of documents presented, this protection is by no means absolute. Where circumstances exist which should have served to put a bank on its guard it may be held to have been negligent in its duties as agent of the applicants if it nonetheless pays fraudulent beneficiaries; negotiating banks should be ever alert for signs of possible fraud. In a work of this size it is impossible to enumerate all the possibilities which are open to fraudsters in their never-ending quest to obtain money to which they are not entitled and since they are always at least one step ahead of the banks, merely by virtue of the fact that they know that they are dishonest whereas the bank does not, it would probably be counterproductive to attempt to do so. There are, however, a number of factors which, although not in the least suspicious in themselves, gain significance where they exist in combination with each other.

The foremost of these is the amount of the drawing. When fraudsters go to considerable trouble and risk to obtain money by false pretences, they tend to look for substantial returns from their wrong-doing. What constitutes a large amount is for individual banks to decide and any attempt to define it here would merely serve to indicate to the criminal element what might be a "safe" amount to aim for. As was stressed at the beginning of this section, the size of the drawing is not important in itself but only assumes such importance when it coincides with one or more of the other factors to be mentioned below.

Almost as important as the amount of the drawing is the status of the beneficiaries. Where this party in unknown in the commercial world but is nonetheless apparently dealing in high value contracts, the question arises why they are not better known. Often the answer is that they are a company which has been formed with the specific object of procuring a large supply contract from an unsuspecting overseas buyer and then using the basic principle of the documentary credit, that banks deal in documents and not in goods, either by shipping worthless goods and presenting the resulting genuine documents, or by presenting documents which are wholly or partially forged.

Another factor which is often seen in cases of fraud is the involvement of numerous countries in the transaction. There may be good reasons for a credit issued in Bangladesh to be advised through London to beneficiaries in Greece covering goods being shipped from the USA, but another possibility is that fraudsters are trying to put as many national boundaries as possible between themselves and any pursuing police investigators.

Mention of Bangladesh leads to another, particularly deplorable, facet of international trade fraud, in that very often it is the poorer nations of the world who are the target of such deception, in reliance on their lack of resources to enable effective action to be taken to recover their loss. This lack of resources also makes such countries vulnerable to offers of cheaply priced goods, since criminals are easily able to undercut the quotation of genuine suppliers, as they have no intention of supplying the goods anyway.

Other signs of possible danger, if they co-exist with the above, are:

(a)   the use by the beneficiaries of one of the recognised tax havens, which may be from financial motives but may also be from a desire to confuse the pursuit following a fraud;

(b)   use of a chartered vessel, since at the lower end of the market it is frequently possible to find owners or masters willing to collaborate in the production of fraudulent documentation; and

(c)   the beneficiaries being traders rather than producers of goods, which, although an honourable and essential profession, can attract the less-than-honest by virtue of the ease with which a business may be set up without significant outlay of capital.

Where the suspicions of a negotiating bank have been aroused in circumstances such as those outlined above, or for any other reason, provided that it has not confirmed the credit it may exercise its option to refuse negotiation and it is not obliged to give any reason for such refusal. Where it has confirmed, its position is a little more difficult since it is legally liable under the credit, but if it has certain knowledge that a fraud is being attempted it would be in little danger from a similar refusal. Usually, of course, there is not absolute conviction but a nagging suspicion and the only course open to the bank is to make further enquiries. No-one is completely immune to fraud and, provided that a negotiating bank can show that it has done all in its power to verify the transaction, it should be well protected by UCP.

Fortunately, perfect forgeries of documents are exceedingly rare and the eye of an experienced checker will quickly identify anomalies in the document and departures from the usual format. In most cases the issuers of the documents can be contacted for verification of their authenticity, but some, particularly bills of lading, may prove more difficult. In such cases, publications such as *Lloyds' Shipping Index* can prove invaluable in checking on the existence, capacity and whereabouts of the vessel named in the bill, and may also provide information regarding the ship's owners or agents who can be contacted for further information. Failing this, resort may be made to the International Maritime Bureau, based in Barking, Essex, England, which is the arm of the International Chamber of Commerce specialising in the combating of marine fraud. The IMB may well be able to verify the existence of the cargo described in the bill of lading, and its loading on board the stated vessel.

Payment and reimbursement

Negotiation having taken place, the negotiating bank must then follow carefully the instructions contained in the credit in order to obtain reimbursement of the amount paid by it. If it is a paying bank it will have paid without recourse to the beneficiaries and will either debit the account of the issuing bank in its own books, thus securing immediate reimbursement or, if the credit is not expressed in its home currency, will claim such reimbursement, plus interest, from the issuing bank or from a third bank nominated in the credit. Such a reimbursement claim should not require to be accompanied by a certificate of compliance and should be honoured without delay. If it is not, the issuing bank is responsible for interest payable as a result of the failure of its paying agent to reimburse in good time.

Acceptance

If the bank has accepted the beneficiaries' draft under a usance credit, the accepted draft will, according to the instructions received, either be returned to the beneficiaries or held in a safe place until it becomes due for payment, either on a safe custody basis on behalf of the beneficiaries or on its own behalf if it has discounted the acceptance. In any case, acceptance and maturity must be advised to the issuing bank.

Disposal of documents

As regards the documents, unless the credit states otherwise, these will be sent to the issuing bank, which has a reasonable time in which to examine them and to decide whether or not it considers that they are in accordance with the credit terms. This, of course, is the crucial factor which determines whether or not the negotiating bank has been successful in keeping to the narrow path mentioned at the beginning of this section. It is not obliged to acquaint the issuing bank with any discrepancies which it has found in the documents, but in practice if it had considered them important enough it would have rejected the drawing.

Rejection by issuing bank

If the issuing bank refuses the drawing for reasons which the negotiating bank considers spurious and these objections are maintained after reference to the applicants without adequate justification being proffered for such rejection, then it is evident that the issuing bank is seeking to avoid its obligations under the credit in order to please its customers, the applicants. This may be because they have lost interest in the goods or because they are in dispute with the beneficiaries regarding this or another consignment of goods. Whatever the reason, this situation is one of the most deplorable which can occur in connection with a credit and resolute action is called for from the negotiating bank. Often communication at high level threatening to refuse in future to handle the issuing bank's paper and to make clear to presenters the reason for such refusal, will bring about an astonishing reversal of policy on the part of the offenders.

Where, however, the rejection is justified, the position of the negotiating bank will depend on its true status in terms of the credit. If it has paid the beneficiaries there is little that can be done other than to attempt to dispose of the goods which it has, by default, become the owner of, at the best possible price and to revise its procedures to preclude future repetition of the mistake which caused the loss. If it has negotiated in the true sense of the word, it may seek to exercise its right of recourse against the beneficiaries, but the attendant admission of incompetence and the resulting bad publicity may well lead it to dismiss this remedy.

Discrepant drawings

It remains to consider the position where documents are presented which do not conform with the terms of the credit and the percentage of all presentations which fall into this category is amazingly high (and one of the more important reasons for the writing of this book). Technically, the mandate implied in the credit is to honour the beneficiaries' drawings provided that all conditions of the credit are complied with: if they are not, then the mandate falls away and there is no obligation upon the bank to take any further action. In practice, however, there are a number of options which are open to the negotiating bank between the extremes of outright rejection of the documents and total disregard of the discrepancies.

The first of these, and the most satisfactory to all concerned, is to have the documents corrected. Whether this can be done will depend upon the nature of the discrepancy (nothing can be done to correct late shipment, for instance) and the time which remains available before expiry either of the credit itself or of the period allowed after the date of the transport document for presentation of complying documents. In most cases, correction will involve the beneficiaries taking the documents away again, although the bank may be prepared to co-operate in allowing properly authorised and identified persons to make and authenticate alterations to certain documents on its own premises. On most documents, authentication of alterations is essential, though minor alterations to such things as typing errors on purely commercial documents such as invoices and packing lists, may be made without such authentication and may even be made by the bank itself with the agreement of the beneficiaries. Obviously, great discretion should be exercised when such an action is considered, the criterion being whether the alteration is of a nature which could mislead subsequent holders of the document and whether it is relevant to the interests of such parties.

The next most practical action is to telex the issuing bank detailing the drawing, the underlying shipment and the discrepancies found, and ask for its authority to pay notwithstanding those discrepancies. It is important that, when such a telex is sent, it gives the issuing bank all information which will be relevant to its decision. For example, there is little point in telling the issuing bank that late presentation has been made without including details of the carrying vessel in order that the applicants may calculate whether or not the documents will be stale by the time they are received.

An alternative course which is often followed as a "soft option" is to pay under the protection of an indemnity, either from the beneficiaries or from their bankers, in which the givers of the indemnity undertake to refund the amount paid if the documents are rejected by the applicants on the grounds of the named discrepancies. This course of action has a number of drawbacks. Although it facilitates the processing of the drawing it is of no help to the issuing bank unless the negotiating bank in turn extends its own indemnity. This involvement in multiple indemnities creates much extra work at a later date in the monitoring of continued validity and release of the indemnities, and from the beneficiaries' point of view involves them in additional expense if the indemnity is required to be issued by their bankers. More importantly, it leaves the amount of the indemnity outstanding in the beneficiaries' books as a contingent liability. More than one company has had its annual accounts qualified by its auditors by reference to numerous such indemnities, casually given and unrecorded in its books.

Finally, the option exists for the credit to be disregarded altogether and for the documents to be sent to the issuing bank on a collection basis. Where this occurs, usual practice is for reference to be made to the credit in the covering schedule and for the discrepancies which have been found to be listed. This is not really necessary, however, since a collection is a collection and should be treated as such. In this, full instructions should be given to the collecting bank (the erstwhile issuing bank) and the provisions of the Uniform Rules for Collections should be regarded as applying to the item. For full information on the treatment of collections, see Chapter 8.

17
The avoidance of loss under documentary credits: the beneficiaries

It has been stated before in this book that the beneficiaries have less responsibility under a letter of credit than any other party and this is true insofar as it concerns their duties to others. If they so choose, they are perfectly at liberty to ignore the credit completely and this in fact happens on a surprising number of occasions. Their obligations under the commercial contract are, of course, an entirely separate matter. On the assumption, however, that they wish to carry the sale through to a successful conclusion, their prime duty is to themselves in making absolutely sure that they will be paid by the buyers.

We have already spoken many times of the paramount need in an international trade transaction for sellers and buyers to be in possession of the fullest possible financial information on their opposite numbers and for that information to be constantly updated. Sellers should not be under the impression that because the buyers have agreed to provide a letter of credit to cover payment for the goods that they have nothing further to worry about. Even with all the safeguards provided by Uniform Customs and Practice and by the banking system itself, abuses do occur whereby buyers find an excuse not to pay for the goods. The usual result of this is that the goods are eventually sold to the highest bidder, invariably at a substantial loss and frequently to the original buyers. The issue of impossibly complex credits, inclusion of "built-in discrepancies", equivocation over trivial discrepancies, all these are ruses which can be, and are, used by unscrupulous applicants to deny sellers the payment to which they are entitled and should have been certain of by virtue of the letter of credit.

We have seen that the chief advantages to sellers to be expected from
the use of a letter of credit as the means of settlement are certainty and
immediacy of payment, yet as much as 70% of all drawings under
documentary credits are rejected by banks on first presentation and the
time of payment is frequently postponed even for complying documents,
by credits being made payable at the counters of the issuing bank and
similar ploys. The purpose of this chapter is to put sellers in the position
of being aware of these dangers and able to identify them in time to
avoid loss.

Forged credits

Although there is nothing to prevent a credit being sent by the issuing
bank direct to the beneficiaries it is highly unusual; the issuing bank
normally employs the services of its agent in the sellers' country to "advise" the credit. This provides a great safeguard for the beneficiaries since
it is the duty of the advising bank to check the apparent authenticity of
the credit and if it transpires that it is a forgery that bank is liable for any
loss which occurs if it has been negligent in such checking. Where a
credit does appear to have been received direct, therefore, it should be
viewed with suspicion, since such credits frequently turn out to be
forged. The credit should immediately be taken to the beneficiaries' own
bankers who should be asked to take steps to have it authenticated.
Other tell-tale signs of a forged credit are repeated communications from
the "applicants" stressing the urgency of the order and requesting immediate dispatch of goods, requirements in the credit that goods be sent by
air and consigned direct to the applicants, requirements that any
acknowledgement or request for amendment be addressed to the applicants rather than to the issuing bank, and the use of false or incorrect
addresses or post box numbers (although this would not be apparent to
the beneficiaries). The first two of these are, of course, not suspicious in
themselves, but become so where the credit is received direct.

Checking the credit upon receipt from the advis-
ing bank

Though it might seem obvious, the single most important piece of advice
which can be given to beneficiaries, and the most frequently ignored, is

that immediately upon receipt of a credit they should read it. It is easy to breathe a sigh of relief at having received a "guarantee" of payment and to file it away until it is needed at the time when documents are ready to be presented to the bank. By this time, of course, it is far too late to do anything to remedy any deficiencies and the expected payment is postponed, perhaps indefinitely.

Contract terms

Ideally, none of the requirements of a credit should come as a surprise to the beneficiaries, since the type of credit, payment terms, goods specification, contract terms, delivery dates, documentary requirements, responsibility for payment of bank charges, should have been agreed at the contract stage and the applicants should not have incorporated any additional requirements without first obtaining the beneficiaries' agreement. Provided that this has been done, it becomes a simple matter of checking the terms of the credit against the contract and requesting an amendment to the credit in case of any discrepancy. Such a request should be direct to the buyers, since the banks will in any case have to refer to them; a request routed through the banks will only be unnecessarily delayed. If a request for an amendment required to bring a credit into line with previously agreed contract terms is refused the buyers are already in breach of contract and the sellers would be well advised to take heed of this warning and refuse to ship the goods.

Type of credit

The first point of which to take note when checking a credit is the type of instrument which has been issued. A revocable credit can be amended or cancelled at the behest of either the applicants or the issuing bank without the agreement, or even the prior knowledge, of the beneficiaries. It is therefore of little use as a guarantee of payment and is normally used only where the buyers and sellers have a long-standing relationship or perhaps belong to the same group of companies and are obliged to use a credit as the means of settlement by regulations in one or other of their countries. Most sellers, in specifying a credit, will be expecting an irrevocable instrument, which cannot be amended or cancelled without their consent. The type of credit will be shown clearly at the top, usually preceding the credit number. If it says "confirmed irrevocable letter of credit", this is an indication that the issuing bank does not understand credits and great caution should be exercised with the rest of the credit's terms. Other adjectives which may be used here include "revolving", "transferable", "red clause", and "standby", each of which was defined in detail in Chapter 10.

Time and place of payment

Probably the next most important matter to be checked is the terms of payment; these must be read carefully and understood and where any uncertainty exists the advising bank should be asked for clarification. If usance drafts are called for, their tenor should obviously be the period of credit agreed in the contract, but most problems in this area arise from the actual place of payment rather than the time. The majority of sellers expect to be paid under a credit by the bank in their own country to which they present conforming documents, but where the issuing bank has used words such as "available at our counters" or "payable on receipt by us of conforming documents", what should be a right is being denied to the beneficiaries. Unless such an arrangement has been previously consented to they should treat the credit with suspicion. In fact, such an instrument is flattered by being called a letter of credit at all; it is really a conditional guarantee of payment of a collection.

Amount

The credit amount is the next thing which should be checked. Not only should it be sufficient to cover the agreed price of the goods, including any variation in quantity which may have been allowed for, but it should also represent the full value of the goods under the contract terms which have been agreed. For a CIF contract, therefore, the amount must cover the full CIF value of the shipment, including freight and insurance premiums. If the quantity of the goods is specified as being approximate, then a variation of 10% either way will be allowed, but where the quantity is exceeded this will be of no use to the beneficiaries unless the amount is also expressed as approximate.

Dates and time constraints

Next, the dates stipulated in the credit should be examined and considered in the light of whether they can practicably be adhered to. The time required to procure or manufacture the goods and the frequency of sailings or flights to the specified destination will be the chief factors affecting whether or not the latest date for shipment can be met. If any doubt exists, it is preferable to obtain an extension now rather than to take a chance and risk delay in payment later. The other import-ant time constraint is that which restricts the number of days after the date of the transport document which are allowed for presentation of documents. This should also be carefully considered in the light of the usual delay in obtaining the transport document and the formalities, such as insurance or legalisation, which will have to be attended to between that time and the stipulated date. If the credit does not stipulate this period of time, UCP automatically apply 21 days as the period allowed. The difference between the latest date for shipment and that for presen-tation of documents should automatically determine the expiry date of the credit if it has been properly drawn up but beneficiaries should beware of credits to which such professionalism has not been applied. Many drawings have been rejected because the beneficiaries looked only at the expiry date of the credit without realising that the time allowed for presentation effectively nullified the credit several days prior to its stated expiry. Finally, while on the subject of time constraints, beneficiaries should be especially cautious where the credit provides for shipment in instalments at specified intervals. If one such instalment is shipped late, the credit becomes null and void for future drawings even though they represent goods shipped on time, unless it is specifically reinstated by the issuing bank at the request of the applicants. This can be a serious problem where shipping opportunities to a particular destination are few or where cargo space in the available vessels is heavily booked.

Goods and shipment

The description of the goods as given in the credit should now be con-sidered and its exact conformity with the contract verified. Applicants are discouraged by banks from including excessive detail in the credit description but instead should require just sufficient detail to identify the goods as those ordered and call for the beneficiaries' certificate that the goods supplied conform with the specification in the order. The brief description, however, should not indicate any deviation from the type or specification of goods which were actually contracted for. If, by their hazardous or bulky nature, it is likely that the goods will be carried on deck, the credit should specifically allow for bills of lading to indicate that this has occurred or the documents will be rejected. Similarly, if it is likely that the bill of lading will be claused by the carriers regarding defects in either the goods or the packing, the credit should specifically allow for this, provided, of course, that the applicants are prepared to accept such clauses.

The stipulated voyage should be considered, including whether it is in fact possible without transhipment, if the credit prohibits this. This is particularly troublesome where goods are sent by air, since airlines tend to tranship goods as is convenient to their purposes without prior reference to their customers; their prime consideration is to get the goods to their destination in the shortest possible time. The relationship of the stipulated voyage with the stated transport document should also be checked and if, for example, the voyage is between two points, one or both of which are inland, yet the credit calls for a marine bill of lading, this should be amended to a combined transport document.

Documentary requirements

The transport document is an important point to consider from other aspects. If the intention is to entrust the shipment of the goods to forwarding agents, they should be consulted in advance to ascertain whether they will provide the carriers' bill of lading or their own house bill. If the latter, the credit must specifically authorise such a document or it will be rejected, unless it is the FIATA FBL described in Chapter 4. Even where a FIATA FBL is to be presented, an amendment may be necessary, since the decision of the ICC which authorised the use of this document where the credit stipulates presentation of a marine bill of lading has not yet been enshrined in UCP; the advice of the envisaged negotiating bank should be sought. If the credit requires any particular clauses or information to appear on the transport document which would not normally be present, the carriers should be contacted to ascertain whether they are prepared to comply. Generally speaking, carriers are unhappy about including information on bills of lading which they have no means of verifying. They quite properly consider that such information, if really necessary, should be provided elsewhere. They are also understandably reluctant to provide the many certificates demanded by paranoic buyers, or their governments, regarding the condition, age, flag and route of their vessels, and periodically rebel and simply refuse to issue them.

Regarding the other documentary requirements, it should be checked that they are in accordance with the contract terms, eg that an insurance document is not called for where the shipment is CFR, and that they will all be obtainable, since if one is missing or incomplete, payment will not be made. If any are to be issued by third parties, other than transport or insurance documents or regularly-seen papers such as certificates of origin issued by chambers of commerce, then the prospective issuers should be contacted at an early stage in order to confirm that the documents will be obtainable at the time they are required. Beneficiaries should beware of any credit which makes it a condition of payment that a document be presented which has been issued or countersigned by the applicants or their agents, since in such circumstances mere inaction on their part is all that is required to frustrate payment.

The credit should be examined generally to ensure that it contains no contradictory or nonsensical requirements. The beneficiaries' own name must be spelt correctly or this may cast doubt upon whether the right organisation is claiming payment. Any requirements for action such as dispatch of documents or telexing of shipment details "immediately after shipment" or similar should be reworded unless the beneficiaries are absolutely certain that they will be able to comply, since shipment details are rarely available in time for such compliance and interpretations of the word "immediate" vary. The advising bank's covering letter should also be read. This will often be the vehicle used for the addition by the advising bank of its confirmation of the credit and may also state for whose account bank charges are to be presumed.

Amendments

Provided that beneficiaries carry out all these checks, they should have little to worry about as the time approaches for negotiation other than gathering together all the required documents and remaining within the time constraints imposed by the credit. During this intervening period, or indeed at any time during the lifetime of a credit, they are under no obligation to accept any amendments which may be received, nor are they, despite anything they may be told to the contrary by the advising bank, even required to formally reject such amendments in order for them to be inoperative. The beneficiaries cannot, however, accept part of a multiple amendment contained on the same advice whilst rejecting the rest.

Presentation of documents

On the assumption that all the documents required by the credit have
been obtained, if the procedures outlined so far in this chapter have been
followed there should be a very strong chance of their being accepted
by the bank and of negotiation being effected in consequence. It is not
recommended, however, that the documents are simply lodged with the
bank and the detailed checking left to them. Banks vary widely in the
time they take to process documents under credits, some providing a
same-day service whilst others take up to a week or even more. This
means that if any discrepancies are found which can be put right, the
time available for this to be done may be short or even expired; therefore
it is very much in the beneficiaries' interest to check the documents
themselves before they are presented.

Even though every care may have been taken to produce precisely the
documents called for in the credit, it does no harm to check them once
more when they are gathered together in the form in which they will be
presented to the bank. Also at this stage it will be possible to check the
documents against each other, for if they are inconsistent they will be
rejected. This is particularly important in the case of the shipping marks,
which in all other documents must correspond with those shown on the
bill of lading. Any alterations which have been made to documents
should be properly authenticated by the issuers and the documents themselves properly signed where necessary. The bill of lading, the insurance
document and the bill of exchange, if any, will probably need the beneficiaries' endorsement, and if an insurance certificate is used it may need
to be countersigned by the insured party on its face. It is as well to check
that the cover is adequate, not only in terms of the credit requirements
but also in the light of any restrictions on cover which it may itself detail
in its preamble. These usually affect the type of goods, the value limitation on goods shipped together in any one vessel and the places of
departure and destination. At the same time the expiry date of the open
cover should be checked—these arrangements are normally valid over a
number of years and the inadvertent continued use of out-of-date certificates is not unknown.

Any certifications which are required to appear on the invoice should
be checked for their presence and correctness. Unless the credit says
otherwise and the invoice is signed as a document it is not necessary to
separately sign such certifications. The invoice description of the goods
should coincide exactly with that in the credit, even to the extent of

reproducing any spelling errors which appear in the credit version. Additional descriptive text may appear but care should be taken that no part of this seems to contradict anything in the credit description.

A credit should not make stipulations which cannot easily be verified, such as "shipment by conference line vessel". If it does, the beneficiaries should provide the steam ship company's, or, failing that, their own separate certificate that the requirement has been complied with. Some banks would make their own enquiries or draw on their own knowledge and experience to make this decision, but others might simply reject the drawing through lack of evidence of compliance. In these circumstances, although the credit does not call for such certificates, it is better to provide them.

It is not a good idea to present any documents to the bank other than those called for in the credit. Any other documents should be sent to the buyers direct. This is because, although such documents are gratuitously presented, some banks will nonetheless examine them in terms of the credit and, if they appear to cast any doubt upon the information contained in the credit documents, will reject the drawing.

Discrepant documents

If, despite all these precautions, the bank discovers discrepancies which cannot be rectified, it may be prepared to take any one of a number of courses of action. Its mandate to pay has, of course, ceased to exist, because it depended totally upon the lodging of correct documents. However, most banks are prepared to assist the beneficiaries as far as they are able, bearing in mind that, even though they may be the beneficiaries' own bankers, they are in this instance acting as the agent of the applicants and their priority must be to protect the interests of their principals.

Unfortunately, all the options available where discrepant drawings are concerned are likely to cost the beneficiaries money. The quickest, and usually the most satisfactory, solution is to ask the bank to send a telex message to the issuing bank asking for authority to pay notwithstanding the discrepancies. This will involve payment of the telex costs, possibly of both banks, but will usually produce a relatively speedy decision and thus reduce losses through interest charges. Much slower is the option of asking the bank to send the drawing to the issuing bank on a collection basis, which is in effect setting aside the letter of credit altogether. This option is not really to be recommended because it may involve a lengthy wait for remittance of proceeds and collection charges will be payable by the sellers whatever the credit had to say on the subject. It is sometimes unavoidable, however, as when in response to a telex for authority to pay the applicants state that they wish to inspect the documents before reaching their decision.

The bank may offer to pay the drawing under the protection of the beneficiaries' indemnity, or one issued or countersigned by their bankers, in which an undertaking is given to refund the amount paid if the applicants refuse the documents by reason of the discrepancies listed. A similar alternative is for the bank to pay under reserve, which means that it reserves the right to reclaim the amount paid if the documents are rejected. Neither of these is very satisfactory, however, for although costs are limited to the commission which may be charged for a bankers' indemnity, plus a small interest loss whilst it is being prepared, it should appear in the beneficiaries' books as a contingent liability and the transaction cannot be regarded as finalised until the indemnity is released by the buyers taking up the documents.

If what takes place is a negotiation, ie the bank is paying the beneficiaries against a credit which is payable elsewhere, such as where drafts are on the issuing bank or the applicants, the bank may deduct from the amount paid a sum representing interest for the period for which it will be out of funds. This also applies where a reimbursing bank is named in the credit. In such cases, the bank has recourse to the beneficiaries if the draft is not paid. Where payment takes place, as where drafts are to be drawn on a paying bank nominated in the credit, or where the negotiating bank has also confirmed the credit, no such right of recourse exists and the transaction is completed when payment is made.

18
Bank finance under bills and credits

In this final chapter we shall examine the various ways in which banks provide working capital to exporters and importers where such arrangements are directly related to either collections or to documentary letters of credit. Sellers of goods, particularly where a bill for collection is the agreed method of settlement, frequently require assistance during the period while the collection relating to those goods is outstanding, while buyers may wish to defer payment for the goods until they have concluded an onward sale.

Negotiation of collections

When a bank negotiates a bill or documents it in effect makes a loan to the drawers against the proceeds which they may expect to receive in the future. As with any other lending proposition, the bank will require negotiations to be part of a prearranged facility and, before granting it, will require its customers to provide it with full financial information in order that it may assess the extent of the risk which it is incurring by doing so. It will normally call for lists of drawees to be submitted in advance and will seek financial reports on them which it will continuously update, since they will be the prime source of repayment of the loan. It will exercise limits for each drawee, beyond which it will not be prepared to be exposed, and those limits may well encompass the collections of more than one drawer. It will often also be a condition of the facility that the customers' exports are covered by an appropriate export credit insurance policy.

Export credit insurance

It is perhaps appropriate at this point to include a few words of explanation of export credit insurance. While ordinary marine insurance can provide protection to exporters against maritime risks such as damage by fire or sinking, loss by breakage or pilferage and against the risks of war, perhaps the greatest risk of loss to exporters lies in the failure of the buyers, either through their own insolvency or intransigence, or through government intervention, to pay for the goods. Such risks can form a strong disincentive to companies to enter export markets, with a resulting adverse effect on a country's balance of trade and therefore on its balance of payments and its foreign currency reserves. Many countries, therefore, have established government-backed agencies which exist for the purpose of providing insurance cover to exporters against these credit risks which they are unable to cover under their ordinary insurance.

In the United Kingdom the government agency involved is the Export Credit Guarantee Department (ECGD) which provides a variety of types of policy designed to foster the country's export trade, and also provides lines of credit which are available to specified countries or for specific projects to provide finance to overseas buyers to pay for imports from the United Kingdom. Many other countries have organisations providing similar services to their own exporters: COFACE in France, the Hermes organisation in Germany and so on. Although their prime consideration is facilitation of their own country's export trade, the commercial possibilities of the cover provided have been recognised and some of these organisations, such as that of Singapore, have begun to compete for export credit insurance business on a worldwide scale; commercial insurance companies also now offer competing cover in this field.

ECGD

The main types of policy offered in the United Kingdom by ECGD are the Comprehensive Short-Term Guarantee covering credit periods up to six months; and the Supplemental Extended Terms Guarantee covering credit periods of between six months and five years. Under these policies, the exporters are expected to declare all their exports (not just the bad risks), in return for which ECGD bears varying proportions of the risks of insolvency of the buyers, non-payment within six months for accepted goods, failure of the buyers to take delivery of the goods, a general moratorium on external payments by the buyers' country, delay or exchange loss in remittance of proceeds in negotiable currency and certain other risks. For larger capital projects specific guarantees are available on negotiation. The External Trade Guarantee offers reduced cover where the United Kingdom company is a merchant or confirming house and the goods are purchased in one overseas country and sold to another without entering the United Kingdom in the process.

Negotiation or advance?

Many banks differentiate between collections against which they negotiate the full value and those for which they advance up to an agreed percentage of the collection amount. Technically, in the former case the bank may become a holder in due course of the bill whilst where less than the face amount has been given the bank merely has a lien over the bill to the extent of its advance and can only be a holder for value. In practice there is really very little difference, since the bank will have taken a general right of recourse in its agreement with the customers and so does not have to rely on its recourse under the bill. The general right of recourse is necessary because this type of finance can be applied to collections where no bill of exchange is used, as is often the case where either the exporting or the importing country levies heavy stamp duty on bills.

Interest will be charged on the amount of the advance and may be debited to the drawers' account when proceeds are received, estimated and deducted from the amount paid at the time of negotiation, or deducted from the balance of proceeds if less than the full amount has been advanced.

Unless the drawers are absolutely undoubted and the bank is consequently content to rely solely upon its right of recourse if the collection is unpaid, it will consider the individual aspects of each collection against which it is requested to advance, taking into account the limits it has set for both drawers and drawees, but also looking carefully both at the documents and at the goods themselves. This is because it may have to rely upon its title to the goods to recover the amount of its loan if the bill is unpaid and the drawers are unable to repay when the bank seeks to exercise its recourse. To this end, the customer will normally be required to sign a general letter of hypothecation and pledge of goods, which gives the bank a right to sell its customers' goods if necessary in order to secure repayment of the loan.

Documents

The documents will be examined for their completeness in the light of the bank's knowledge of import regulations in the country to which they are consigned, for the security of title which they convey to the bank and of their adequacy for the purpose for which they are intended. In particular, the bill of lading will be examined to ensure that it is made out to order and is endorsed in blank, is not stale, does not bear any detrimental clauses relating to the goods or the packing and generally does not give any indication which might have an effect on the marketability of the goods. The insurance cover, if any, will be evaluated for its adequacy and the policy or certificate checked for any errors which might affect that cover.

Goods

The goods themselves are important and banks prefer to lend against collections covering shipment of merchandise which would be readily saleable in a stable and constant market. Goods which are subject to the whims of fashion, which enjoy only a seasonal demand, which are perishable, or which are of a highly specialised nature, are unpopular because of the possible difficulties in realising anything like their invoice value in a forced sale situation. For different reasons, banks are sometimes reluctant to be involved in the financing of transactions relating to commodities such as armaments, drugs and the like, particularly where those goods are bound for sensitive areas.

ECGD backed finance

In the United Kingdom, since the demise of the ECGD Short-Term Comprehensive Bank Guarantee scheme, many of the commercial banks offer non-recourse finance to exporters backed by the banks' own ECGD policies. ECGD Bank Guarantees remain available for credit periods in excess of two years, however, and a beneficiary bank of one of these guarantees can reclaim in full amounts advanced to exporters where the cause of loss is covered by the Supplementary Extended Terms Guarantee or by a specific guarantee. This greatly reduces the risk of the lending to the bank and consequently its interest rates are reduced to reflect this.

Discounting of bills

When a bank discounts a bill of exchange, it in effect buys that bill from the holder at a discount on its face value; the amount of the discount represents the interest from the date of discount until the maturity date of the bill. Unlike a negotiation, discounting is not possible when no bill of exchange accompanies a collection. Furthermore, it can only apply to usance bills and they must have been accepted. As was seen in Chapter 8, a bill drawn payable at a stated number of days after sight does not qualify as a bill of exchange within the meaning of the Act until it has been accepted and its maturity date can therefore be determined. Since with discount the source of the right of recourse lies in bill legislation, it is essential that the discounting bank acquires the rights of a holder in due course.

Because acceptance obviously takes place in the buyers' country, discounting of accepted bills under collections is usually carried out by the collecting bank acting upon instructions received from the remitting bank, which may also have negotiated the item. In most cases the bill would be expressed in the buyers' home currency to enable the bill to be rediscounted in the local bill market, if one exists. If it does not, in very rare cases, and in total reliance on the standing of the drawers rather than that of the drawees, banks may agree that the collecting bank be instructed to return the accepted draft for discount by the remitting bank. Such a discounted bill would, of course, have no value for the purposes of rediscounting in the bill market, because the name of the acceptor would be unknown in the exporting country.

Exchange as per endorsement

A specialised form of discounting, this type of finance was developed to enable sellers to obtain finance for credit periods granted to their buyers whilst taking advantage of low interest rates applying in the buyers' country and putting the buyers in the advantageous position of having their liability denominated in their home currency. At the time of presentation to the remitting bank the amount of the bill, plus collection charges and interest, is converted into the currency of the importing country and the resulting figure endorsed on the face of the bill, which then becomes payable for this amount. The item is then sent for collection in the normal way, perhaps being negotiated by the remitting bank, and presented for acceptance. When this is achieved the collecting bank is asked to discount the acceptance and the proceeds are remitted back, either to be paid to the drawers or used to repay the loan, as the case may be. EAPE finance was once common in trade between the United Kingdom and Australia and South Africa, but tended to fall away as the interest rate differential was eroded. There is, however, no reason why it should not be used again where similar circumstances exist.

A forfait finance (forfaiting)

As the name suggests, where *à forfait* finance is provided, something is forfeited, and that something is the right of recourse to the drawers which would normally be enjoyed by the discounting bank. This type of finance is generally reserved for larger contracts where buyers are obliged to request extended credit terms. It was nurtured in trade between the West and eastern Europe where the chronic shortage of hard currency with which to pay for imports was discouraging trade because of the huge contingent liabilities which would have arisen in sellers' books even were they able to finance the transactions. The geographical scope of forfaiting business has broadened considerably but the tendency remains for the buying country to be one with foreign currency reserve problems.

On receipt of an enquiry, the sellers approach a bank specialising in forfaiting business and request a quotation for a financing package, advising them of the full details of the proposed contract and of the credit terms requested. The forfaiters' quotation will be based on the sellers' basic price for the goods but will be increased to allow for the interest payable for the credit period requested and will be further loaded to cover various factors including exchange risks, credit risks, interest rate risks and political risks. The total price will be that quoted to the buyers for supply of the goods on the requested terms, with a stipulation that bills of exchange accepted, or promissory notes signed, in respect of payment for the goods will carry the aval of an acceptable bank in the buyers' country. The subject of avalisation was touched upon in Chapter 7, but what it amounts to is a guarantee by a party, otherwise unconnected with the bill, that it will be paid. Since in forfaiting the guarantee is frequently given by the central bank of the importing country the degree of security thus afforded the forfaiter is high and dishonour of forfaited paper is extremely rare.

Once the contract is signed, shipment of the goods and presentation of the required documents proceeds in the normal way. This may be by means of a collection but is more likely to be under a usance letter of credit. The resulting acceptances or promissory notes are presented to the avalising bank which adds its endorsement "por aval", whereupon the instruments are returned to the forfaiter, who then discounts them at the previously agreed rate which has been calculated to achieve payment of the sellers' basic price in full. As has been stated, the forfaiters surrender their right of recourse to the drawers, and thus the latter have no contingent liability and as far as they are concerned the transaction is at an end. From that point on the forfaiters carry all the risk, presenting the bills or notes as each falls due and taking the difference between the bill's face value and its discounted value as their gross profit before interest charges.

To summarise, the advantages to the sellers of using *à forfait* finance are that they are able to grant extended credit terms to their buyers whilst obtaining payment without recourse on, or soon after, shipment of the goods, without bearing the portion of risk which would remain uncovered if the deal were financed with backing from an export credit agency. The buyers have the advantage of being able to obtain the capital goods which they require on the credit terms which best suit their requirements.

Acceptance credits

An acceptance credit is an extremely simple arrangement whereby buyers or sellers of goods have the right to draw usance bills of exchange on the issuing bank in respect of payment for goods which is either awaited by sellers or due to be made by the buyers. The bank accepts the bills and then discounts them, the proceeds of the discount being paid to the drawers. The tenor of the bills will have been calculated to cover the required financing period but there is often a subsidiary agreement providing for maturing bills in respect of which covering funds have not yet been received to be provided for by a temporary loan. This type of credit is unique in that applicant and beneficiary are one and the same.

Back-to-back credits

Although a back-to-back credit is not necessarily a financing arrangement, this is in fact most frequently the case. It arises where merchants are buying goods from their suppliers and have contracted to sell those goods to the ultimate buyers. The merchants will usually have no physical contact with the goods, their function being to act as intermediaries between manufacturers and end buyers. Where the merchants are the beneficiaries of a letter of credit from the ultimate buyers and are asked by the manufacturers to provide them in turn with a letter of credit, the problem arises that because documents will have to comply with the terms of the first credit (the "master" credit) the back-to-back credit must be issued in such a way that it will produce such complying documents.

Where the merchants have a previously agreed facility with the bank for the issue of letters of credit, the issue of a back-to-back credit may be made under that facility and no financing is required. The technical problems remain, however, since it needs but one small mistake to be made, or for documents to be delayed in transit, for the back-to-back issuing bank to be faced with an unavoidable duty to pay on the one hand and a non-complying set of documents on the other. Where the purpose of the transaction is not finance, however, this risk should be offset by the customers' creditworthiness, which it is to be hoped was taken into consideration when the facility was granted.

Most frequently a request for the issue of a back-to-back credit takes place in circumstances similar to those giving rise to many transferable credits, where the merchants in the middle of the transaction are not of sufficient standing to warrant the granting of letter of credit facilities and cannot cajole the manufacturers into parting company with the goods unless they can provide them with a credit as an assurance that they will be paid. Some countries' regulations do not permit the issue of transferable credits, or in some cases the merchants would prefer that the ultimate buyers remain unaware that they are not dealing with the manufacturers of the goods, lest in future transactions their own services are dispensed with.

They therefore approach a bank, usually either their own bankers or the advising bank of the master credit, and ask that they issue a credit in favour of the manufacturers, not under a facility but against the security of the money which will become due when they present complying documents under the master credit. If the bank agrees (banks' attitudes to back-to-back credits vary widely) a credit will be issued showing the merchants as applicants and requiring dispatch of the goods to the end buyers and presentation of the documents called for in the master credit. Unlike a transferable credit, it is essential that the dates for shipment,

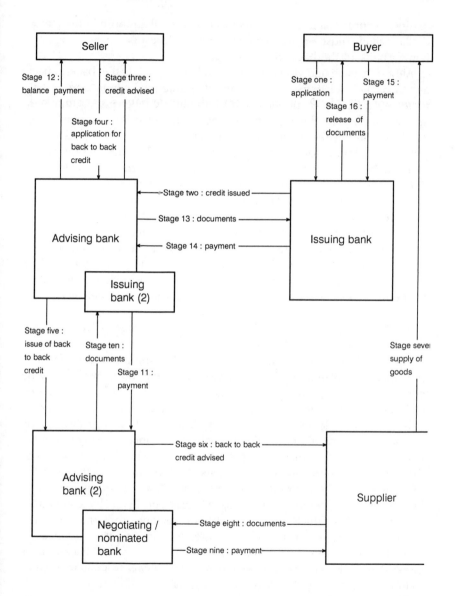

Back-to-back credit

expiry and presentation of documents are earlier than those in the master credit, which must on no account expire before documents reach the issuing bank of the back-to-back credit.

Although each individual credit is subject to UCP, the back-to-back aspect of their relationship is not, and therefore banks indulging in their issue can look for no protection from the articles. Because of this they are not subject to the restrictions which UCP place upon transferable credits regarding requirements which may be altered. This gives rise to numerous requests for variations in the terms, all designed to prevent the ultimate buyers and sellers from being put in touch with each other. These only serve to increase the danger that a discrepancy will arise between the documents presented under the back-to-back credit and those required in order to obtain payment under the master credit.

For the merchants, the attractions of back-to-back finance are that it serves better than a transferable credit in enabling them to maintain their pivotal position in the transaction because it is potentially more flexible and it is far cheaper than the alternative, even were such a course open to them, of borrowing the money with which to obtain delivery of the goods.

For the banks, it is difficult to see what advantages could possibly accrue from this type of business. If a bank which issues a back-to-back credit has advised the master credit it is withholding information from its principals which may be of vital concern to them and therefore may be considered to be in breach of its duties as an agent. If it has not advised the master credit, the beneficiaries may accept amendments to that credit without its knowledge. It is frequently dealing with an organisation on whose behalf it would not under normal circumstances even consider the issue of letters of credit, yet it is implying to the suppliers of the goods that a very different relationship exists. Its "security" is subject to the possibility already referred to of being nullified by postal delays or human error. Its return is small, usually pathetically so by comparison with the profits which the merchants are making from the deal. The wonder is therefore that banks are prepared in any circumstances to entertain such business, but in many countries of the world back-to-back credits are quite commonplace; whether this stems from ignorance or optimism on the part of the issuing banks is impossible to tell.

Where a bank does agree to issue a back-to-back credit and reimbursement for drawings thereunder is obtainable from no other source than the proceeds of a drawing under the master credit, its first action should be to ensure that it remains in possession of the original of the master credit in order to make certain that negotiation of documents cannot take place through any other bank. Alternatively, the original should be marked indelibly, on its face, to the effect that it is the subject of a back-to-back agreement. The bank should then insist upon the first beneficiaries supplying, in advance of the issue of the back-to-back credit, their commercial invoices and drafts in accordance with the requirements of the master credit, fully completed as far as possible and signed. Careful consideration should then be given to the dates for shipment and expiry and the time allowed for presentation of documents under the back-to-back credit, to make it as certain as possible that the similar dates in the master credit will be complied with. It should always be borne in mind that any variation in the terms of the master credit may well put the bank in a position of total reliance on the ability of the first beneficiaries to rectify the differences before presentation under the master credit and that if such differences relate to the bill of lading the bank may have no option but to release the bill (and with it, of course, *prima facie* ownership of the goods) to the first beneficiaries in order that the alteration(s) may be made and authenticated by the carriers. Sometimes, requirements of the master credit, such as the sending of documents by the first beneficiaries direct to the applicants within a specified period from shipment, may make the issue of the back-to-back credit totally unviable, and the bank must weigh up each of the master credit's requirements with this in mind.

Usance letters of credit

Normally a usance credit is an indication that the buyers are being granted extended credit terms by the sellers, but they can be used for the provision of import finance to the buyers by the issuing bank. This is achieved by requiring the beneficiaries to draw usance bills under the credit but including a provision for those bills, when accepted, to be immediately discounted at the expense of the applicants. The sellers, therefore, are effectively paid at sight while the buyers benefit from the usance period in order to process and/or on-sell the goods. From the sellers' point of view there remains the question of recourse, but as the bills are usually drawn on a bank the likelihood of this right being exercised is minimal.

Buyer credit guaranteed by exporting country

In furtherance of their basic aim of encouraging their own country's exports, the export credit insurance organisations of many countries (including ECGD) are prepared to issue guarantees to overseas banks in support of loans made to buyers for the purchase of goods from the guarantor country. This means that the sellers receive immediate payment for their goods and do not need to concern themselves with such matters as the granting of credit terms and the contingent liabilities attaching to negotiated or discounted bills of exchange or promissory notes. Such arrangements may be either for specific projects involving one contract or may be under a line of credit involving multiple suppliers and buyers concerned in a particular trade, usually in goods of a capital nature.

Produce loans

A traditional form of finance provided by banks to importers is where the bank advances the money to the buyers which is required to pay an inward collection or a drawing under a letter of credit and as security for the loan retains control over the goods until repayment occurs. This means that the documents must include either a negotiable bill of lading made out to order and endorsed in such a way, either specifically in the bank's favour or in blank, as to allow the bank to take delivery of the goods on arrival, or a transport document showing the bank as the named consignee.

On arrival of the carrying vessel, the bank will arrange with its agents for the goods to be cleared, warehoused and insured in its own name. In effect, the bank is *de facto* the owner of the goods until it is paid for them. When this happens, a delivery order will be issued to the warehouse keepers instructing them to release the goods to the buyers or their nominees.

Trust receipt facilities

Under a trust receipt facility the bank pays an inward collection or a drawing under a letter of credit in the same way as for a produce loan but instead of warehousing the goods on its own account releases the documents to the buyers in exchange for their signature to a trust receipt. In this document the buyers acknowledge receipt of the goods, which are identified by shipping details and by a bill of lading number, and undertake to hold them in trust on behalf of the bank, whilst admitting the bank's continued ownership of the goods pending repayment of the loan, and to sell the goods and to account to the bank for the proceeds, in the meantime insuring the goods for the benefit of the bank.

This arrangement has the advantage from the bank's point of view of making it unnecessary for it to become directly involved with the goods. The disadvantages are that the buyers have physical possession of those goods and may abuse the bank's trust by selling them without its knowledge and without using the proceeds of sale to repay the advance. Alternatively, they may use the documents of title as security for further advances from other lenders. It is well established in law that in the latter circumstances the second lender's interest takes precedence over the first. The operative word in a trust receipt facility is therefore the first, the transaction being wholly based upon the degree of trust which the bank feels it can place on the buyers.

Index